PATCHWORK JUNKIE

Donna -
I love you! I miss you!
I cherish your support.
Thank you for never
giving up on me!
Kyle Dean

KYLE DEAN HOUSTON

www.kyledeanhouston.com

Ordering Information:

Quantity sales. Special discounts are available on quantity purchases by corporations, associations, and others. For details, contact the sales and publicity team at booksales@kyledeanhouston.com.
Orders by U.S. trade bookstores and wholesalers. Please contact: booksales@kyledeanhouston.com or visit our website at www.patchworkjunkie.com

Printed in the United States of America

First Edition, 2020

ISBN: 978-0-578-73521-4

Disclaimer: In some instances, details such as names, dates, locations and scenery have been altered in order to protect the privacy, feelings and freedoms of characters in this book.

DEDICATION

To Dylan and Sean: Being locked away when you needed me most is an emptiness that will never be filled. Neither of you will ever know how perfectly you fit in my arms in those too-few, brief moments when you were little. If a bunch of fancy words could somehow give back a childhood with me in it, I would write a thousand books—but the only words that matter are, "I love you."

CONTENTS

Why do I do it? I guess I know the answer to that naïve and silly question. Why I do it is easy. As I sit here watching the pure white flakes materialize in the tempered glass, the petroleum scent of acetone starving my brain cells yet feeding my mind, feeling the ache in my head…no, my bones…no, my spirit; as the fractured, crystalline lines form across the liquid, turning into something beautifully dangerous, I know exactly why I do it…

Who I am; now that's another question.

PART ONE

BURN

1

THERE IS THAT one night I'll never forget. Not exactly the beginning; but fuck it, I've got to start somewhere. How none of us saw the fire coming—not the tweakers, not the biker bitches, not me, as I stand trapped in the center, flailing my arms, feeling my flesh boil and my own skin burn, as I frantically look for an open space to stop, drop, and roll.

The whole memory is still a blur of toxic fumes, volatile chemicals, and coffee tables full of ingredients that could put us all in jail for a very long time. People running around everywhere, eyes wide, voices screaming because the flames are out of control and I know there is hell of a metaphor inside all this for the dumpster fire my life had become.

How incredibly fucked up it all became so fast, so deeply. How in such a short amount of time, I went from a young entrepreneur with a bright future to putting my life in danger for people I have nothing in common with.

Yeah, this is the spot where I have to start, when it still seemed like someone else's life, not mine. That night, where the addiction became something different—something much worse—in spite of how impossible the idea of worse seemed.

A memory of so many firsts. First fire, first time letting the old heads know I had arrived and could make the precious substance that was the currency of the underground, and the first time I realized that, quite possibly, there would be no event too life-threatening, too earth-shattering, for me to ever want to stop using. Because although none of us could see the bottom or how close it ever really was, the fact that my life was in grave danger and it still wasn't enough to quit, made me realize that the worst, no matter how vivid my imagination, would always be something unimaginable to me.

And on this night, I was relatively unknown, I was definitely in over my head, and I was already a consummate liar, because I was an alchemist who was convinced he was simply just passing through.

You know what, let's rewind. Not much, just twenty to thirty minutes, so I can give a proper introduction.

It's called a burn. That spellbinding process of taking over-the-counter chemicals and turning them into the pure white powder that consumes far too many of my thoughts these days. And it really is a complex set of formulas and reactions with scientific terminology that I'm not quite qualified to understand. I mean, I know my way around a hydrocarbon as well as the next guy but I don't really give a shit about all the Methyl-this and the Chloro-that. I give a shit about meth. I'd love to tell you that my pursuits are noble, that I'm driven by science, but although it is all fascinating stuff, without the incredible euphoria of this drug I probably wouldn't know the difference between a Bunsen burner and my a-hole.

Note to self: never get those two things mixed up.

To me, the science is simply a necessary, albeit interesting, evil. A means to an end. Sort of like the way physics helps scientists master drag, lift, and propulsion in order to send a human to the moon. As cool as all that might be, I remain content being the primitive man, standing in my loincloth out beneath the stars, staring up at the same glowing orb and writing poetry to get in some girl's pants. It all depends on what trips your trigger. Rocket scientists are motivated by numbers or moon studies or the advancement of our species, but I don't possess the attention span for things like that. But if those same scientists sent a colony of bikini-clad women to that same glowing orb, you can bet your sweet ass I would retire the loincloth and somehow Forrest Gump my way to the moon.

Where there's a will there's a way, I guess. As long as you're prepared to accept that with this drug, the will that finds the way is no longer your own.

But at least meth isn't heroin, right? Although, heroin does have those cool-ass poetic nicknames like Chiva or Smack or China White. Almost sounds romantic, huh? This is meth. And what we call it changes with our moods. Like when I've been up for three days and I'm tired, and my back is killing me from the stress of too many people, and I need a hit, then I call it dope or shit. But the minute I get high, the minute that circulating smoke filters through the base of a clear glass pipe, past my lips, and into my lungs and that glorious full cloud of smoke billows from my mouth like a Pittsburgh smokestack on a cold winter day…well, then I call it by its biblical name: Crystal Methamphetamine.

Oh, and down in this basement around these assholes, it's all just shit.

After four months, six at the most, of getting high, I'm not really sure what I am at this point—habitual, dependent, a fiend—hell, take your pick. It's all so new to me and I'm no expert. Not yet. But one thing's for sure, as I sit in a cloudy, unfamiliar basement with oversized ashtrays brimming with half-smoked Camel Wides and Marlboros while the people who smoke them are watching me like some nervous kid setting up his eighth-grade science project, I know I'm definitely no longer experimenting.

There's a name for people like me but I don't think it matters. Because at this point, I've lost track of time, of everything. The proverbial water that has run under the bridge since I last spoke to my mother and to the girl in Chicago, who I swear I love, is definitely measured in months, not weeks. There's a voice inside me that has gradually gone quiet and meek that suggests I'm doing something wrong, something evil that infringes on trust and love and the implied laws of possibly humanity, but what that something is isn't exactly clear.

The drug does more than control me; it hides my way back in those same places it hides my self-image. It tampers with all three dimensions of a normal existence and distorts reality like a funhouse mirror, so the world as I knew it becomes impossible to recognize. It has brushed away the footsteps on the path, the breadcrumbs I was planning to trace back to something normal after the binge was over.

At least that's what I've been telling myself.

And I don't know exactly how long a binge is supposed to last, but I know it's not six months. I know binges aren't supposed to be so long that my mother is left sobbing in the middle of the night, wondering if I'm alive. Or leave her wringing her hands and watching the evening news to see if I've been killed in yet another meth lab explosion, which seems to be the top story almost nightly.

Or so I'm told. I don't watch TV. I'm addicted to meth.

I don't worry about paying bills or eating vegetables or getting my share of vitamin D from the sun. I don't use the phone or check in with friends or consider the pain I might be causing any of them. I don't look into the horizon or think about the future or see beyond the zip-lock bags of pure, white flakes because I am hopelessly obsessed to know everything I can about doing a goddamn burn.

And I taught myself to cook, although no one believes it because, truth be told, I look like a cop. I have short hair, no beard, no mustache, and my sideburns are trimmed, ending just above the earlobe like James Dean in the *Boulevard of Broken Dreams* painting that hung from the wall in my living room.

Before the foreclosure.

Actually, the skinnier I get, the more I look like Brandon from *Beverly Hills 90210*. And although there's nothing wrong with looking like Jason Priestley, I'm not exactly blending in with this bunch. But meth has an endearing way of bringing people together, I guess. As long as you're skinny and borderline insane—borderline being optional—and you don't mind blankets on the windows twenty-four hours a day, chances are someone in this godforsaken town is going to let you in.

And in exchange, you get to plow through their food, overstay your welcome, and pilfer all their shit. The true Tao of the meth addict.

But I had some help developing my affliction; a short, freckle-faced, white trash girl from the wrong side of Independence made the necessary introductions, and I took to it all like a duck to water or a bee to honey or, I don't know, a virus to a host. I somehow parachuted right smack dab into the middle of the meth capital of the world: Independence, Missouri. But somewhere along the way I graduated from getting "high" to getting "spun out", which translates to "really fucking high".

And once she decided my drug abuse wasn't fun anymore, she pulled a power move and cut me off. But joke's on her.

Because voilà, I have my own meth lab now.

I've been hovering over a sweltering waffle iron for God only knows how many days now. The room is cramped, pockmarked with working stations—small Tupperware containers full of tinted liquids, Pyrex cooking dishes with white powdery residue caked across the bottom, and commercial-size coffee filters scattered and waiting under oscillating fans.

And here I am in the center of it all— at a too-low coffee table with a chemically discolored 2000-milliliter flask and this hot-ass waffle iron that I'm assured will "do the trick". The alkaline fumes that used to stink, but now just dull my senses, are all around me. How strong those fumes are is anyone's guess. Looks like sleeping and eating aren't the only things I'm immune to. Still, breathing poison is probably bad.

"People don't give a shit about anything but the drugs in Independence anymore," this kid named Evan passionately explains to me as if somehow this doesn't apply to him, doesn't apply to me.

This dingy basement, with the windows covered, is hot and sticky and I am nervous, trying desperately to concentrate as Evan stands behind me talking way too much. He has been yammering on about how becoming a meth cook was something he would never let himself do, never go down that path because it just "comes with too much trouble".

I understand why he says this. Let's face it, saying it's your choice not to become a meth cook is much easier than saying, "I'm a dumbass," that you aren't smart enough to figure it out after countless nights of watching the process or that you need a scapegoat to point the finger at and say, "I might sell meth but at least I don't cook it."

Claiming you never want to be a cook is much easier than telling a bunch of people that you have no backbone or that your back up plan when the DEA finally arrests you is simply to snitch. And if you're the cook, then who the hell do you snitch on?

"Don't you agree?" Evan asks and blows out a long plume of cigarette smoke.

The room is crammed with far too many of these sons of bitches. Distressed, anxious, annoying caricatures of people whose sunken cheeks and red-rimmed eyes that rarely blink remind me of the haunting black-and-white images of World War II concentration camps. Everyone's name altered, different from their driver's license I imagine, except mine.

"I mean, it's not like I'm addicted to this shit," Evan says, probably trying to convince himself. "I can quit anytime I want."

"Yeah." But that's what everyone says.

Women in Harley Davidson jackets chain smoke long cigarettes and come and go as they please. Their words are sweet but their faces are mean and weathered like old salty sailors who have been out to sea for most of their lives. They shoot me impatient glares every time I look up so I know if I don't produce a batch soon, I'm going to meet a different version of every woman in here. I am not like the other men they know and weirdly trust. I have a baby-smooth face and fairly good teeth and a vocabulary that extends beyond "motherfucker" or "shut up, bitch".

At least, I used to.

And Kenzie, the nineteen-year-old girl—who I met only a week ago but is somehow now being introduced as my girlfriend—sits across from me on a barstool, swinging her legs into the wooden footrail with soft taps. She's wearing a short red skirt and white shiny boots that come up past her thighs. She is cute still, with color in her face, straight white teeth, and life in her eyes that seems so out of place in this crowd of shitty, hateful people. I wonder which category I fall into inside her mind and then feel silly because my new gauge has become what I may or may not look like to a girl who isn't even old enough to drink. She reaches for my hand and giggles, and I pretend it's because we are different than these people. But what does she know?

I am the one standing here, fighting to ignore the shadows dancing on the walls. I am the one who sees things in my peripheral vision that make me question everyone in the room. I twitch, jerk to the right, and hope no one notices…like the three guys who have said very little but study my every move. Are they cops? Are they dangerous? Are they waiting to kill me for my dope? I blink and remind myself I've been up for at least three days. I'm exhausted and paranoid and desperate at this point.

Clearly, I have a problem.

Otherwise, how could I remain unemployed? How could I let my home go into foreclosure? The corner lot with friendly neighbors where we eventually resorted to burning candles at night because the electricity was disconnected, and we parked in the garage with covered windows so no one could see if we were home and knock on the door to tell me to "mow the goddamn yard".

And maybe if it wasn't such a shitshow, I could see the burn as some kind of accomplishment. As if there was a category for Most Successful Meth Cook at high school reunions. Even as a powerless piece of shit, I still have the resolve to figure out the alchemy of volatile chemicals, the dance of the skulls and crossbones that warn me how easily it can all ignite—a warning that, if I'm being honest, I don't pay a lot of attention to. Who needs training? I have proven that I can combine the ingredients just right to create my own supply of these beautiful crystalline flakes. I'm Kyle Fucking Houston and I will never run out again, never have to ask or wait or beg or sacrifice my dignity to people who are shittier than I will ever be.

I hope.

This burn won't just be a couple of 8-Balls to ease the suffering. It will be the one that makes sense of what I've become. And something better make sense soon before I think too much about what I gave up to be in this basement.

"It's been two days," I hear Sweeney, the owner of the house, yelling down the stairs. "You always do this, Evan. How much longer?"

Evan darts up the stairs and meets him halfway, hands held out in a stopping motion, to explain. "The ephedrine wasn't easy, Sweeney. Goddamn pharmaceutical companies are putting carnauba wax in it now."

He's right. The over-the-counter diet pills get harder and harder for us to extract the ephedrine, which adds an extra step, makes the burn take longer, and pisses everyone off. But it's really just some chemical version of cat and mouse. Because the cooks will always figure it out. Chemistry and degrees are no match for the ache of addiction.

I listen with my back to the stairwell as I pour Red Devil Lye into a container of Coleman fuel.

"Well, there's too many fucking cars parked outside my house," Sweeney continues in a whisper loud enough for everyone to hear. "You know my neighbors. They're old and nosey."

"No problem," I hear Evan tell him. "We'll take care of it."

And I hear Sweeney's grumpy footsteps stomping up the stairs and across the kitchen floor over my head. The women with the cigarettes are sitting on swivelling bar stools now and saying they aren't leaving until they get "their dope", and I think to myself how Evan was right; nobody gives a shit about anything but the drugs in Independence anymore.

"It's cool," Evan tells me as he comes back down, offering me a cigarette, his forehead damp and shiny and his eyes wider than before. Two guys sitting on the couch in the next room casually flip through porno magazines.

I decline the cigarette and point to the container of fuel. Evan shrugs.

Kenzie tries to say something but she's interrupted by another woman, I think her name is Sadie, with a hoarse, smoke-stained voice. "Does this one even know what he's doing?"

As if I can't hear them, Evan replies, "I've helped him hundreds of times." He's lying but I let him as Sadie babbles on about how some guy named Dalton never did it this way.

She starts in on a history lesson "back before the laws changed" and how glorious things were in the "good old days". My neck is stiff and my nerves are shot, and I hear myself yell slowly, annunciating every syllable, "Shut. The. Fuck. Up!"

The room goes quiet. I hear her mumble words like "asshole" and "faggot", things that say more about her than me as Evan snaps his fingers at her. For a split second, I wonder how she would feel if I stood up and slapped the shit out of her like I'm sure this Dalton character would've done by now. But that's not me, not how I was raised, but still I'm thinking about it—and that says something about the person I've become, right?

I want to remind all of them that I'm cooking meth here, not having happy hour at the local pub. And although I might not know the way people did it "before everyone got sent away", I'm pretty sure nobody wants the guy handling explosives to be nervous and pissed and on edge. Don't poke the bear, bitch. He just might make really good dope.

Evan stands over me. "What should I do?" he asks. He's fidgety and wide-eyed and useless.

He's driving me crazy, they all are, and I want to be alone. I miss my house. Something that rarely registers until I want to be alone. Or when I am left to wonder where I'm going to sleep or bathe or keep my things. A place where I could close the doors or sit on my deck in my backyard again and barbeque and drink and still have dreams. Where the neighborhood children would still run up to my truck when I pulled into the driveway and tease me because I was funny and safe and full of strength. Not the man they saw towards the end.

The place where my son, Dylan, slept and took his first steps and demanded my attention. Where I could never get along with his mother, my ex-wife, who lied about everything and held tightly to codependency just like her parents did with her. Where I eventually lived with friends and talked over bottles of beer and music after midnight, after restaurants had closed and the bartenders and waitresses showed up to fan the embers of still being young.

But I quickly cut off those thoughts because my conscience might not be able to take it if I dwell in those days of Dylan's smile, and my house, and who I used to be for one more second.

"Kyle," Evan says, and I want to punch him.

"Yeah."

"I'm here for you, Man," he tells me. "Whatever you need."

I walk over to the bar, light a cigarette, wipe my palms down the front of my pants, and stare at the chaos. My fingertips are stained red-orange, the same color as the filthy rags that smell unlike anything I've ever smelled outside a meth lab, outside these clandestine moments. A stain I've noticed for weeks. I wonder vaguely if it'll ever go away.

Kitchen chairs scoot overhead, feet shuffle, and someone behind me whispers something I don't hear or care about. Kenzie and I share my cigarette. I can tell she doesn't really smoke. She leans toward me every time she takes the butt from my fingers, trying to get closer.

"Yo," Evan says, "we should have Sweeney come down and watch you finish the cook. He's never seen this part."

I take a drag of my cigarette and blow smoke toward the ceiling. "Tell him he has to be quiet," I reply. "And ask if he has a better shaker jug."

"He doesn't, but I'll ask."

Kenzie pulls me closer, in between her legs. Her hands are warm and clammy on my skin as she puts them up underneath my T-shirt. "You're so sexy," she tells me as I stamp the cigarette out in the ashtray beside her.

"I'll bet you say that to all the —"

She leans in and kisses me, making me uncomfortable, self-conscious. A side effect of being around the non-addicted. A result of my atrophying self-esteem.

And Sweeney lumbers into the room, a big man with a congenial smile and greasy curly hair and a facial expression that screams something important is missing behind his eyes. "Thanks man," Sweeney nods and holds his hand out to shake mine. It seems so out of place in this moment but I oblige and shake it anyway. He seems pleased.

I ask Sweeney how many times he has used the waffle iron to burn off the fuel and he says, "All the time," although Evan just told me he has never seen this step. Evan reminds me there's no flame to the iron so he "guarantees it", and it makes sense.

I don't care that they're all lying because, God willing, we'll all be high soon.

"Cool?" Evan asks.

"Cool," I reply and grab a long glass eyedropper and a bottle of hydrochloric acid. I slowly twist the lid off and dip the eyedropper into the acid. Smoke drifts up from the bottle and into my face. It burns my nostrils and the back of my throat; it's probably permanent damage. I drop the acid into a shaker jug full of fuel, close the lid and shake it three times, like an oversized martini. The acid collects and grows and falls to the bottom of the jug. I repeat. It gets bigger.

"What's that?" I hear Sweeney ask.

Then Evan says, "What do you think?"

But the oversized hole has Coleman fuel dripping slowly down my arm, soaking my hand and arm like a Molotov cocktail. And when I pull my thumb away, I instantly remember the warning signs on the sides of those cans.

The meth falls to the pan, sending camping fuel splashing over the side of my Pyrex dish. Once it hits the surface of the waffle iron, like an egg on a hot skillet, everything in the world goes silent except for my heartbeat and this sizzling of volatile, flammable fuel. But hey, no open flame, no danger, right?

Wrong. Holy shit, what was that? I stare at the image of bubbling liquid on a hot surface that's no longer there. It's my mind unable to catch up. I register the explosive flash of light that hits my face, which is suddenly hot, and the deep-bass boom that sounds like my head is inside a furnace when the pilot lights the gas. I feel it all in my body and my only passing thought is overwhelming fear.

To say fire is fast is like saying shoving your hand into a garbage disposal could give you some scrapes and bruises. When surrounded by fumes, fire is instant, like the speed of thought. And it forgives nothing, it surrounds everything and it wants all the oxygen, all the fuel, all the heat that it takes to burn forever.

I'm enveloped now, panicked and swatting wildly. Quickly, I stand and back away, driven by the things in my body that tell me to blink, tell me to breathe. The things I don't consider but just do. I'm in some kind of survival mode.

And just like that, the fumes die down as quickly as they appeared and leave small fires in their wake, in every corner of the room, threatening to reach the dangerous chemicals.

Shit! To every overlooked warning sign on every can of fuel in here, I think, *You win, you have my respect now.*

Everybody's in crisis mode, moving with purpose, as if they've trained for this occasion or at least seen it before. People running, people yelling, people grabbing towels and leaping over flames. I look down and realize

I'm on fire, with flames burning my flesh, stuck in the middle of iodine and acetone and fire and addiction, frantically looking for somewhere to stop, drop, and roll.

The pain is killing me. Nowhere to run, it just doesn't work like that, so I swat at my clothes and try to double up and smother the fire myself but it is too painful. Behind me I hear the extinguishers hiss and smoke with clouds swirling through the air. And then I'm tackled. It's Evan and he hits me hard from behind with the power of fear and he's clearly shitting his pants. *There you go buddy, another reason not to be a meth cook.*

I hear myself thank Evan and then feel firm hands forcing me up the stairs. Everything in slow-motion, detached, deniable. The bubbling raw skin, the throbbing heartbeats of pain build now. Holy shit this is starting to hurt.

Running up the stairs now. Skipping steps. I think I'll live but, goddamn, it hurts.

"Back here," someone yells. "Get his arm under water."

Pain builds as I follow the sound of running water, the sounds of unfamiliar voices. How close to death had I really gotten? What have I done? What are the consequences? Am I safe? I test the water. It is cold and soothing and clean; it is all that matters in this moment.

"I'm sorry," I repeat to Sweeney and he says things that don't register, although he doesn't seem mad.

"Keep your arm here."

"Don't worry about me," I yell. "Hide the evidence."

Suddenly I'm alone, in a strange bathroom, in a strange house, standing in a shower with my boxers getting wet. I think of her, the girl in Chicago. The girl who invested, who believed; who, if she could see me now, would shake her head, would hold nothing back, and would slap the shit out of me. And you'd think that with everything going on, I'd stay on task inside this unfamiliar tub with cool water running down my arm; but I love her, I miss her and I make a solemn vow to call her just as soon as I get to a phone. Oh right, and if I'm not high.

My skin is pink with oversized blisters full of liquid. Downstairs I hear loud voices and quick, impatient movements. I hear people leaving as the front door opens and closes. I think of the chemicals and glassware and how everything I own is now downstairs being thrown around, disposed of, hidden. I think of the burn and how I could do it better, how if I could pull my arm away from this cool, clean water, I would go down there right now and finish what I came here to do. No regard for danger or my life or the law. Forget who I was or the people who miss me or the girl I love in Chicago, I need to be high.

There is no denying it. I'm a meth cook now.

2

A WOMAN NAMED Sam wakes me up. I struggle to remember where I am—the strange surroundings, the sound sleep.

"Sorry to wake you," she says, her voice compassionate, concerned.

I sit up and feel the throbbing pain in my arm, the gauze now melded with the puss and blood. She hands me a Vicodin. "Sweeney had these," she says. "You really need to see a doctor."

"Sure. Thanks." I take the pill. "It's not as bad as it looks though."

She disapproves. I can tell.

"Kenzie and Evan took your car," she blurts and then studies my face.

"Who was driving?" I ask but I'm not sure why. What does it matter?

"Kenzie said you didn't care if they took it, but I didn't believe her."

I pat my chest, looking for cigarettes and realize I'm not wearing a shirt. "Do you know where my—"

Sam hands me a pack of cigarettes from her purse. "She took your wallet, too."

Of course she did. Fucking Kenzie. I light the cigarette and take an extended drag. I exhale and wait. My thoughts are cloudy. I thank this woman I barely know.

"What about the meth?" I ask. "Who got that?"

"Sweeney says it isn't meth. You didn't do something right."

"And where is it now?"

"You really should see a doctor."

I take another drag. The tip glows in the dimly lit room. "Where is it?" I repeat.

"They took that, too."

"And it wasn't meth, huh?"

She doesn't know how to respond so repeats that I should have my arm looked at.

"It's only been a couple of hours," I say. "They'll show up."

"That's the other thing," Sam says. "It's been eighteen hours. Sweeney needs you gone." Then punctuates the request with, "Sorry." And I believe her.

But I don't care what Sweeney wants and ask for another cigarette from her pack. I don't care that it's been eighteen hours since I've been conscious or that I'm around unfamiliar people who didn't ask for the burden of me, a strange man with burns on his arm who is lucky to be alive. Or that the blisters on my arms are huge and full of fluid that will probably leave scars, a reminder of the binge I took when I was twenty-something, or that I feel my heartbeat underneath the pain. I don't care that my pants fall below my hips now, or that the business I had started, that was doing well, is gone along with the house, the truck, the respect. I don't care that a nineteen-year-old girl has stolen the final remnants of my possessions and ran off with a boy who will use her to open doors, use her every way he can and then feed her to the wolves. I don't care that they will turn her out and leave her soulless with a new set of rules, a new set of morals. I don't care about the car or that I was almost a statistic, a story on the ten o'clock news, an answer to my mother's questions.

I oddly don't care about life or death or the carbon taste in my mouth from too many cigarettes, two packs a day if I try to control it; three packs if I don't. Or that the porno magazines are slowly getting more hard-core and widely accepted. Or that the stories of people who used to be sweet and sympathetic to everyone's curse are now stealing credit cards from the elderly members of their own family who slipped on the ice and were put into the hospital believing that all their belongings were being taken care of…believing in the ghosts of these people before there was meth. None of it. Nothing. At this point, as I lie in the darkness listening to a rational lady trying desperately to be the voice of reason, all I can think about is the drug and how in the hell I get it now.

I look at Sam for a moment. She smiles and looks away. The thought of sex enters my mind but leaves when I move my arm and feel the excruciating pain. And I wonder how bad this is going to be and how long I will let it go before I get it looked at.

"Got any shit?" I ask.

"No. I wish."

I exhale, trying to relax, choosing my next words.

"I'm sorry I had to be the one to tell you," she explains and again, I believe her.

I gingerly remove blankets, hang my legs over the side, and feel for the floor. I take a long hard pull from the cigarette and look up, "I guess it really is true." I sigh.

"What's that?" Sam asks.

"That nobody gives a shit about anything but the drugs in Independence anymore."

Sam is gone and I sit on the edge of the bed contemplating my next move. I have no wallet, no car, maybe third degree burns, and a pack of Marlboro lights. I hear my name faintly, said loudly from another room. Who could it be? Kenzie, I bet. Frightened, ashamed, no longer untouched—perfume like a stripper, makeup fading, the traces of regret streaking down her face. But I'm not one to give two shits. I'm not one to accept an apology because I'm not mad. I strangely don't feel wronged or abandoned, or even disrespected. On this side of life, emotionally, spiritually, I can chalk it all up to the game. On this side of life, it doesn't take long to understand that loyalty is a lie that only a sucker believes. Rare are the connections that run deeper than anyone's degree of separation, their proximity to the drug.

You don't owe me an apology, Kenzie. I knew what you were before I picked you up, what you had in you, what you would become. Because whether you like it or not, you are an addict now.

You're staying true to your nature. Besides, I'm the one who brought you in, opened this door. The unimaginable possibility is that it is me who should be sorry, who should feel remorse. But you'll soon find out that I don't.

Not that I wish you any ill will, I just don't care. Just like the one who opened doors for me and the one who opened doors for her and the one who opened doors for him. It's perennial, it's perpetual, it's potentially infinite. And there's no room for feelings like that. So, don't worry. Don't cry. Don't give it another thought. Just fuck off because nobody cares…At least no one in here.

"Who is it?" I call out, lightly squeezing my arm. The wound is tender and moist, the pain dulled by the Vicodin.

"Kyle?" I hear and the voice is familiar now, but unsure and anxious. For a second, I wonder if I'm hallucinating, but there it is again, her voice, the first voice of my existence. The one I have run to my whole life. The voice I forget to miss until its unique vibration enters my heart and warms me, soothes me, reminds me that suddenly I am sorry.

"Mom?"

"Kyle?"

And now she's there. Sturdy but not without effort. Broken but open, soft but prepared to fight.

I lower my voice, look behind me. "Mom, you can't be here. How did you know where to find me?"

Instead of answering, she says simply, "Come home."

"I can't." I hesitate, "I need to—"

"I'm not asking. It's been long enough." A tear runs down her cheek, dropping to the floor. She wipes her face, clears her throat, and holds her head high. "I'm NOT leaving without you."

I can't answer that right now, can't think about that or what leaving with her means. "Where's Dad?"

"What does that matter?" She holds her arms out and steps towards me. "Come home, baby."

I meet her halfway and squeeze her in my arms. "I'm sorry, Mom," I whisper.

"Of course you are," she says against my cheek. "Of course you are."

She's always been my den mother, my cheerleader, my biggest fan. There was that time when I was six and she told me not to move the typewriter because she was going to do it later, but I was 'a man' and she was my mom, and six stitches later she knew I was always going to try to help. Then there was the time I cracked my head wide open across the street at the park. By the time she got there, I couldn't stand, I couldn't speak and blood was everywhere. She screamed as she tried to carry me but she was less than a hundred pounds, not even five feet tall, yet still she tried her best.

And as we share this surreal moment, standing at the front door of a meth addict's house, staring at one another, I know, once again, that no matter how much I fuck up, no matter how many times I push her away, no matter how many times I choose the drug over her love, she too is always going to try to help.

"You need to see a doctor," she says, pointing at my arm.

"I need a cigarette."

"Don't be an asshole." She takes a step back and motions for me to follow alongside the sidewalk, I can see her car, curls of smoke coming from the exhaust. "Everything worth keeping is this way."

"I don't even have shoes," I utter more as a question.

"You need a doctor," she answers.

It's nighttime now and I wonder how many nighttimes have passed, have I missed. The porch light casts shadows out into the yard, almost guiding us to her car.

"You shouldn't leave the car running unattended, Mom. Not here. Not with these people."

"Shut up and come on." She fakes a smile.

"I'm sorry," I tell her, my voice cracking. My heart is torn between this substance that I've known for a very short time and the love of my mother that I've had since conception.

"I know."

"So sorry." I wonder what it means, why it isn't obvious.

"Kyle. Get. In. This. Car."

I chew at my fingernail and glance behind me then back at her. Here's the woman who has been to every wrestling tournament, every football game. Here's the woman who has kissed every scrape and bruise, every heartache and failure. Here's the woman who has taught me to be a fighter, to dust off my britches and climb back up on the pony. And now I'm....what? Not sure. Fuck that.

As I move toward the car, she reaches over and squeezes my hand. "How did you know where to find me?"

"I got a call from someone's mom. Said she always liked you, always felt like you would take care of her baby girl when she couldn't."

I rest my hands on the roof of the car and look at my mother across the cold, burgundy metal. "What girl?"

My mother shrugs. "Someone named Kenzie."

And just when I think I can't be surprised anymore, there's that. I glance up at the house, and feel the pain of the burn in my arm, and wonder why this doesn't feel like goodbye; to these people, to this house. "Let's get out of here, Mom," I say climbing into her car. "Dad's gonna be worried."

3

LET'S GET ONE thing straight: I never saw myself as broken, or hurting, or missing some key ingredient to being whole—I mean, if there was something missing, I didn't know it. We didn't discuss that airy-fairy shit when I was a child. I grew up in a tougher time, not so much the black and white photo days, but certainly the dog-eared Polaroids with coffee spills and cigarette ashes days. A simpler time when a boy wouldn't be caught dead wearing a helmet riding a bike. Back in the days when a good ass-whipping meant your parents cared. But sometimes it would have been nice to feel the softer side of love. A smidge of tolerance, an explanation instead of so much anger.

I realize there are lots of people who have reason to complain about their imperfect childhood—broken family, fractured relationships, extreme dysfunction, alcoholic father figure, classic shit—but I'm not trying to do that here. The fact is, I love my parents. It's just that it's complicated, that's all.

Before I get into all that, I want to be clear that by no means am I throwing my parents under the bus. Turns out I had some personality traits that didn't quite "mix" with their ideal of the perfect child. How was I to know? But fair or unfair, here we are.

Now, Jerry Sam, my biological father, left my mom—or so the story goes—when I was three, and Tom Runge, the man who my Mom picked to take his place a year or so later, didn't really know what he was signing up for. I was a high-energy, impressionable carbon copy of Jerry Sam—the man we were all supposed to hate, that "son of a bitch", as Mom would say—and whether they intended to exhaust so much attention on this middle child or not, I certainly demanded as much as I could get.

Mom still tells the story of how I vomited every day for a week after "Jerry Sam left us". And it brings a lump to my throat every time just thinking about how attached I must have been to this man for my little body to have had that sort of reaction.

I craved attention from anyone and everyone, and only felt happy when I was the center of it. The incredible joy that I felt when I was able to make people laugh sustained so much of my life that I grew up scared that the day I wasn't funny any more was the day everyone would figure out I wasn't worth their time. My desire to please, although not obvious, was crippling. And my disappointment in two men—my two dads, who clearly never signed up to protect my heart—was an extension of this desire.

But before we start casting stones, let's not forget that nobody had a playbook that taught anyone how to navigate unchartered waters like stepsons, or divorce, or how to love a boy who reminded you every single day of the mistake you married because you were young and dumb. And as much as I'd like it to be different, I learned early on that my role in life was to push the boundaries of my parents' love and I took that responsibility very seriously. Whether I felt loveless or discarded, or was simply just a little shit from the beginning, I think at a certain age none of that matters any longer.

So, if some overeager therapist thinks I'm going to sit here and connect dots from my childhood to addiction, I'm not. But I am going to tell you that, ever since I can remember, I have had this deep sense of emptiness… probably from all the vomiting when Jerry Sam left.

But we all have our thing.

The truth is, since my earliest memories I was never able to find happiness in simple things. I never felt I belonged within my family. I never felt wanted by a single one of my parents in a way that was significant or empowering, and for that reason my self-worth was doomed from the beginning.

But don't confuse self-worth with confidence. I always had a huge dose of God-given confidence, whether it was justified or not. I was popular and funny and grew up in a small town where I became a big fish in a very small pond.

All I know is, when I was younger, I used to bump my head on purpose so that my mom would come pick me up, wrap her arms around my body, draw me against her bosom with warmth and love and kisses, and rock me until I was done crying. Could that have been a gateway to something? Could my love-starved little body have grown into a love-starved man who needs to be rescued, who needs to be saved because that is the way I was taught you get love? Maybe I was a pretty savvy codependent even back then when all I had to do to score my mother's affection was create a life of pain.

There you have it. Mom was my gateway drug. Can I just skip to the part where we all get in a rocking chair now?

Don't get me wrong, I care. I care about my mom, I care about people's feelings, and I'm not going to gloss over the fact that a fire in a strange basement around volatile chemicals that could not only kill you but could also get you God only knows how many years in prison, is fucked up by anyone's standards. *Anyone's* standards.

And as we drive down the road and Mom is talking about how much I need help; I realize her heart's in the right place but she doesn't know what she's talking about. So I had a fire, so what? I'm probably lucky to be alive but "need help"? Bullshit. What some people call rock bottom I call a stretch of bad luck that was going to happen either way.

I'm not going to lie to myself, this doesn't feel like addiction. This is more like a strong curiosity, a confusing pattern, whatever. Every time I hear my mom mention treatment or rehab or getting clean, I think about sitting across from assholes who ask me where I think it started…Where was the beginning of the end? And my answer is going to be, "I have no idea, I'm not that kind of an addict. I'm not like you!"

Was I a meth addict when I bought candy by the pound from Huscher's drugstore or had an uncontrollable need to play Pac Man every time Jerry Sam and I stopped at a truck stop? Was I a lost cause back when I stole quarters from my new dad's nightstand so I could ride my bike to the convenience store in order to get my video game fix? Who fucking knows? What about the poor sons of bitches who can't function without their coffee or the stress eaters with grease-smeared lips and sadness in their eyes as they clutch a half-eaten fried chicken leg in one hand? Are they on their way to a meth binge?

I lean my head back against the leather headrest and say very little so that I don't upset my mother. The truth is, I like crystal. I like crystal a lot. And I had a fire, which I am gathering means a lot, so nobody better fucking ask me where it started. Because I'm not willing to go any further back than the first time someone folded up a piece of tinfoil like a paper airplane, dropped a couple rocks of speed in the middle, heated it up, and told me to chase the smoke with a hollowed-out ink pen. That was the beginning of the end. That moment when my hair stood straight up and my pupils grew so fast and strong that you could almost hear them expanding. Almost. If the sound hadn't been drowned out by the freight train running through my head.

Mom and I never really talked about the night she picked me up in Independence. It just became an assumption that rehab was the natural direction for a fella in my shoes. Everybody thought I would somehow get the tools and understanding from total strangers who were committed to turning wayward sorry sacks like me around, like some Disney film with a sunset and a castle.

She got no push back from me. I just nodded my head and went along, because it's what you do when you are super fucked and get wrapped up in the warm fuzzies emanating from your very own mother. Maybe it was when she cried, because I know, with me, there are so many damned things to cry about and that makes me feel shitty every time. And, well, I do things that aren't quite what I want. And so my mom, with her belief in the integrity of systems and institutions, and I, approaching all of this with a cynical eye but a burning desire to take control, set out toward a place we both believed was going to bring back the boy she thought she was picking up at that house with the burned-up meth lab.

4

Did I mention I hate rehabs yet? I do. Standing in line at the intake counter of this ridiculous rehab in the middle of the foothills of Southern Missouri, amongst the hillbillies who probably have car parts in their front yard and white trash girls who are honestly sexy as hell but will probably be pregnant three times before they're even old enough to drink, I realize I didn't think this through. I hate addicts. I hate recovery. I hate groups. I hate clichés. I hate being in the same room as people who want to open up, who think their shit is so interesting, who feel strongly that they have to compete about whose life has been the most fucked up.

Hi my name's Bill, and I'm an addict. My life's events are worse than any of y'all's so I'm going to talk longer than I should and probably cry like a snivelling bitch in front of every stranger in here.

I hate them all. Every fucking one of these unoriginal bastards. I hate the way they look at me, I hate the way they fake it to make it with contrived bullshit smiles and this make-believe ideal universe where we are all in this together. And I know what I'm talking about because Mom and Dad put me in rehab back when I was sixteen because I drank beer and smoked pot too much, right alongside the kids who were shooting heroine and the cheerleaders who were blowing their dealers for cocaine. Clearly, I didn't belong then and I don't belong now. Still, if I'm being honest, I hope someone can help because something inside me wants to be different. I think.

I take a Marlboro from the fresh pack that Mom bought me, a pack that signified new beginnings or an olive branch or common ground, it wasn't clear, and as I light the cigarette I notice the overweight man standing in front of me is pale and sweating, nervous. Unlike others who are engaging with people around them, he has this look like he is being chased. Like there are demons that only he can see and they are clearly closing in.

Then a second later he's on the floor, sweating and convulsing, with spit boiling up from his lips, and I see that his demons have caught him. I want to do something, I want to help, I want to be involved. Maybe it's because that's the way I am or maybe it's because I would want him to do something for me if the shoe was on the other foot. Or maybe I am already beginning to realize the strength of powerlessness, although I don't want to admit it, and I see myself in his passing life and I need him to show me survival is possible.

The counselors rush from behind the counter and push through the mob. They move efficiently and quickly, repeating codes into walkie-talkies, louder each time—this is obviously a scenario they are prepared for.

And seeing this man's reaction makes me realize how incredibly deep the addiction to alcohol might be. I try to wrap my mind around how much you have to drink to be physically addicted, but my experience is lacking. He's not the first man I've seen with the spider web of purple blood vessels on his cheeks and the tip of his nose. Or his bloodshot eyes that earlier seemed so apologetic and unable to make contact with anyone else's, as if shame had taken on a human form.

This quiet man, who looked all alone and frightened when he was standing in front of me, is by no means the first late-stage alcoholic I've seen in the throes of alcoholism—hell, I was raised by a man who had his fair share of clear alcohol, the kind with the least amount of odor, the kind you could easily conceal from your wife by secretly drinking it undisturbed and alone out in the workshop—but this might be the first drunk I've seen brave enough to try to quit. My hat goes off to this poor lost soul dying in front of me. And as the paramedics arrive and do what they do when faced with someone who might be dying, I feel sadder and more empathetic and humbled; and reaffirm that this place isn't for me because I'm sure I'll never be as bad off as that poor bastard.

It has been at least three weeks since the fire, three weeks of sleeping at my mom and dad's house, eating normal food and living with this ache before checking into this shit hole. At times, my body has the urge to move, to exert energy with muscles and fuel and strength. I want to kick things hard and swing punches late at night when I watch TV. When I'm lying on the couch, I feel pent-up electricity kicking inside me to just move, but I don't. My teeth itch in ways I can't describe, like they are too close together. And my gums feel like the hard plastic of a mouthguard, and I brush them to no avail.

Mom and Dad didn't talk much about it, didn't try to figure out what was going on with me while I was at their house. But they didn't lay on a guilt trip either. For Mom to get a call from some strange woman telling her where I was and that I was physically hurt from a fire must've been the answer to her prayers, finally knowing where her baby boy was. Like God's end of the bargain, I guess.

God just let me know where he is, dead or alive, just let me know.

The alcoholic man is gone now. Whisked away on a stretcher to hopefully live, and heal, and find the will to carry on in spite of his broken spirit. And I am here being processed into a facility, a system that is just a series of boxes to check.

Ten minutes into this place and the only box I want to check as quickly as possible is 'Relapse'. Something we all can agree on.

5

I AM FOUR *years old and Mommy has started dating a man named Tom. He seems to be like some sorta knight in shining armor for her and my older sister, Kelly. For me, he is more like a giant fist crushing the happiness out of being a little boy and making it hard to breathe. The words in my head, the ones I don't say, tell me I'm not good enough for him. My tummy feels nervous now when it's time to eat—he always has this look like he's going to attack. I don't know how to hold my fork the way he tells me and I often chew with my mouth open, and he freaks out when I rest my face in my hands with my elbows touching the table; just like that, he kicks my shins.*

When I say anything, Mommy gets mad at him and then I have to for sure keep my distance because he says I caused a fight.

I just want my Daddy, but I think Mommy really likes this guy.

6

"MAKING AMENDS IS really all I want to do," Cam tells the group. He's doing that thing where he plagiarizes the soundbites of speakers before him and says the words that help his case file. He is clearly a ward of the state or here on some court-ordered *get out of jail free* Monopoly card.

"That's great, Cam. How do you plan to do it?" Sandy, the counselor, asks as we sit in a circle facing one another. Her posture is perfect; a stack of folders balanced on her lap and knockoff Gucci glasses on the bridge of her upturned nose.

I hate the counselors with their ridiculous phrases and their condescending ways of looking down on me. As if they have a better story. As if they know so much better than me. I don't trust any of them to guide me towards self-realization because I am smarter, I'm sure of that, and my situation is different than what they typically see. Fuck 'em all. These counselors have issues or why would they be here working the program? They aren't as fancy as they think. Listening to the counselors' false, contrived compassion is like fingernails scraping down a chalkboard to me. And I just want to hear one goddamn original thing come out of anyone's mouth in this stupid hillbilly rehab.

"I don't even care about jail," Cam continues. "Like, I'm really sorry man. You know what I'm saying?"

"You don't care about jail?" A man named Spider snorts. "Man, everyone cares about jail."

But Cam shakes his head, sticking to his guns and I can tell he realizes maybe he's laying it on too thick. Even Sandy looks at him suspect.

It's day three and I hate my life. My daydreams are incessant and out of control like ADD on a three-day binge. I sit here in these meetings yearning to be different, wishing to never hurt anyone again, but knowing there's going to be more. The replay in my mind comes up constantly with all the ways to cook better, safer, yielding more.

But I realize I'm also a little crazy. A few weeks without the drug is not enough detox to find yourself alive beneath the rubble.

"Don't get me wrong," Cam says to Spider. "I don't want to go to jail. I'm just saying making amends is important." This Cam kid is a joker. Pretty adept at lying. He's even good at lying to himself, but aren't we all? He has long hair and seems to be my age, mid twenties, and we both know we haven't seen our last bump of meth.

Spider takes a sip from his coffee, swallows hard and mutters, "Uh-huh."

Who am I kidding? This shit isn't going to work for me. This is the program for the 'others'. I see the depth of my creator and my challenge, my cross to bear, is more existential than anyone who sniffs glue or uses needles or drinks alcohol in a way I never have. I am happy that these people find breadcrumbs to their better lives somewhere in the Twelve Steps, but it's not going to help me.

I just really like meth.

I admire the commitment of some of the people in here—the older people who cling to their styrofoam cups and watch the clock, biting their nails while waiting for the next cigarette break. They are who this is for. They seem committed. But not the court-ordered patients, the ones checking the box to appease some judge somewhere who has a little faith that some of this clinical bullshit works.

And certainly not for me.

But don't get me wrong. I mean, I'm all in, I swear to God. Well, I think I am. As long as it's easy. I'm committed to never feeling the shame or the unrelenting pain of hurting another soul that cares for me as long as that commitment doesn't take work and pain and crying about all the loss. Or facing what I have left in my wake—like my child.

I mean, come on, there's way too much of that. To be honest, I'm good at seeing my addiction patterns; I'm good at feeling powerless and even good at admitting it. But sobriety is new, as individual as the path to salvation, and a part of me wants to be changed or woke or whatever it's called. So, I hope it all goes well, but something inside me knows that sobriety is but a philosophical concept. But relapse? Now, that's something I can wrap my mind around.

Sandy scribbles in a folder. "What about you Kyle?" she asks without looking up.

"What about me?" I answer.

Her listless eyes drift up from her folder and land on me. "What's important to you?"

I think about the alcoholic man and how his booze-inflamed veins across his face were like a heavily traveled roadmap to the dark places only he has seen. Although I'm still not sure if I witnessed the passing of a man's life, I'm a hundred percent sure I witnessed his rock bottom. And I hope he gets his second chance because I haven't seen him again. I haven't heard if he lived or died. He's not sitting in this circle and his life hasn't been talked about. I will never know if he sobers up or falls in love. I will never know if his convictions save another tormented soul, someone like him, because he fought to be clean, to be proof, to be alive. Never. I will only be left to imagine the pain and torment of his existence and how he fell so far down or how his mother must've cried herself to sleep at night wondering how her baby ended up with such an unforgiving curse. Now, that's authentic to me. That's original and personal yet universal to me. And I hope God forgives him because the man was lost and broken and deserved a fucking break from that love-shaped vacuum in the center of his being.

Yeah, but don't we all.

And I wonder if everyone here is just checking boxes. The addicts, the counselors, hell, maybe even God. Maybe God is like me, telling himself that all of this getting sober business is a hopeful and precious concept, but it's not real. God knows better than any of us how impossible it is to put down your vices by visiting this place and having faith in anything other than "you'll get there when He decides." When sobriety becomes the final box on his clipboard left unchecked, just below the fucked-up shit like rock-bottom and humility and complete and utter loneliness.

But we all know I'm not going to get to that point. Don't we? I've only been at this for less than a year. The addiction part anyway. But at least until any of us get there, we will always have the sanctuary of our substances. Unfortunately, the most original thought I have is the undeniable fact that, for me, clarity is going to be directly proportional to how cynical my outlook becomes.

And who the fuck needs that?

"Kyle?" Sandy's voice is a nudge.

What do I want? I shrug. "I guess more than anything, I wish I could find the desire to even want to quit."

The room seems to gasp. Oopsie. I don't think Sandy has a box to check for that.

She shuffles through the stack of folders, opens my file, and thumbs through the papers. "What do you mean by that?"

"Just what I said."

"Do you hear yourself when you say that, Kyle?"

Yeah, I hear myself, Sandy. I'm not fake like these other fuckers. I want to tell her and her condescending tone that a week into my detox at Mom's, I had a tiny square baggie fall out of one of my shirt pockets and send me down a path I'd never experienced before. I mean, five seconds before that happened, I was committed. The loving, nurturing moment with Mom was still fresh. The tiptoeing around my feelings with my father was very new and real, but when I saw the pink tinted miniature Ziploc with a fat half gram of pure white oblivion, my blood changed direction in my body. My heart pumped something thicker, my lungs moved faster, heavier, and my palms started sweating even before I picked up the bag and pinched it securely between my thumb and index finger.

At first, I thought, "No way." I've never lost track of my stash; therefore, this must be a gift from the universe. God knew about the itch and the commitment I had made and knew I couldn't just go cold turkey. Nobody does that. You need to know when your last hit is being taken. It's part of the process, the ritual, right?

And as I quickly hid the bag before Tom noticed I was salivating over some dope, I knew this internal dialogue was probably horseshit but I still couldn't get over how perfect the timing was.

And in the end, I let myself believe the lie. That it was a gift from heaven so who was I to question God's plan? Make no mistake about it, the more you try to quit, the worse you find your addiction. And whaddaya know, I was high for four days. Much respect, God.

"Do you think you probably misspoke?" Sandy slowly nods her head in a yes motion like I'm a child.

My blood starts to rise. I feel the room staring at me and consider retracting, suppressing the anger, but remind myself that this is real. That I'm the only person here who cares about being honest and authentic. That my anger is a pure expression of telling the truth in this moment, in this room full of bullshit users going through the motions to find leniency for their crimes.

In this moment, true or not, it feels like I'm defending the weak, I'm defending everyone too impotent to speak, everyone who has ever cowed to these bullying bastards with their listless looks and superiority complexes and textbook terms to deflect real meaningful dialogue. In this moment, I guess I am still a little scared and uneasy about the frothing alcoholic that nobody seems to talk about.

"Do I think I misspoke?" I repeat the question. "Let me ask you, do you think your approach works?"

I ask because we talk about cooking meth in the dorms and how I can use the phosphorus from the striker on matches to make the chemical reactions—all theories I read in books that infected my mind with the chemistry, as well as the history, of this insidious drug. Both pieces of information that an addict doesn't need to know or talk about when he's in a rehab full of condescending counselors he can't stand. If anyone here is truly getting clean, I'm not seeing it.

Sandy looks over the frames of her glasses and pauses for what feels like five minutes. "I follow the procedure of this institution."

"Is it procedure to try and intimidate people?"

"You might want to be careful, young man."

"What do you mean? I'm just trying to be honest." It comes out sarcastic, but I am sincere. This anger building in me is causing something to crack. Like molten rock below the Earth's crust, the boiling current has found a hotspot—a place where the hate and guilt and pressure can be released… right in the center of this fucking ridiculous circle.

Sandy makes a sour face. "We can talk about this in private."

"No. I want to talk about it now. While I feeeeel it." I stand up from my chair. "Isn't that what would make sense?"

I feel the other twenty people on the edge of their seats. They probably want to cheer for the guy who's disrupting the whole inane process.

"I see that you are passionate, Mr. Houston." Sandy closes my file and moves the stack of folders from her lap onto the table next to her. "But there are more appropriate ways to deal—"

"Like what? Sit around in a fucking circle and listen to more bullshit?"

That sour face reappears. "Watch your mouth in the circle, please."

"Why?" The tension in the room is almost as intense as it is within me. Something needs to break, something's gotta break, but I'm not sure what that something is.

Then I realize it's me, and how I can't hold back. My voice is high and my mouth is spewing uncontrollable emotion. "I want to quit this shit! I don't care any more, don't you see? I don't care about your files or your checked boxes or saying what you want me to say. I just want to stop hurting people and feeling like shit. Doesn't that mean something?"

Sandy is pissed. "It might, if you weren't screaming."

"Fuck you," I can feel the tears welling up, the lump in my throat, "I'm here for help. Just like the guy you hauled out on a stretcher the other day." What about that poor bastard? Can't anyone see that he matters, goddamn it?

"That's quite enough, Kyle." Sandy stands and turns to leave, her stack of files now tucked neatly beneath her arm.

"I'll tell you when it's enough, Sandy. And we ain't even close."

"Calm down."

"You're supposed to help!"

"I do." Her face is calm, and I wonder if maybe she does have some answers I need.

"Then help me," I scream. "I want my fucking life back!"

I have flashbacks of my mother rocking me to sleep as a child, my father teaching me to play baseball, and I want to hug them both and tell them it's not too late, that I found the will to change because love is stronger than addiction right now. I want to fix it all because it feels like there is time, still so much time to become the man they knew I could be. I'm ready to get clean, to quit.

Without turning around, Sandy says, "I'll give my recommendations to the staff and we'll figure out what to do with you."

"Good! Maybe next time we can talk about it in the fucking circle." But I know I'm fucked. These counselors don't get talked to this way, from the heart, from the pain. I'm sure they have some bullshit box they check for assholes like me, but what do I do? With everyone telling me my life matters, maybe I need someone to prove it. Just a little. Because I don't feel it and I don't believe it. And as Sandy walks out, I want to kick something, I want to scream at her and tell her that she would act exactly like me if she had this itch, this confusion, and most of all, this guilt that grows louder each day I am without my drug.

But in *this* circle, I'm on my own.

7

"I TRIED EVERYTHING I could," Darius assures me. "Sandy is adamant that you were violent."

It's just after lunch and Darius, the one counselor who—up until this moment—I believed had a backbone, is now standing in the doorway to my room, shifting from one foot to the other.

I shove my stuff into my bag. "Did you tell them I had a..." I catch myself because it sounds so clinical in my head.

"What?"

"A breakthrough." There, I said it. What's it matter now?

"Look, Kyle, I don't like this decision. Between you and me, I think it's wrong."

"So, don't do it." I want him to make it better because I'm in this precarious place and we both know if they kick me out, I'm going right back to that white powder in those little Ziplock baggies.

"It's out of my hands."

I believe him. Darius is a genuine guy. Although we weren't allowed to discuss his past, I can tell he has some scars. He's one of the good guys, a true convert who understands the consequences of turning me away. He's compassionate and tough and someone I could have admired if our paths had crossed at a different time.

"I'm sorry," he tells me.

"I know."

"This can be a powerful moment in your life, Kyle. You get to decide how this plays out."

"I know."

"You can turn it around, find a good chapter, live a happy life."

"I know."

"Or you can continue down the path you were on and end up in a morgue."

I say nothing.

And I wonder if Darius is supposed to give me a rah-rah speech before he shows me the door. Did the sweaty, convulsing, alcoholic guy get the same speech in his past? Did he believe it? Did he do a damned thing that brought him closer to that happy life? I just wonder where that poor son of a bitch is right now.

Darius and I shake hands and I know this will be the last time I ever see this man. I wonder if maybe I failed here. Maybe I should have put more effort into the program for the sake of my mother, I don't know. All I can tell you with complete certainty is not much has changed. I still hate addicts, still hate recovery, still hate groups, still hate clichés. I still hate these counselors, with their ridiculous phrases and their condescending ways. I hate them all. Every fucking one of these unoriginal bastards. But the only thing that seems to matter, as I continue shoving clothes inside my bag, is the uneasy fact that this will be the last time I ever see Darius again.

Later in the day, as my mother and I drive through the winding landscape of the southern Missouri foothills, I think about the events of the last three days. I think of the words of Darius and my whatever you call it—breakthrough, I guess. What would thirty days have been like with those people? What would I have been like on the other side? And for a brief moment, I consider feeling remorse for my outburst.

But I'm mad at those sons of bitches, shocked by the lack of compassion from kindred spirits who have actually walked a mile in my shoes. They know what happens with lost souls if you send them away. And now I'm...what? Discarded by the very people who are obligated to give a shit? Congrats, Sandy. I'm triggered. Back to this familiar sadness that reminds me how we got here in the first place. Lucky for me, I don't care, not really. A weaker person might feel rejected or unimportant or not worth the time, but not me.

Because I am reminded of how unnecessary feelings really are when you can manufacture methamphetamine. Suddenly, without warning, it's all better.

I'm excited and trying to look contrite for my mother, but inside, I'm anxious and ready. I'm on my way back to a world that will help me find my last burn, my last hit, my last three-day binge. Because it will be different this time, under control, willful after all. Just a few more hours and the answers will be circulating back through my bloodstream.

But as we meander down the road, trying to sing the songs that are on the radio, taking in how green everything is around us, how impossibly green it is in springtime, I know there's a good chance that I'm going to understand the fate of that alcoholic man better than I ever wanted to.

I look over at my mother and wish I could just say what I'm thinking. *I'm so sorry, Mom. It would have been so much easier if you could have just given up on me.*

8

WHAT IF I said that addicts don't just abandon their dreams? What if I claimed that us gaunt skeletal shadows of human beings with bloodshot eyes and stolen dignity really were just hopeless romantics who believed in the same future as anyone else? Would you believe it or think I was full of shit?

Well, it's true. We still believe we'll fall in love, get married and have children, and live in the house on the corner with the white picket fence that we mend every few years. We still see a world where we finish college and start our careers of a lifetime and maybe even rule the world. We cling to all those dreams we've put on a shelf because our talents, our opportunities, our luck are all waiting for us to pick them right back up tomorrow.

Tomorrow: the most common word in an addict's vocabulary. It's the comfort in our hearts, the redemption in our path, the promise in our future. More than a moment in time and space: its an emotion that we touch, that we hold.

Because tomorrow, we'll kick this habit. We'll quit for good. We'll pick ourselves up, dust off our boots, and start getting fucking real.

But the problem with all of this is that tomorrow never comes. And while we're too busy chasing the high, we burn through a vast sea of precious tomorrows to the point where two months becomes two years, two years become five, and so on and so on until we wake up one day and we've been clutching to these plans for "tomorrow" for the past twenty years. Those are all the lies that the drug sells you in that warm and cozy oasis called "tomorrow".

The echo in the addict's mind.

9

I'VE BEEN OUT of rehab for all of twelve hours, and all day I've struggled to ignore my conscience, trying everything to distract my thoughts. Like I'm dealing with two sides of me, both equally clear and nagging and difficult to ignore. On one side is better judgement that illuminates the path to my inevitable demise if I concede to the drugs will; and on the other side is my affliction that promises I won't give a shit once I get there.

And I know it is futile, and I know it runs deep; I am angry with the counselors for not valuing my life and for kicking me out just as I danced on the edge of new feelings, new thoughts. Now, far from the sterile halls of that rehab, my body screams for the drug. My soul whispers, "No, don't do it!" but my heart is broken and my spirit weak because every part of me knows that 'No' isn't an option.

'No', at this point, is nothing but a philosophical construct that only makes the truth more painful.

I pull up next to Kitty's car just as she parks in front of her house. She's always been some weird liaison between the users who parachute in and out of the drug world for a weekend and the committed bastards who ain't never getting out.

"Look at you," Kitty says, eyeing me out of her open driver side window. "You clean up nice."

"I've been away for a while, I guess," I say and realize I haven't seen her since before the fire. "So glad I found you."

"Yeah. Found me." She stares at her hands, interlaced above the steering wheel, for a few seconds, before cutting her gaze to me. "Where have you been?"

"Figuring shit out."

She scoffs. "How's that working out for you?"

"Fuck it. I don't know. I'm here." I put my car in park and light two cigarettes. I offer her one.

"Don't worry, sugar." She takes the Marlboro, draws deeply, and lets out a ring of smoke. "Everybody comes back in the end."

"Don't say that to me." I jerk away from the window, take a long drag off the cigarette, and fidget with the rearview mirror.

"Hey, honey, I just meant—"

"Just don't say it." My words are sharp and her lips clamp in a tight line.

The sound of the engines hum and tick as we idle in the middle of Kitty's street. I avert my gaze to the floorboard and notice my shoes: they are clean and current and too new to be on this street. Too clean, too new if I want to blend in.

"Who's got shit?" The question hangs between us—a clear division of which fork in the road I chose. Fuck rehab and all their happy bullshit clichés. I guess.

"I…I'm not supposed to—"

I give her a smile, a reminder of times past. "Kitty, it's me."

"They think you're a cop."

"Fuck you. Everybody thinks everybody's a cop."

"These guys are not the same ones you know. I mean, you've been gone, and no one knows where and…" She shrugs.

"Everybody's different. Do you know how many times I've heard this shit? You know I'm not a cop."

She thinks for a moment. "Come in. Let me make you something to eat."

"I don't need food, Kitty." I hit the cigarette hard and fast; it is hot and moist. I flick it out into the street. "You know what I'm here for."

"I have some of that, too." She smiles.

And instantly, I am different. The funny thing is, it's not an act. In that instant, I like her more; in that instant, I care about her more; in that instant, the minute I hear she has some speed, I want nothing but the best for her. It all feels real and has no boundaries, but the truth is we would cut each other's throats in that same instant if we thought one of us was holding out.

The schizophrenic law of attraction between addicts—complex in its nature but easy to predict.

"Holy shit, Kitty, why are we sitting out here?" Trying not to act too excited but suddenly I'm alive and confused and I'm not sure I give a shit how I'm acting. She knows what it's like. "Let's go to your bedroom."

"Oh, I hear you, Casanova." The joke falls flat because both of us know we're not going to her bedroom to have sex. "Just don't park on my street. Pull around back." Then she smiles. "You'll like this shit. It's wet, but it's got legs."

"We'll see," I tell her. "You know I can make better."

"Fuck you, Kyle. I heard about your fire."

"That's what I love about this town. Nobody minds their own fucking business."

She opens her mouth to speak, but pauses and stops herself. Instead, she smiles and repeats, "Just pull around back."

As I pull into the alley, I think of the talk I had with Darius and how he seemed so caring and compassionate as he sent me on my way with no defense, no real tools. And it seems like months ago since I left, although it has been less than twenty-four hours. It seems like months since that lost and broken man collapsed in the lobby.

Everyone comes back in the end.

Why did Kitty's words make me feel so uneasy? Why were they so hard to hear? I think of the alcoholic and how all the stories and places and people intertwine and seem prophetic. I feel anxious and hurried, and when I step out of the car, my foot sinks into a puddle.

And I think of the girl in Chicago again. I am here, in Independence, Missouri, dogs on both sides barking, one of my clean, too-new tennis shoes is now covered in dripping mud, but for whatever reason, she enters my mind. Maybe it's because if she were here, I'd have my reason to never walk into this house and my shoe would never be dirtied. Maybe. If she were here, I might break down into tears and swear I was sorry and she would forgive me as we turned around and went back to our lives, before the fire, before the foreclosure, before any of these people knew my name. And I would never think about meth again and I would never wage losing battles against my own conscience and I would never have to question why I am so weak or where I have hidden any of my better judgment or why I can't say no to this insidious white powder.

Maybe.

The thought of her flits away like dust, a flickering memory of someone who knew a different version of Kyle Houston. A person who is as unreal as the thought of that different version of me. And what is real is the mud on my shoe, the incessant pangs of my conscience, and the thing inside this house that will make it all go away.

I scurry across the yard and up a small flight of stairs with a wobbly railing. The door is cracked open and I know it's for me, so I walk in. I wipe my shoe on a threadbare mat so thin the word "welcome" is a blur of swoops and head for Kitty's bedroom. The house is empty, and dark, and quiet, and I am electric and nervous and in a rush.

When I walk into the bedroom, Kitty says, "Your shoe, it's dirty."

And I casually reply, "Whatever."

Her room is a dim, tangled mess of sheets and clothes, with a scarf draped over the lamp, making everything glow with an eerie shade of purple. She's sitting cross-legged on the bed, her eyes wider in the low light. "The dope, Kitty," I say, a little more aggressively than I mean to.

"Hang in there," she tells me as she reaches under the bed for a tray.

Why the fuck wasn't she ready? She knew I was coming. Her hands seem to move in slow motion. "Where's your shit?"

"Where are your damn manners?" She shoots me a glare, then tosses me a sandwich bag of pristine, white, glass-like powder; probably a couple of ounces. "This ought to shut you up."

I have already stopped listening to her. The room disappears from view and Kitty becomes an afterthought while my heart hammers in my chest and my brain begins to salivate. I hold the bag into the light. It is beautiful and quietly demanding as I feel the weight in my hands. I see the flakes and the sparkle and feel the grip around my throat the longer I hold it.

"Here, load this," Kitty hands me a pipe. "It's never been used."

I bury the pipe deep into the Ziploc bag and pull it out. Full. I grab my lighter, then hold it just beneath the Pyrex tube. The flame glows beneath the glass bulb, turning powder into liquid.

"Kitty," I say, still staring into the pipe. "Don't let me stay here forever?"

"Sweetie, that's up to you."

"Just promise me. Two, maybe three days max." I pull the flame away and twist the pipe back and forth.

She's laying across the bed, her voice soft and dreamy. "Where did you say you'd been again?"

"Just one last time," I say, more to myself than her.

I stare at the perfectly round glass bulb as I teeter the clear yellow liquid back and forth across the bottom of the pipe. I bring it to my lips, then inhale, the burning cloud chasing down my throat, into my lungs, and when I exhale, the room is filled with thick, white clouds and oversized pupils.

Home. I am finally fucking home.

"Good shit," I affirm and swallow hard and swallow often as I sit there and feel everything inside me change. The guilt, the shame, the struggle—all gone as the smoke dissipates and absorbs into the ceiling.

I think of Darius for a moment and what he told me just before I left rehab. He said, "Turn it around. Live a happy life. You get to decide," but he had to have known better. I'm not the one in control of my decisions.

And as I look down at my right shoe, the white now imbued with the dirt and grime of this place, I see it all as a metaphor. It doesn't matter how clean you are when you arrive; because if you stay here long enough, you'll get dirty. And the stains you pick up always seem harmless in the beginning, but eventually they become impossible to wash away.

How could you do this to me, Darius? How dare you be kind? You know the injustice of kind words better than anybody. Because when kind words are spoken to an addict at the wrong time, those words ricochet inside the guilt like a bullet in a steel chamber and become the very reason we *have* to use so much more. *So how could you so irresponsibly leave those words with me on my way out, knowing I was just like you?*

Knowing damn good and well that everyone comes back in the end.

10

I DON'T ADVOCATE the use of a deceptive drug that clearly steals lives from decent people but I can see how someone might think I do. I mean, how in the hell can I break my mother's heart, agonize over why I can't quit, compromise so many things about who I am, and still not be able to just walk away? How does a rational adult like me become part of the zombie herd with rotting teeth and horrible looking skin, who pick at their arms and waste away day by day, yet still have this sick codependent love affair with meth?

Don't mistake the hideous physical image of a tweaker with what's going on inside that magical interior world full of light and positivity and euphoria. In a fucked-up way, I guess I could say the shit's kind of spiritual. At first. But to all the people looking from the outside in, explaining what meth is like is easier to do by explaining what it isn't like.

Imagine the most broken piece of your existence. Don't worry about how it broke, just think about the unyielding negative emotion that comes from being broken. Imagine shame or grief or sorrow to a depth that drives destructive behavior, or stress that doesn't allow you to sleep. Or better yet, imagine the pit in your stomach and lack of energy you experience because you walked in on a spouse or a lover who is cheating on you. Try to imagine the pain and agony of all the years it takes to get over that. Any negative emotion you can think of—abandonment, insecurity, even hopelessness.

Now, what if I said that not only is using meth the complete opposite of experiencing any of these emotions, it will instantly cure what ails ya', a hundred percent. Abandoned by your father at a young age? Check. Convinced nobody could ever like you? Check. Best friend just hung himself in the threshold of a doorway in a Kansas City apartment? Check. No matter how deep, how long, or how much a part of you these emotions truly are, they instantly dissolve; and poof, you're shining like a diamond in a goat's ass again.

And for those of us with the loudest internal voices, meth not only puts a sock in it, but it also graciously replaces the negativity with courage, hope, and the belief you can literally do anything. Meth creates a beautiful reality of personal power and ability, so that whatever you have been putting off not only *can* be done tomorrow, it *will* be done tomorrow. The problem is there's that fucking word "tomorrow" again.

Think about all the reasons why people drink alcohol or spend a month's salary shopping at the mall or shove fistfuls of chocolate in their face to change their state of mind. Meth is no different. Well, except for the mystical powers, the disregard for your appearance, and the proverbial headlock it puts around your neck. With a slight shift in perspective, we start to see why intelligent people get addicted. The psychology of methamphetamine use is such a circular trap that the idea of quitting is an impossible concept, even for people who were raised to know better.

Ask anyone—if they could erase guilt simply by sprinkling magic dust on it, would they try meth? Of course not, at least that's what the people driving SUVs in the suburbs or the promising college graduates or the teenage football stars tell themselves. But what if their best friends show up and proclaim, "You've got to try this!" And what if they do try it, just once (at least that's what they tell themselves), and positive things came from that moment? What if even the pain of a friend's suicide could be set aside by spending a week locked inside your house snorting lines?

I did. And it worked. The problem is that pain and suffering are nature's worst predators. Before you know it, your guilt expands. Suddenly you're hiding from your mother's voice, or your baby boys' tears, or the girl you abandoned in Chicago. And you have no idea how it ever got this far; you just know you can't run out of dope, so you do more. And more. And more.

And the wheels on the bus go 'round and 'round.

11

JUMPING BACK IN is surprisingly easy to do. One hit smoothly transitions into a three-day bender; the three-day bender quickly morphs into three months of cycling dealers in and out of small caravans of familiar faces. Anyone who has the strength to stiff-arm their conscience, like some animated Heisman trophy, just one more time, will always find themselves sucked right back in exactly where they left off. It's how the machine is built.

Unless you're me. Because I cook the dope.

Me? I possess the keys to some lost kingdom, so I'll always get to come back in, but it's never where I left off. These people need me where they need me, position me where I can be leveraged, and used, and molded. They do what anyone would do if they had the affliction.

Time is not linear here. It's more like a wormhole puncturing through the universe. On one side, I was cordial and healthy, with new shoes and color in my face; and on the other, I am forty pounds lighter with new connections in every corridor of the unlit underground. On this side of the wormhole, I am instantly notorious; I am instantly the source. Like fire to the Neanderthals, I carry the torch and they all bow down. And as long as it stays lit, I am their King.

So, in a short amount of time, I am set up inside a distorted Play-Doh™ factory, where we all shovel chemicals and sex and felonies through plastic shapes and what comes out is addiction—the purity, the defeat… the impossible shape of addiction. Everyone contributes something in this world and we are all predictable and self-centered, lying about everything to everybody. Including ourselves.

In the eyes of the law, I am the supply chain. I create a drug that feeds an addiction that then perpetuates crime in every way. When affliction takes over, that's when liquor stores get robbed, that's when people get shot, that's when the good people of the world are introduced to breaking and entering. And that's my fault now.

In the eyes of the law, at least.

What people don't understand, viewing from the outside in, is that it's not a pyramid in my world, it's a circle—no beginning, no end. And this never-ending cycle and the economics in this world where they interchange faces and names of cooks like marquees on a billboard was established far before I ever arrived. It's the addicts who perpetuate cooks. Not the other way around. Like some twisted version of *The Farmer in the Dell*, the cooking and the using never stops. The supply and demand keeps in time with the rhythm of the hunger, the pulse of the addiction; and if it ever slows down, the addicts will find another cook, create a new supply, and do what it takes to always keep the music playing.

Which came first: the chicken or the egg? Both, I suppose. Because without me, the cook, none of this is possible in the eyes of the law. Yeah, right.

My conclusion: The only thing it takes to transform people into bloodthirsty instruments of evil who gladly perpetuate the deterioration of another man's soul is a firm belief that their mere survival depends on it. And if killing the boy inside me is what they are doing, then I am certainly returning the favor.

And now I'm obsessed with bigger and better, and I'm sure I'm insane based solely on my unflappable belief that if I can have that one last burn of an undetermined size, one last burn at an undetermined time, it will be enough to satisfy me for the rest of my life.

Then, I'll quit. Then, I'll break free. And life will pick right back up where I left off.

Tomorrow.

Whatever happened to just wanting to stay high?

12

"ARE YOU SURE we are safe?" Josh nervously runs his hand through his hair, making it stick up and out. His eyes are wide and he's shifting from foot to foot.

"As safe as we ever are." I concentrate on stirring the mixture of methanol and ground-up diet pills inside an oversize glass jar.

"I don't like it, man," he continues. "Right smack dab in the middle of the hood."

"Goddamn it, Josh, nobody can tell we're here," I tell him for what feels like the twentieth time. And it's true, even if Josh doesn't believe me.

The warehouse is huge. Three stories high and a few blocks from the police station, with only one way in. It's my new sanctuary, hidden in plain sight; and for the first time I'm a part of a larger network. Anything I want or need is brought to this location through my new acquaintance Nate. I'm still not sure how I met him. I have a lot of "friends" like that now. But I can tell he likes having a cook in his possession, gaining access to quantities of powder and status and respect and the entire array of misinterpreted fringe benefits of never running out. Nate walks taller since I came around, with his head up and chest out. He talks differently, too, but no matter how connected he really is, no matter how long he's been in the meth game, having control of a meth cook is like dating a supermodel—seems like a great idea until you find out how needy they truly are.

The parking garage we pull into is big enough to test the sights on the guns that Nate loves to bring me on a daily basis. And we shoot guns, and we barter our worth, and we cook meth to our heart's content.

But I'm pissed that I have Josh here, another fucking person who "wants to help". Because I can see the future, I can see the felonies that collect in the periphery of this warehouse. Stolen cars, the kind I start with a screwdriver, and the guns and the girls and the thousands of dollars worth of power tools that are nothing more than pictures in a scrapbook because all I do now is cook. But Josh insisted and Nate okayed it, and I told myself I didn't give a shit.

"Just stay on task, Josh. Nobody knows we're here." I glance at the twelve-gauge standing in the corner of the room while Josh paces like a nervous cat.

Normally, this is the fun part—the prep, the pills, the first of two beautiful powders I make before the finished product. But Josh is annoying me and we need to hurry. I ate a quarter gram in a couple of time-release capsules about twenty minutes ago. My hair is starting to crawl, my vision is getting blurry and my patience is nonexistent with this asshole.

"I heard the door open. You know, to the garage," he says, biting his fingernails.

"Probably Nate…Or Nicki."

"What? You gave her the code?" Josh stops and stares at me.

"She can get cases of pills. She got these." I point to our supply.

"She'll take it all or snitch you out, I guarantee it."

"You don't know her, dude."

"*You* don't know her, Kyle. Why give her the code?"

"Because I can, motherfucker!" I stand up and kick a bucket across the room. It echoes against the concrete. "Now wash the dishes. The reason *you* are here."

I remember the first time I met Nicki. It was at a party when people were still in the open about the drugs. No blankets on the windows yet, or hiding in back rooms for days. Just fun and the occasional quarter gram. She was quirky with a boldness that was out of place and she came crashing through the front door. Her makeup was misplaced, her clothes a little too nice, and her arms were full of pizza and CDs. She giggled and said, "Sorry I'm late, I just spent four hours listening to Jane's Addiction and masturbating."

Some people found her funny. Many ignored her. But she was unashamed, she was unapologetic; for lack of better words, she was so Nicki. And I just found her weird and fascinating and memorable.

We didn't have sex that night, although she definitely extended the offer. For reasons I can't remember, I was pissy and I think we both yelled at each other in ways that would hurt most people's feelings, but she is impervious to all that. Nicki is good at two things: sticking to her guns when it comes to a lie, and laughing at herself. Two things I should probably get better at if I'm going to give my life to this drug.

Josh is still pissed, but doing what he's told. I don't care. As long as the shotgun is in the corner and ephedrine is separating in methanol and I know Nicki's on her way, my universe seems right. All day long she's been on my mind. I'm not sure why. There's no mystery to why Josh says what he says, but he doesn't know. The reality is that she's sleeping with all the right people and filling in the missing pieces—the hard-to-get ingredients that would normally take forever to procure. So, that's why I tell myself she is here. But I think of her way too much and it gets harder to deny it and I know what kind of trouble that leads to.

"Hello?" I hear her voice now, calling from the stairwell.

"Holy shit!" Josh whispers.

"Nicki?" I call her name and it seems to echo in the huge building.

"What other self-respecting meth whore would come to this shit hole?" She calls back, then giggles. It's misplaced and I look at Josh and smile. He shakes his head.

"Up here," I yell. "Watch your step."

She climbs the three flights through empty, unlit hallways. And with every step I hear her take, my chest is tight, my breath shallow. Probably from the time capsules releasing into my system, I tell myself. Because that's easier to say.

She breezes in, giggles again, and holds up two bags. "Anybody want McDonalds?"

"Hey, Nicki," Josh says, his tone nicer, calmer, a stark contrast from a few minutes ago.

"What are you two homos up here doing alone?" She looks over at me and winks. She holds my gaze for a long second. "Making meth?"

"I'm not," Josh says. "Kyle just wanted some company."

"Looks like he's got that now," she says, still looking at me, her eyes full of those things that Nicki likes to do, the type of things that make most woman blush. "Hey, Josh, wanna borrow my car?"

"But where would I—"

"Somewhere safe. I don't care where you go." She dangles her keys from one finger, her gaze still on me.

Josh looks at me. I shrug my shoulders. He takes the keys, but hesitates.

Nicki walks over to a bucket, turns it upside down and sits. She unhooks the straps on her shoes, slips them off and rubs her heel. She has long legs, and a curvy body that is as unique as her giggles. "When is this shit going to be done?" she asks. "I've got kids to feed."

"Just getting started," I tell her. I open one of the bags and pop a fry in my mouth. It tastes like cardboard to me, foreign and unwanted.

She giggles again, like a teenage girl, the one she holds onto to remind her life didn't start with this version of Nicki. "Josh," she says firmer this time, "why don't you take my car to Independence. Just hang out at my house, you know? Watch porn, drink beer, and uh, get my kids to school in the morning? I think Kyle and I are going to be here a while."

In another world, putting meth ahead of your kids and pawning them off on a total stranger is wrong. But we are nowhere near that other world. Because in this world, everyone does what it takes to stay close to the source, to never run out. And although I can tell you that mothers should never act like Nicki, for the life of me, I can't remember why.

Nicki jerks to her feet and crosses toward me, her body swaying with each step. She's touching my shoulder now, inviting me closer. We are in a meth lab, with a shotgun in the corner and a cornucopia of felonies scattered throughout the warehouse. We are in a place where souls will decay and lives will be stolen and new addictions beyond using the drugs will be birthed.

And she makes it feel like a teenage sleepover, fun, light, with barely a care in the world. She is good at that, creating alternate universes. The thing that I love, what nobody sees but me.

"Josh," I say, as I close the distance between Nicki and I. Everything else is forgotten. "Why don't you take a couple of eight balls too? Nicki and I can take it from here."

13

IF ANYBODY CALLED Nicki a whore, I'm not the guy who would rescue her honor. Why would I? I mean, how could I? I'm no knight in shining armor and she's no Guinevere. If anyone asks me what I am doing with her, what I am thinking by being there, I won't waste any time explaining. None of that matters. Not the neglect of her kids, or the neglect of mine. Not Josh, not Nate, not anyone else in our lives. Because they've never seen how she looks at me, with her piercing, grey eyes, in the dimly lit room, skin on skin, where words can no longer affect either one of us. We've all abandoned our former selves, every single one of us, and connecting to someone in this environment all boils down to who is going to see your lost and hidden intrinsic value, and who is going to reveal theirs? We cling to what makes us feel good, what makes us feel safe. Opinions and ego have all been rendered to something much, much worse than love, so in a world bent on destroying everything in its path, why not lean into something reckless and wild and alive? When you already know you'd give up anything for drugs, who gives a fuck what you'd give up for love?

And maybe I do love her. For the time we spend together, nursing each other's wounds but making life worse. She is not pretty, she is not kind, she is not loyal—not in the traditional sense —but her affection for me is obvious and deep and we do what we can to ease each other's pain. She becomes a place to hide. A place to forget. A place to rest my head. A place to feed any addiction while I hide in her basement and listen to intimate music, the kind that started Lilith Fair, while candles flicker and burn down to their final moments, and while we whisper in the dark, pretending we are better than the others.

We make love irresponsibly and our passion is heightened by all our needs and our abandonment. She is fragile and soft and feminine, and in those secret moments of escape, she is open.

Our universe is designed to implode, our paths set on destruction. With every character in my story bent on taking, on using, on pretending to care in order to get what they want, I choose to believe she actually adores me for who she imagines I was before all of this.

But it's never clear to me, what is the truth, what is a lie, because she'll use my circumstances and soft heart to her advantage, to maintain a steady supply, yet…I always forgive. It's how she has learned to survive. Still, she finds me behind decay, behind defeat and that's hard to ignore.

And in the end, I decide it's her lies I need the most.

14

I'm five. And I'm a stepson now. I'm not sure what that means exactly except what I've been told. Mommy says things like love and family and it seems to make her smile so I believe in her words because that's what good boys do.

Tom is my new daddy and Mommy tells me he's the one who will protect me, that he will make me feel safe and strong because that's what daddies who love their boys do. And everything is changing so fast but I'm excited for this new life. And I wait to find out what it's like to be loved by a daddy.

I keep on trusting, and believe this promise, running towards it with love and joy and hope that this is where I might fit. A place where I could belong and discover 'normal' with a new daddy who knows how all this is going to work. I run headfirst with a smile into arms that look open but never close around me, never hold on. But I'm learning that big boys don't need to be held. I guess.

I think my new daddy is confused too, and doesn't know how to do what Mommy promises. 'Dad' and 'son' are weird words for both of us. And sometimes when Tom looks at me, I wonder if he only loves me because my Mommy told him he does.

I am so proud in my new suit with a clever little clip-on tie; the tiny, smiling ring bearer. But still, I miss my real daddy, Jerry Sam, and wonder when I'll see him again. When will he hold me on his knee or let me lay my head on his shoulder with the sweet smell of aftershave and cigarettes on his shirt? When can I wrap my arms around him, the strongest man in the world, with my eyes squeezed tight because this time I'm not letting go?

When will he come back? Once he sees that my new daddy and I love each other? Will he come then and tell me I'm important?

I miss Jerry Sam. I love him with all my heart and something hurts deep inside my belly. I try to believe what everyone says, that this new daddy loves me, even though he frightens me and makes me nervous to be the little boy I've always been.

It's not my fault, Tom Daddy. It's not my fault that Jerry Sam was first or that Mommy still talks about him all the time. It's not my fault that I don't have table manners or that it makes your face red when I try to eat and do it all wrong.

It's not my fault that I'm an anxious boy who shouldn't be your problem or that I keep reminding you of the son of a bitch in Mommy's stories.

Mommy pushes so hard to make us fit, to make us a family, but something is wrong with me because I can't get it right. I don't know what I'm doing wrong; I just know I feel like it's all my fault. Now around you, I am always sorry.

And so, I secretly hope that my real daddy comes back around soon. But I don't tell anyone my secret hope. Sometimes, not even myself.

15

THE TWIRLING LIGHTS from the cop car register differently to the driver than they do for me. I can tell because he's yelling, "Shit," and "Motherfucker, I don't want to go back to jail," more to himself than to me. I sit in the passenger seat of a beat-up pickup, and keep looking ahead. On the outside, I'm calm and collected, seemingly trying to figure out the next move, a move I've never been faced with in my life. But on the inside, I'm questioning how in the fuck do you get in this deep. But I am. And I'm here. And I better think fast.

From the rearview mirror, I see the flashes of bright blue coming in fast like some UFO locking in with a tractor beam. I only met the driver a couple hours earlier, and he's pounding the steering wheel and freaking out while I'm contemplating something more existential like fate or destiny or whether anyone could've seen this happening to me.

I mean, the truth is I've only been in this game for a year and I'm already on a two-lane blacktop in a suburb that could be anywhere in the Midwest—they all feel the same to me—with a person I barely know who apparently has done an unknown amount of time, which may or may not explain his dated mullet.

I think of Nicki and the fight we just had, and I wonder if I will have a chance to fix it. I think of my mother and that time when she asked me if I smoked pot. I was fourteen and didn't want her to look stupid defending me all over town if I lied, so I told her the truth and in return she called me 'scum'. I think of the Lutheran pastor who baptized me at seven and how he was caught years later soliciting a male prostitute and the whole town thought, "Oh yeah, I guess we always knew he was gay." And for some reason I think of my football coach who taught me how to dig deep and plow through and win.

How surprised would they all be to hear about this episode of my life? Or would the whole town just say, "Oh yeah, I guess I always knew Kyle was like this."

And what is this? What do you call a guy who travels from town to town setting up meth labs? Out in the fringes of city life, out where the good people live, where children throw baseballs to their fathers and buy tickets to see the Royals. Where the intoxicating scent of the grill washes through the air on the weekends and families drink Anheuser-Busch beer and talk about their love for Jesus. What labels will get bandied around at the police station, or in the truck stops, when people hear that Kyle Houston is in trouble and facing an unknown amount of years in prison? What do I say I am then?

How do I look Tom in the eyes and say, "I'm sorry, Dad?"

What's that? *Why did I keep doing it, Dad? Why didn't I stop after the first fire I started or the first time I went to rehab that lasted for all of three days? Why did I get out after I swore I'd never do it again, after I swore I'd never break Mom's heart again, and meant it all when I said it? You want to know how I live with myself, knowing that this isn't how I was raised or even remotely the path I was meant to travel? Knowing how honorable you are, and how you put yourself last when we lost the family business a couple of years ago. Or how you saved hundreds of jobs but we lost the house, and your retirement, and the memories that were built, but maintained your integrity? Or how many times I created bags and bags of the beautiful crystalline flakes from these household chemicals? I don't know, Dad. I swear, I try to understand. I swear this isn't my decision. I swear I'm in agony. Because I can't say no. And clearly, I should want to say no but I just don't possess whatever it's going to take to stop. I am out of control, pissing away my future and crushing your hearts in the process, still I swear I'm sorry every single fucking time I blow thick, white clouds of euphoria from my lungs.*

Trust me, I can't explain. Not to you, not to mom and for sure not to the cop who is going to have an orgasm once he sees how much shit we have in this truck.

And I think how underqualified I am to be in this situation as the cop chases us down this dark road. Me, a small-town boy who once bailed hay in fields just like the ones surrounding us now. How unlike the boys from Independence or Northeast Kansas City I am. How they would know exactly what to do, probably start shooting out the window and how horrible it would be if someone had to die because of this addiction.

The driver starts to slow down, starts to pull to the side of the road, surrounded by cornfields and barbed wire, but I'm not ready to throw in the towel. That's not the way I'm built. The one thing that I still know about me is that at least I'll go down swinging.

"I thought you didn't want to go back?" I turn around, look into the brightness of the spinning colors behind us, and then face forward to see the darkness ahead.

"I don't."

"Then go," I say, my voice dry and quiet.

"What?" the driver asks.

"Go! Goddamn it! Go! Go! Go!" I scream as I slap the dash.

"What do I do?" he yells, as if I have some handbook.

"Drive fast," I answer and it sounds right so he does, and we accelerate—fifty, sixty-five, eighty—the needle pinning itself against the numbers, the truck shimmying with the effort.

The roads are winding, somewhat dangerous and desolate at two o'clock in the morning. It is hot and the sky is clear with stars like pinholes in the night of the rural back roads. And although we are approaching speeds above a hundred on the straightaways, the flashing lights just inches behind our truck make everything seem like slow motion. Like the Frankenstein scenes in the haunted houses on main street.

"Whose truck is this?" Gauging my next move.

"Mine. It's legal." His eyes are wide, his chest pumping for air.

Shit. I hope he's not too attached to the truck.

The truck's tires squeal as the grip between rubber and road give way around the winding curves of the country blacktop. If there is a silver lining to this moment, it's that we are in the middle of nowhere. Good. Because although I don't know how, I do know I'm getting into one of these cornfields and running as far and as fast as I can until I make it back to Nicki. Even submerged in flashing lights and a high-speed chase, every desire is to get back to her basement and its closed, locked door and the placeholder boyfriend upstairs and the candles flickering and her warm soft body that can't say no. I need her. Who knew? I don't know if this is sudden or has been building for months, or even what you might call it, but it guides me now and I will let it. As if I have a choice.

I have no movie, no book, no memory to refer to while formulating this strategy. I am a boy from a small town where we respect the police, where more than likely we went to school with the officers and they know my mother, my father, and my grandparents by their first names. Therefore, there is no model for me to follow, there is no training, there is no preparation; so I do what anybody would do in this situation—I take inventory of my strengths and weaknesses.

The ground is soft from the rain, the corn is high, I'm wearing flip flops. We're outside city limits, which means the county sheriff will be involved, the driver won't make it far, and I'm in the country…my element. It's early morning, still dark, and nobody's as motivated as I am. And most of all, I'm still a fast son of a bitch on foot.

At least, I better be tonight.

The truck hits the soggy bank in between the highway. The tires spin as we go from high-speed to barely moving. I can hear the mud flinging, feel the truck sliding sideways and without another thought, I pop the door and bail. My first two steps are out of the flip flops and I'm barefoot and running like Carl Lewis out of the blocks, only probably faster and with no finish line. The cop car, determined and angry, hits the median directly behind me. The sound of RPMs and the spinning, wet slap of mud from his tires are so close I can reach back and stiff-arm the grill of the car. It is clear to me this is personal. It is clear to me he doesn't care if he runs me over and kills me. It is clear to me I better be the fastest I have ever been.

Because I grew up with a cornfield in my backyard, I know how much distance there is between the rows of barbed wire. Not in inches, but in body parts, and I'm prepared to make this seamless, I'm prepared to accelerate where my instincts would normally say slow down and therefore, I'm prepared to take on damage. I think.

My strategy remains vague, but the next step is to dive between the first and second row on this barbed wire fence, clear my body and roll into the cornfield. For some reason, I'm reminded of Mike Tyson's famous quote, "Everybody has a plan until they get punched in the mouth," and I now know that the only thing that has been revealed about this strategy is the unavoidable fact that I'm going to get punched in the mouth. I'm going into this as the underdog with nothing but a puncher's chance to win and for some reason I'm finding comfort in at least knowing that.

Now, let's find out who wants it worse—me or the cop.

The plan works but not flawlessly. The barbs catch my shirt, tearing the flesh on my back and the bottom row hooks my trail leg like a marlin on a taut line. My body stops abruptly, without warning, and I face-plant into the soft outer fringes of the cornfield. Air leaves my body in a loud, painful whoosh, and I have no doubt the damage to my shin will hurt much worse when my adrenaline isn't pegged. I stumble to my feet and plow through the field, head down like a fullback churning through the line. Dig deep! Find pay dirt! At this age, at this size, the cornfield is a worthy opponent. Unlike the six-year-old version of me, I no longer fit between the corn stalks. I'm forced to combine my way through this field, clear my own path, as the leaves from the stalks slice tiny lacerations all over my face. The cockleburs intertwine into my hair tightly and the spiderwebs—which are the homes of Garden Spiders, some of the biggest spiders in North America—cling to me and scare the shit out of me but there's no time to give into fear. I swat at my face and pull frantically at the webs and continue running like a bull in a china shop.

Imagining dogs now, like Paul Newman in *Cool Hand Luke*, and in spite of how badly it all hurts, I continue to dig deep and reach the other side of the damned cornfield. Finally, I gather the nerve to stop and listen. I'm not only high but adrenaline is coursing through my veins like rocket fuel, causing hallucinations that manifest like a slideshow. The shadows, the sounds, the phantom images play in my peripheral vision and seem so real. In this world in my head, a pack of hound dogs quietly sniff through the path I made behind me, I can hear gravel ricocheting under slow-moving, covert tires, and any minute a team of snipers, who I hear rustling in the bushes now, will flip on the lights and tell me to come out with my hands up. So I wait, an agonizing, excruciating endless amount of time.

I drop into the small, short stalks on the edge of this new side of the field and army crawl forward to get a closer look. I imagine how I look—muddy, torn, too thin, and trying to hide in a field in the middle of the night. Me, the son of international business owners. Me, jersey number three on the Higginsville football team who made two touchdowns during homecoming against the Lexington Minutemen. Me, that loving child who once waddled the floor of his mom's kitchen repeating the words 'happy, happy, happy' is now desperately hiding from men sent to protect the world from people like me.

I have broken laws in ways I never would have imagined, have broken laws in ways I don't even know, and I'm running from the good guys, knowing that I'm not one of them any longer, with the alarming realization that they would probably kill me or at least beat my ass until I wished I was dead. I know these guys are dads and sons and husbands who go to church and watch the games. These men who chase me would never believe I was once one of them. And they would never believe that I had potential, that I was the star athlete, that I dated the cheerleader, that mothers once liked the idea their daughters were with me. But this cornfield, surrounded by hungry officers that want nothing more than to find me, is a long way away from that letter jacket and that class ring that created my identity not so long ago.

And I want to stand up, wave the white flag and explain that I'm not who they think. I want to walk over with my hands up and tell them they have the wrong guy. Because deep down I'm a good person who made a left turn last year and I can't seem to find my way back to start.

They would never believe that I once went to church every Sunday, never believe I could recite verses with the best of them because of my grandmother, Tina Bacon-Houston, and never believe that I am going to call on the strength of the Lord right now, the mercy of the Father, in Jesus' name, amen, to get out of this shitstorm any way possible. I'm going to pray to Buddha, Mohammed, and the gay preacher who baptized me to lift me up and guide this Hail Mary.

These prayers in the middle of a dark, wet field are my only strategy. The cops have guns, they have the law, and they have strength in numbers.

And out here, right now, I only have God, my motivation to stay out of jail and a burning desire to be with Nicki. And I'll be damned if that's not going to be enough.

Dig deep. Stay focused. Have faith.

I'm growing tired of trying to figure out what's real and what's meth brain. There's no turning back anyway, so I decide to move. If there are snipers lurking in the bushes, if there is a posse of vehicles waiting to hit the spotlights like some 1940s jailbreak, then I'm fucked either way. Gingerly, I stand up. Nothing happens. I step into the middle of the gravel road. Nothing happens. From my new vantage point, I can see them, still on the other side of the cornfield, searching like giant lightsabers sparring through the field. They think I'm still in there. Oh yes, I have faith.

Patrol cars drive up and down the road, the road I have to cross to head to the lake I know is somewhere around here. There is a break between cruisers, a distance of maybe six seconds, and I think I can sprint through this and dive into the bushes without being seen. But what if I can't? Then come the dogs. Then comes the ass-kicking I probably deserve.

My thoughts are like confetti, going in a hundred directions at once. Wait, can they shoot me if I'm unarmed? I mean, one tried to run me over, which could be seen as an accident, but can they get away with shooting me? And does Nicki even know I'm out here? How could she? I wasn't with her. Oh God, I can't screw this up.

The field on the other side of the highway is perfect for an escape, no corn and large, round bales of hay, like tents on the open range. Plenty of places to hide, nothing to impede my running, and I know there is a body of water in that direction. Besides, I'll be halfway through the field before they see me. And if God is truly on my side, they will all be fat and overweight, and not have one super-fit cop who just completed an Ironman.

Dear God, don't give me that guy, because I don't have it in me. I'm already breathing hard, fast. My legs are numb, except for the deep gouges on my shin.

In football, I ran the forty-yard dash in well under five seconds. But because my eyes are blurry, because it seems so far away, I don't know if this is a forty or fifty or sixty-yard dash. I only know I have approximately six seconds. Coach always knew I was quick, which is why I made varsity my sophomore year; it's why he held onto the number three for me, because he was so sure I'd make varsity. Because I had talent, because I had heart and will, and I would practice until I was perfect. Running sprints just like this when I was tired, when most people would give up, was my wheelhouse. I'm so glad Coach can't see me now.

Go!

I run with everything I have in me, terrified I'll trip or be one second too slow. Once on the other side, I'm breathing heavier and my lungs are starving for air. I don't have the stamina to carry on but I'm sure the dogs will be on the way soon, so I need to get to the water.

I was the captain of the wrestling team, set the pace for football practice, and a four-year letterman, but I have never pushed myself harder than this very minute. I run ten yards and dive headfirst into the tall veil of grass. I don't want my head up when the sweeping light swings through this field. Don't sit too long, continue to rinse and repeat, as the lights pace the tempo. And as long as I stay in rhythm with these cops, I'll get over this hill and I'm home free. But where the hell am I? When was the last time I ate?

The lights seem to sweep the field I'm in more often now. Do they know I'm here? Are they toying with me now? Did the driver get away? Or is he on his way back to the very place he never wanted to see again?

Keep moving. I hear the bullhorns now, or maybe I'm making that up, but it's loud and there are dozens of squad cars and I am not fucking qualified to escape from this situation.

I think of Nicki. What is she doing? Who is she with? I think of her, then I run another ten yards and dive. If I get caught, will I see her again? If I go away, would she come see me? Would I want her to? Oh God, don't let our last kiss be over, without my knowledge, without saying goodbye. Don't let our last fight be what we remember of each other because I didn't mean it, I need her to know that. If for no other reason, let me get back to her. *You know, God, how she eases the loss and loneliness, the shame and agony and how I don't understand any of it, but I don't care. You know what's in my heart and maybe it's all codependency, and we all know we are only together because of the drug abuse, but I don't care. I need to be held, I need to be less lonely, I need to be forgiven and I will get none of that if I'm locked away for years.*

Keep moving.

I'm twenty yards from the top of the hill and at least a hundred yards from the road that they continue going up and down. A football field separates me from them; a football field once again allows me to escape my true identity. Even in this moment, in this shape, the irony of a football field being part of my destiny is not lost on me. And although I don't know what's on the other side of this hill, I do know they won't be able to illuminate what I'm doing.

Keep moving.

I'm here now, over the hill. I can walk slowly and focus on direction because the night hides my movement. I see fences, I hear dogs—farm dogs with low, content bellows, and I feel my heartbeat soften a bit, move from my throat to my chest. These are familiar sounds to me—the crickets, the frogs, the sound of God's country at night—as I try to stay away from the duskto-dawn lights spotlighting large farm equipment. I'm safe, although I'm somewhere I don't belong, and I feel like I have an advantage now, especially because I finally see a small lake or pond, I can't tell. If there really are dogs sniffing out my trail this water will prevent them from finding me.

At the banks, I walk into the cool calm water, in toward the middle of the pond for a moment to think. Now that the weight is off my legs and the adrenaline is starting to subside, I feel the scrapes and bruising and swelling on the bottoms of my feet. I am thirsty, I am dry, and I am surrounded by water, so I cup my hands together and take a sip. It tastes so sweet and refreshing and needed, like a gift from God; so, I lower my head and drink until my stomach bloats and cramps.

And I wait.

There is an engine to something running off in the distance, but it seems natural, like it belongs; and at this time of the morning, I'm banking on it being unmanned. Again, I drink. So thankful for this gift, so thankful for the liquid, so thankful to feel so undetectable as I swim like a frog in a pond looking for a place to hide. I am tired, to say the least. I am winding down from the chase and need a place to rest my head as the horizon changes from pitch black to lighter hues. There is a drainpipe large enough for me to sit up in and I'll be able to sleep without a helicopter or a dog or a farmer being able to find me if I crawl in twenty feet or so.

Thank you, God…how in the hell did my prayers transgress to this?

Inside this drainpipe, like the cave of a hibernating bear, I sleep. Off and on, I wake and see the hole that is twenty feet away has turned a new color. First black, then grey, then orange and now blue. The hum of that engine in the background, like a lullaby, helps me sleep soundly and I think I'm safe, I think I've done it, but I still need to get back to Nicki. My movements hurt as I slowly scoot across the floor of the drainpipe toward the exit. My ass is wet and asleep, and I'm already trying to figure out how I can get to a phone looking the way I do. The deputies must still be looking for me and if anyone has ever conjured up the poster child for an all-night cop chase, I'm it.

My jean shorts are torn, basically now just a waistband holding together strips of cloth that attach to the smaller band around my thigh. My torso is bare and bruised and I feel my face has cuts, raised and scabbing. And as I slowly climb out of the drainpipe onto dry, uneven ground, I not only see the gash in my shin now but that my bare feet are swollen and sore and impossible to put my weight on.

Thank God my coach can't see me now.

And it's oddly cold because I'm wet, but the sun is shining and I'm not in jail wondering what she is doing. I see that the mechanical noise that sang me to sleep comes from a machine shack that looks like a miniature house with pumps and pipes with valves on the end. The pipes seem to tunnel under the water and although I'm fuzzy and not well versed in big green pieces of equipment, I'm sure this isn't good. I drank the water, no, I engorged my stomach with this water with a thirst unprecedented in my life and it looks like the punchline is that this is the lagoon of a sewage plant of some sort. Note to self: when running from the cops on a hot summer's morning, thirsty, tired and scared—pray for bottled water.

Because if you simply pray for any old thing to drink, you just might get what you ask for.

The car is quiet; her unspoken judgment is loud. Mom is terrified or disgusted or appalled, I can't tell, but one thing is for certain, she is confused that she had to drive three hours to pick me up from yet another insane situation. My shorts are in shreds, my face lacerated, my body muddied. I look like a savage and I live like a criminal with my head on a swivel, looking in mirrors and back windows for any sign of what chased me, but all that I really care about is Nicki.

Standing on his porch watching us leave, without a glimmer of farewell in his stance, is the farmer who reluctantly let me use his phone after listening to a thick, yet semi-plausible, crock of horseshit about how I had blown a tire miles up the road and was chased by dogs, 'big dogs', into a field where I wasn't so lucky.

"And well, that's why I've got this hitch to my get-along, Sir," I told him trying to be cute. "Even got my shoes."

"Uh-huh," the farmer grumbled as he brought me his phone, "Make it quick, boy. I got dogs, too."

Now, in the car with Mom, she glances sideways at my shirtless, gaunt torso, but she puts the car in gear and I'm thankful for that. I don't mistake the silence for not having anything to say. We both know there is no protocol for something like this. What does a mother say when she gets the call to come pick you up 'before the sheriff finds out where I'm at'?

I know her. She probably concocted every excuse she could think of on the ride here—he's not that bad, he's just a little confused, it's all my fault. And all the memories of rushing me to the doctor with a cracked skull or a broken bone or torn skin never prepared her for this. She's heard me coo, changed my diapers, picked me up from every practice for every sport I've ever played, but there will be no talk of how I snagged a fly ball or broke free for a touchdown or did my first double flip off the high dive at the public pool this time. Because, although this story has far more amazing feats, I will bury it deep inside a hard-to-reach place because, quite honestly, I'm not sure I believe it myself.

"Thank you, Mom, for not asking questions." I say as I sink a little lower in my seat. "Let's get out of here."

She looks at me as if to say something, pauses, and slowly accelerates away from the driveway. As we leave, the farmer turns and goes in his house, his door shutting with a loud thud.

Based on my mother's initial reaction, it's no wonder the man didn't invite me in; I'm just thankful I got to use the phone at all. "I know what you're thinking, how this must look." I break the silence as my mother drives and focuses on the road ahead of us.

Her eyebrows go up. Still no word.

There's definitely no use in lying. This is my mom; she can smell my bullshit a mile away. Always has. Besides, this is the second time in less than—shit, I don't know—four months, five maybe, that she's rescued me from some life-threatening stunt like this. And will there be a day when she no longer comes, a day when she stops rescuing me? I can't bear the thought but realize I'm pushing her too far.

I pause for a moment then say, "I'm in trouble, Mom. A lot of trouble."

"What kind of…trouble?"

"Drugs," I answer.

"No shit," she replies sarcastically.

"Well, drugs and the law." I run a hand through my hair. I'm so fucking tired. "I don't know how to describe it."

"And what do you suppose I do about it?" I hear the edge in her voice. I know what's next. "What do you expect me—"

"Drive," I interrupt and turn to look behind us.

"Where? Who's coming?"

"I told you." I pause to gather my composure so she doesn't see the fear in my eyes. "Over the phone, Mom. The, ah...sheriff's department." I say. The words are clumsy and uncomfortable and seem to float or linger or maybe echo, now that they're in the air.

The curves of the road are sharp as the car winds its way through back roads that are different from the one I crossed in a panic last night.

"Do you have any idea how that sounds? Do you have any idea how you look?"

I sit up now, pull the visor down and open the mirror. My eyes are wide, alert, maniacal. The cuts on my face, now scabbed and bright. I look like I was attacked by cats.

"I can imagine," I say, but that's not true. The truth is I can't see what's wrong, I can't think past Nicki and her messy basement, with trash from fast food littering the hallways and dishes piled up in sinks with orange and brown water stains. I can't put myself in anyone's shoes because my lens is internal, my focus survival.

"Good," she says angrily. "Then you must know that you look like hell, you're wasting away, you're scaring me, and…and…" She's crying now. God, I hate that. But I can't let it affect me. I need to stay on task.

A sheriff's car, headed the opposite way, flies past us as we come around the corner. I think I see the brake lights. I sink further into the seat.

"Mom! What's he doing?"

"Who, damn it?"

"The cop!"

"The what? I don't know." She shakes her head. "This is nuts."

"What's he doing?" My voice is rising now, panicked.

"Nothing! I mean, I don't think he's doing anything. Stop yelling at me, young man."

"We've got to hurry."

"To where? To home, right?"

"To Independence."

"Why?"

I say nothing.

"Why?" she asks louder. She's crying heavily now and I feel like an asshole but what else can I do? I'm jonesing for some shit. Independence is where I belong.

"If you can't, I can call someone to pick me up."

She waves her hand, dismissing the thought, and cries in silence. I check the rear-view window again before sinking lower into the passenger seat. She's my mother, my rock, the vessel of my first nine months and I can't feel any of it anymore. I'm lost, possibly gone, but aware enough to know this is tragic. And I'm scared about the hollowed-out center inside me, and I'm scared about the cop chase, and they both feel like the prelude of something much, much worse.

And I wish it was different—my heart, my life, my feelings in this moment—but I know there's no turning back, there's no bringing her son to the surface. I'm gone, she's here, and if not for anything else other than that, I'm sorry. Because she, like me, doesn't know why she's doing this. Her love isn't logical, not up for debate as she drives her baby boy out of the most surreal experience of her life.

I mean what do you do when you're the loving mother of a meth cook? When you've seen your child's potential, seen what he could become? When at one time, you held this child close and smelled his skin and kissed the soft spot of his head and now you blame yourself for what he has become? What do you do when you love a child who means more to you than air itself, and you want to make excuses, you want to justify it all, but something inside you knows this person is never coming back?

Every time you see him, you die a little yourself. Do you turn your back on him? Do you push him away? What are the rules? What is the equation, the formula, the anecdote? Because when you're that parent you would give your own life; you would stand on the altar and rip your own heart out and offer it to God if he would just spare this precious child.

In this moment, it is maternal intuition that becomes the albatross of a loving mother—protect, shelter, embrace—every instinct a deadfall in a wilderness of what-ifs. And as we drive down the road, in silence, with two different versions of this moment playing out in front of our eyes, I see how this life pulls everyone in. I am her son, the meth cook, and she will never get to be just a mother again.

She is my accomplice now.

16

My mom's burgundy Cadillac looks so out of place pulling into Nicki's driveway. So polished and pristine up against the house with abandoned toys in the front yard and a loosely hung screen door swinging and blankets covering every window. I sit there, looking forward, still wishing I felt worse.

"This is where you live?" she asks.

"Not exactly, Mom."

"But you know these…people, right?"

"Not exactly," I repeat.

She hesitates for a moment, the car running, Tommy James and the Shondells singing *Crimson and Clover* faintly on the radio. A song that would normally connect the dots for her and I. I need to hurry and get high before I think about that too much.

She pivots in her seat and for the first time since we got in the car, she looks at me, really looks at me. "Where does this end, honey? I mean, for you?"

"Not here," I tell her.

"Then when does it end?"

"I don't know, Mom, but not today. I'm sorry, I've got to go." Quickly, I open the door and get out.

"I love you," she tells me, but the words sound like a last-minute attempt to get me to change my mind. We both know I can't do that.

"Please, Mom, not now, okay?" I ask. "I'm sorry. You'll never understand this." And just before I close the door, I stop, all the pain that meth buries starting to surface, my conscience rearing its head.

"Why, baby boy? Why can't I understand?"

And I close the door and walk toward Nicki's house and utter to only myself, "Because I don't."

17

HIS NAME—GET this—is Preston. Quite possible the only Preston in the history of methamphetamine.

The first thing he says is that he thought my biceps would be much bigger, but I don't care what all that means. To him. To me. My arm is bare now, open and exposed as I trust this stranger to know what he's doing. Tacitly we communicate, like primates of a lesser intellect, picking at the fur, submerged within the pack, as he rolls up the soft, red flannel of my shirt, twisting and bunching it just above where the needle will go.

I can't look. My whole life, when I gave blood or got a flu shot, I had to think of something else or squeeze my eyes shut. And down here in this cold, quiet basement with a makeshift lamp casting shadows across the floor, shadows across Preston's face beneath his long, disheveled hair like a witch standing over the cauldron, I sure as shit can't look now.

I can tell he isn't comfortable. He's already told me that after the drug enters like this, you're never the same. And everything inside me knows that's true, but Preston won't say anything else, not another word to change my mind. Because that's not possible. And besides, he knows, and I know, that if he won't puncture my vein for the very first time, I can find a hundred just like him who will.

I've been told about the tickle, like a feather deep within your chest, fluttering in a whispering breeze. It has been described to me, this warm feeling that slowly, deliberately, completely blankets your body from the inside out. And I yearn, and I ache, and I prepare to submit my soul to a feeling I have never had.

I know the needle was what haunted Kurt Cobain. I know the needle was what finally killed Janis Joplin. And I've been warned of the danger, of the depth of evil, of the grip and seduction and of being banished to lonely, dark rooms where there's no turning back. A side of life that no one can teach, a side of life you'd never expect. I somehow sense that it is this that has chased me my entire life, as subtle and committed as death itself. So, to me, a boy who lays prostrate at his master's feet, I know it has to be good.

And what I wrestle with is not what you'd think. It's not this needle, this hunger. But I'm prepared for that to come soon enough. In this moment, the cross I bear is my mother's voice inside my head, screaming, kicking, wailing at me to turn away—but I can't. In this moment, it is worse, more hopeless; I'm standing on the edge of the abyss, melding with the suffering, the darkness, the shame, seeing right from wrong, yet knowing my fate has already been sealed.

I feel the needle against my skin and I hold my breath. The illusion is that I still have a choice.

The agony is this can't happen fast enough.

So, I abandon all judgment and release my conscience because it will no longer serve me as I open up to oblivion. In this moment, as I'm possessed by a singular desire that is stronger than God, something deep within me is crying and afraid and already mourning the loss. Because in this moment, there can be no mystery to what this really is.

The death of my mother's son.

18

RIGHT NOW, AT this point in the game, my favorite place to be is here. With its bare brick walls and the load-bearing pillars that give the building strength and heft and this permanence that doesn't seem to exist anywhere else in my life. Yet another warehouse; three stories overlooking the Avenue, with its loud service elevator and a perimeter of large windows creating a panoramic view of life in this part of the city. The sounds and sights of something alive and busy are so different than the provincial neighborhoods of my upbringing. And I sit on the top floor mixing, extracting, creating the elixir of the addict's soul.

Being in here is impossible to believe—me, completely set up with everything I need to feed the addictions that incubate inside my body. This isn't rehab or my mother's car or some shitty jail. It is the only place that makes sense for a thing like me. Fresh, sharp U-100 disposable needles, cartons of cigarettes that I never purchased, and porno magazines fanned out like a winning hand at a poker table. Lockers in a closet full of a surplus of chemicals now come to me from every angle, from everybody—bikers, junkies and criminals who all seem to know that Kyle Houston is at the top of the food chain now. My fifteen minutes of fame.

And I don't ask for it, but it just keeps coming—the iodine, the phosphorus, the sex, and the infamy. Not even a spun-out meth-head who spends every waking moment clouded by the burden of keeping his machine always turning can overlook that he is wanted by any authority interested in this epidemic.

I don't have the labels for it, but I feel like a fugitive. I live in the shadows. I give my name out less and I deal with a core group of people. I'm smart enough to know that somebody is an informant, probably somebody closest to me, but the irony of it all is that everyone thinks it's me. I'm sure somewhere, on some report, in some case file, there are DEA agents getting a kick out of watching the comedy of this circle.

Unlike my predecessors who built the illusion they made the rules, that they controlled their subjects, I feel incredible pressure to feed the addicts. With great power comes great responsibility, ain't that right, Peter Parker? So, I set my life on a shelf, in a locker, in a meth lab, and feel an unyielding need to please the masses.

This top floor remains unlit—my rules, not anyone else's—as the constant swirl of blue and red from cop cars on the Avenue spin around these brick walls. There are reports on the news of hookers coming up missing and the police are active and alert but looking for someone other than me. What would normally scare any other cook—the sirens and the lights of the men who want to lock you away—brings me solace, brings me peace. Because somewhere out there, in that human cacophony out on the streets, it's somebody's duty to keep order, to enforce the law, just like I do inside my flask.

To the addicts, I am benevolent, I am kind, and I am also so deadly just to be around. I give away far more than I ever sell. So the people who want me now live on one of two sides of the fence. On one side, they build me an altar because I'm generous and caring, because I calm the demand that never subsides. On the other side, they build a case where the end result is a cage for the rest of my life.

The landlord knows what's going on, although we don't share much info. I don't know his name, but for some reason he has confessed to hiding a dead body—one that was crammed into a refrigerator by his dad and sent to a salvage yard when he was a kid. A real father-son moment of his youth. This man has demons. Another story, for another time.

And it's clear that I can't be here when the sun comes up, like the vampire I have become. By night, it is silent up here, full of dust and concrete and these huge out of place half-pipes and ramps like some ghost town skatepark. But when the sun comes up, I have to respect that young boys with skateboards will be all over this floor, and they're curious, and they're innocent—well, at least as innocent as one can be growing up in Northeast Kansas City.

And it doesn't make sense, how I feel so safe, so alone, so untouchable with the noise outside and a killer in here. I wonder why I don't question things more.

But right now, at this point in the game, my favorite place to be is here.

19

For months, I've been putting needles into my veins; well, I guess technically having someone else put a needle into my vein. Whatever. I still can't do it myself, but who gives a shit, there's always someone willing to administer the 'medicine' in exchange for a hit of their own.

The first time I convinced someone to shoot an entire 50ccs into my arm, for a moment, I couldn't catch my breath. I remember the heat and the alkaline taste in my mouth as the meth surged through my body. The only warning of what was coming was this unexplainable cough—a single cough, almost like clearing my throat but still a cough, rising from within to warn me to brace myself because this might be the one that kills me.

I'm not sure what's worse, almost dying because of my insatiable addiction or the utter disappointment of knowing that meth might not be enough to kill me.

And this is my new way now. The way I try to tell myself I don't need, but it's faster, better, more…I don't know, consuming than smoking will ever be. Because the closer I get to feeling like I'm going to blow up, the more my skin burns red, the louder I actually hear my pounding pulse, the higher my high becomes.

Yeah, in a short amount of time, I've graduated to doing shots that felt like they were going to kill me. Yet, here I am, jonesing and not able to get the next one in fast enough.

Right now, all I want is to feel that rush again. The cough. The warmth. The shortness of breath. The spinning wave of euphoria while I bury my head in my hands and ride it out. But who's going to hit my arm this time? It's just me and Carter in this shitty hotel room, and every time I glance at my own veins, I get weirded out at the thought of injecting myself.

"Carter, do me a favor," I say, the room dim as the TV flashes across the walls.

"What's that?" he asks. He barely lifts his gaze from whatever music video he's watching on MTV, VH1, I don't know.

I pick up the clear tube, with the orange plunger at one end and the silver line to my veins at the other. "I don't like needles, man," I say. "Scared shitless of them."

He looks at me, then at the needle in my hand as if to say, *what's that got to do with me?* "Hold up. You hang out at Ruby's. Who the fuck you kidding? You've been using needles for a while, dude."

I shake my head. "They did it for me." It's like admitting I can't take a piss without someone pulling down my zipper.

He starts to laugh, then realizes that I'm not joking. "No shit?"

The room is a mess. Not sure how long Carter has been renting 312, but it's clear he hasn't been letting housecleaning come in. A couple day's worth of carryout clutter the top of the TV, more of it litters the dresser and the table by the window. Clothes are strewn across the floor like a maniac roared through and tried on everything, and by everything, I mean countless black shirts emblazoned with the Harley Davidson logo. Carter has a style, and its biker, although he doesn't even own a fucking Harley.

He shakes his head and laughs, just a little. Who gives a shit what he thinks? I can't put a needle in my own arm, so sue me. I have this fear; no, a phobia of the damn things, and his opinion as to whether I'm man enough to jab at my veins with a pointy metal tube is no consideration of mine.

It's one thing to roll up your sleeve and turn your head while someone else does the dirty work, knowing that once it's all pushed into the bloodstream you won't have to think about what that liquid is doing to your mother's son or picture the haunting image of one of your own future children someday doing the same thing. You don't have to think about it because you didn't see it happen, and all you have to do is feel a pinch, wait for the cough, and ride it out.

There have been people who've refused to push the plunger because they thought the dose might kill me, but they quickly realized that I made the drugs therefore I made the rules, motherfuckers. They'd tap my vein, slide the silver tip into the bulging greenish track, and mutter comments that only registered as background noise. Sometimes I could hear their voices floating somewhere else, in the clouds or another room or another dimension. *Are you going to be okay? Is he going to be okay?*

Yeah, I wanted to say, "*I'll be okay as long as you keep putting this needle where it's meant to go.*"

"I need you to do it," I explain to Carter, who's still staring at me like I'm a stranger. There is an awkward silence for what seems like minutes. "I know it sounds goofy, but I can't do it myself."

"I don't know," he finally says. "I guess I could. I've watched Blake do it hundreds of times." Then he shakes his head and quickly changes his mind. "Can't do it, man. You're on your own."

"No fucking way." His eyes go back to the TV screen. Rob Thomas is singing about how he wants to push someone around. "Come on, Carter. Don't be a prick."

He looks pissy, but the derogatory word barely bothers him. "Then why even do it that way? Like, go back to smoking or something."

I stare at him as if to say *do you really have to ask that question*? I mean, he's seen how this shakes out. The needle touches us deeper than the pipe. In a place that never sees shame or guilt. In a place we wouldn't know existed any other way.

"I hope you never find out, Carter." I reach into the inside pocket of my leather jacket. The cracking of the leather makes me sound like a cowboy in a saloon. I pull out a large Ziplock bag—the batch is fresh, not even hours old, and this is my first stop. I toss it on the table. It's at least a half-pound. Carter looks like a lion who had a fresh gazelle dropped in front of him. I can see him practically salivate.

"Let's cut the bullshit, Carter. I want to get high."

He bites at his fingernail, his eyes fixed on the fresh white powder. "I'll push the plunger," he tells me, "but you have to hit the vein."

Now why'd he go and do that, actually use the word *vein*? Hearing the real, clinical term for where that needle is going just makes it weird for me now. I know I shouldn't be puncturing something as critical as a canal directing blood to various parts of my anatomy. That's reserved for certified professionals, right? Not a couple of idiots with a habit and a fat sack of fresh dope. Nevertheless, I'm perfectly willing to let Carter, a guy I barely fucking know, mess with the bloodstream that powers everything inside me.

I can't shake the foreboding sensation that I'm doing something that feels, I don't know, unauthorized. Something I for damn sure know you're not supposed to be doing in some dark and seedy hotel bathroom. But there's no stopping us now.

"Okay, so I think you should know that I've never done it," Carter tells me, "but don't worry, I'll know if we hit it or not. I'll see the blood swirling before I push the plunger."

The idea of me being okay with someone who has no idea what he's doing coaching me on how to stab a sharp point into my skin, into my vein, is the single, most telling experience of this entire addiction. Even now, as I sit in this disheveled hotel room, asking—no, *negotiating* with—a tweaker to assist me with life-stealing, intravenous drug use, I am fully aware this is that distinct point of no return. I may be an addict but I'm not blind, I'm not stupid. I know that once I have reached that 'whatever it takes' level, there will be no monitor, no gatekeeper, nothing to prevent me from doing it whenever I please. And if sound logic and fear isn't enough to keep a grown man somewhat contained, then the gate is officially open—the bull's out and nothing but the clowns can save me now.

And your guess is as good as mine as to where this ends.

Carter stares at my arms, then takes a deep breath. "We've got this, homie."

"Okay," I hear myself say, rubbing sweat from the palms of my hands. "What's the worst that can happen?" Knowing that the worst that can happen is we actually pull this off. "I think I'm ready."

"Cool," Carter says. "Care if I take a couple hits off this pipe first?"

For a split second, I question whether I care if he's getting spun out before we do this, then dismiss it because I understand. All I care about, as I anxiously stare at the tiny silver tip of this needle, is if I have the guts to stick it in my vein. Carter smokes, then holds the needle while I tie a belt above my arm until my abused and tired veins pop. His hands shake now as he hands it back and I press the tip gently against my rubbery skin. I tell myself it's just material, like a wetsuit, or a patchwork quilt, or the crochet I used to do with my grandmother when I was young, and I hold my breath and I push and I wait.

Carter pulls the plunger as a swirl of crimson-red shoots up into the barrel. Just before he pushes the plunger back down, a fit of survival instinct hits me. Suddenly I'm questioning whether this was going to be it, my destiny, dying in a tweaker's room…or worse, surrounded by people who would clearly abandon my dead body in a rusted-out Toyota in the middle of a white trash salvage yard.

The meth enters me like a slow-burning fuse. Meandering through the trap doors and mechanical levers under my skin. It bottlenecks somewhere in my forearm and it burns. I can almost point to where it is in my veins. And then, like the breaking levy of a dam, it all bursts forth with the unstoppable power of nature and the mercy of a hired assassin. It rushes through my arm—part of me excited, part of me scared at this sudden tidal wave—and I think, *this is too big*. My palate isn't ready for this, the notes of Coleman fuel, the hints of phosphorus that coat my tongue with the mixed taste of diesel and adrenaline. As it empties into my chest, it ignites the cough and I catch myself praying that my heart can handle this one, but then realize I don't really give a shit either way.

Abruptly, I stand and gasp for air, panicked and furious; I brace myself to suffocate with my hand over my heart. It burns in my head, my bowels, now my legs. Then I feel the shift, the mercy, as the panic subsides. The drug is anchoring in, acclimating to the host. My interior life, like cotton candy spider webbing around my mind. Everything fuzzy and light and euphoric. Everything perfect and protected and doable as the shot washes the guilt from my mind.

I am invincible now, suddenly able to fix my life; if I could just pull my head up from my hands, I would do it, too. This is the lie the drug sells me every time. Now that I know I'm going to live, I no longer care how bad I've become because there's still tomorrow.

Always tomorrow.

20

I'm six now and it's happening again. He's towering over me with his red face, his pulsing temples and the faint scent of beer on his breath coming through his nostrils. He's calling me a liar. None of this makes sense to me. He's the only person who has ever said those words, at least the only adult. The only someone who matters.

I know I'm a big boy now and big boys don't cry, but the tears are making it hard for me to keep my eyes open. I'm confused, almost convinced that I lied when only moments before I was sure I was telling the truth, that I could explain what happened, but now I'm so afraid that if I don't admit to this lie I haven't told, it's all going to get worse.

As he squeezes my frail little-boy arm, his hand trembles beneath his skin, like electricity inside his blood. I can feel how deep this is running through his body, I can feel how uncontrollable it is for him. Like a big, scary dog on a chain when the mailman is coming.

"Admit it. You did it. You left the door open," Tom demands after moments of listening to me stutter while crying, cowering.

"But I didn't go down—"

"Goddamn it, boy! Who else could have done it?" His fingers of one hand digging deep into the back of my thin tiny arms while the index finger of his other hand pokes hard, deliberately, into my chest, making it feel elastic, almost spongy.

"I–I can't remember," I try to explain.

"That sounds like you," he tells me and sighs that long, disapproving sigh I have heard so many times. Everything is about blame—I'm being blamed for the door, blamed for crying too long or too loud, and I know I will be blamed for the fight between him and my mother when she finds out.

It is summertime in our new house on Lipper Street—a large gray house on a huge corner lot that overlooks a picturesque park. Trees and tennis courts and oversized swings decorate the landscape outside my front window. I am a lucky kid, afforded so many great things but this is the 70s, and people discipline their children in public. And it is times like these when the spacious and beautiful park could quickly become a front row seat to my 'upbringing'.

I wipe my eyes and cheeks with the palm of my hand, vaguely aware of what the children are doing across the street. I'm still confused but believe this one is over, thankful it is easy this time. And I wonder what my real father is like, the man my mother says 'never paid child support but always had horses'. And I wonder if those are the only choices little boys get—either a dad who pays no attention or a dad who's angry because he has to pay attention.

Is that the way it is for boys whose moms and dads don't love each other anymore? And if the mom doesn't love the dad anymore, will she still find a way to love the boy? Or will she push him onto a German man with hot blood who doesn't like children? Is that what you get when your real father likes horses more than you? Is that what you earn because you weren't good enough for your daddy's attention?

And how long has it been since I've heard Jerry Sam's raspy voice? The voice that instantly makes me proud and excited, the voice that feels far too safe to not have love for me. And although those horses might cost him all the money and all the time it would take to make me a good boy, I know with all my heart he wouldn't scare me or bruise my chest.

And if I ever see my dad again, I might tell him what Tom does but I won't cry when I say it. Because no matter what mom says about Jerry Sam, he would never let Tom touch me like this in front of the kids at the park. My dad would put a stop to it, whether he loves those horses or not. Because I'm his and he's my real dad and I didn't touch the door and I didn't lie and I didn't want a new daddy. I wanted my daddy.

And now all I can imagine is how disappointed Tom would be if I did tell, if I told anybody differently than the way he sees it and I can't and I won't because I want to be loved. I don't want to disappoint him. I want what my mom says is there. Father and son. Love and understanding.

"Now tell the truth, Kyle," he demands, his anger still obvious.

"I will, Dad," I say and look up, careful not to make eye contact for too long. Careful not to push my luck. That will come soon enough.

I hear my mom holler out the door for me to come in. In an instant, life is safe but there's a dark cloud.

"Coming," I yell and start to run.

"Hey wait," he says. "Not so fast."

I'm smiling now, lighthearted and relieved.

"Be. Good," he tells me, staring into my eyes, his eyebrows up.

And I swear, with all the goodness in my heart, I tried, Dad, I tried.

21

DOING A BURN is what drives every thought, every action, every cell in my body. I am intoxicated by the alchemy and its dark secrets. I am infected by the unexplainable scent of the flask, a smell that doesn't exist anywhere but here in a single moment, and I'm convinced that this is as good as life will ever be again.

Not the substance that I seek any longer but the essence of its power, of its beauty, of its destruction that has me now, by my throat, by my heart. This thing that I can't explain. This thing that I can't deny. And it feels far more hopeless than addiction as I swing like a pendulum back and forth between feeling imprisoned and feeling in love.

To me, the beautiful colors of the glass when the red phosphorus chemically burns the deep rich purple of iodine are like the memory of a sunset across a lonely autumn sky. So fleeting and memorable, so captivating and complete, so mesmerizing and easy to confuse with reality. When we learn the laws of abandonment and the art of chemical reactions; excitement is building inside me, like teenagers with wild ambitions in the backseat of an '84 Cutlass. The magic of dry ice and the science of creation through glass bottles that smoke and choke the air are the simple evils of these moments, when I swear I am co-creating something special and unique and important and needed.

I feel peace in that split second when the sun-kissed color changes to a dull and dying purplish grey and I tell myself that God approves of my creation even though I know this is the color of the absence of good. It's the devil we all serve over and beyond the being that creates beauty.

There is a universe inside the meth lab, one that is never lost on me. And at a certain point, I obey, I observe, I lean into the cycles of cooking dope. Where the laws of man don't exist in my mind and there is undeniable beauty and evil and birth and death as unmistakable as life itself. And for the meth cook, who is connected to its nature and at one with its process, what seems like insanity to the untrained eye, is understood by me as pure enlightenment.

Those who know don't say and those who say don't know.

And the epiphany somehow leaves me happy because in a way I understand myself now, and hopeless because it's worse than I ever thought. In an underground that sees cooking meth as the means to get high, I now understand that getting high is simply my means to cooking meth.

That is my deepest desire, and I am happy and hopeless to discover it. And I wonder if trying to find a cure for my obsession would be the equivalent of wondering if God could be less interested in our lives. Though it certainly seems like he found a way to accomplish that.

A still, quiet voice whispers for help, almost unbeknownst to me. Because I want to do it more and I want to do it best and I want to please the people who use the dope. And I also want to die.

Happy and hopeless—an impossible combination that is as real as this unspoken, unchartered addiction. The need to cook, the need to create, the need for perfection. And it is the by-product of my new life's purpose, the care that I put into the taste and the white and the strength of the high, that keeps us all spinning on a single axis and pulls me further into the fray.

And because of my passion we all win.

And because of my passion we all lose.

I give my life to this mission, my life to these people who will never see it the way I do. Nobody will ever appreciate the atonement I feel through colors, through science, through beautiful miracles while I sacrifice everything I could have possibly been.

22

"EXPLOSION?" GRIFFIN IS asking, incredulous. I have his full attention.

"More of an implosion," I confirm. "But not from a chemical reaction."

"But how?" he asks, a little too curious.

In a dry, somber voice, I suggest, "Let's talk about something else right now."

Outside the window is a farmhouse. One I haven't been inside yet because that is outside the parameters of my arrangement with Abby, the owner. Something I have no interest in doing anyway. I have the use of a detached metal shed, on the other side of the driveway, fifty yards or so from the owners' 'normal' life. Abby has a sweet, non-confrontational, and quiet demeanor. She has a wholesome manner that made me talk differently in her presence because she seems like someone's loving and nurturing mother. Like a mom I had imagined once.

With the exception of her meth habit, of course. Yes, it even infects angels.

Perry, Abby's boyfriend, is a firefighter—tall, skinny, boots and jeans. He is the kind of man whose word means something to him, whose profession gives him purpose, and who is attracted to Abby because both of them are good and upright and kind, even in private.

And I trust them both because I felt honesty in their smiles and could see light still lit behind their eyes. These two didn't circle like scavengers, salivating over the drug, waiting for their chance to pilfer the goods. In fact, where most 'landlords' would demand ounces in exchange for harboring me and my lab, Abby and Perry are grateful with a gram or two every once in awhile. They seemed to be doing it out of the kindness of their heart, a twisted benevolence.

In essence, the terms were sole use of the garage in exchange for an occasional supply of methamphetamine. But in reality, I am free to pretend I am hidden and they are free to pretend they keep a very dangerous pet fifty yards from their front door. Bound by the list of felonies we committed knowingly or unknowingly together.

They are making a huge mistake, of course. And as badly as I don't want that to be true, I know how this will play out.

Griffin shrugs his shoulders, "No problem, K. You're the boss in here."

The two of us are alone in the garage, listening to Third Eye Blind sing about some semi-charmed kind of life and wondering how any of it applies to me as we prepare for yet another burn. This will be my biggest to date, a burn I've been thinking about for weeks as I vaguely ran through the possible consequences in my mind. That first fire that seems like years ago, replays in my mind. I glance at my arm, where hair no longer grows, and wonder how many "second chances" I have left.

Griffin knows some things; he spent his share of time with the old heads and I'm counting on him to be my second set of eyes to keep it safe. I need him to be alert, I need him to stay focused on the task at hand, but we've both been awake for the last three days and the shadows are getting hard to ignore.

For the last thirty minutes, we've been blowing glass—heating it up, stretching it out, and creating elaborate pipes from Pyrex tubes. I have an entire case that is new, it still bears the price tag but was stolen, nonetheless. My glassware comes from a guy named Ross, a guy who tweaks for days cutting images from magazines and pasting them all over his house like some cosmic web of the beautiful people. I never know where I'll find one or why he glues them where he does or why he picks the people he does, but he lives around the corner from a critical landmark in Kansas City, a science store in an old Jewish community called Brookside. The tubes were a good deal. I gave him a half a gram.

"Wait a minute! How in the hell…" Griffin's question trails off. He cocks his head, cheeks puffed out, eyes wide open, as he blows into the open end of a tube as the closed end spins inside the flame of a torch. The glowing orange tip inflates into a perfectly round bulb. "…can that implosion even happen?"

I watch the glass expand and glisten and have this thought. Not a new thought, one that always seems to be present, in the back of my mind at least, but it straddles this weird line between a phobia and salvation. It's reasonable based on the volatility of the ingredients. It's reasonable based on what little I know. It's reasonable based on the fact that it happened once before, kind of, and the net result was broken glass and burnt skin and poison in the air. I'm careful that I never screw up but catch myself praying that, somehow, I do. Not to be disfigured, not to just be hurt, but when it happens it needs to kill me because I need something permanent, something that will last.

The evening news brims with storylines of explosions and even I am starting to believe this shit. Because although I've never seen one, at least not their version, I need something to be honest, something to believe in. And if it has to be that I'm always in danger—to be killed in an explosion, arrested by the cops, murdered by the junkies who would kill their own mother for a bump—in order to feel alive, to feel present, then so be it. I just pray that one of them works because I want off this merry-go-round, I want the music to stop. That's what I know; that's what I want.

As long as I can still shoot dope.

Griffin gasps as he holds the tube up like an empty snow globe with a stem. He lays the newly formed pipe on the edge of a gigantic ashtray. It blends in with fifteen others.

I continue with my story, "I put a cork in it, in the flat-bottomed flask, so it had no room to breathe. Then I set it in a cooler of ice and I heard some crackling."

"Huh." He grunts.

"Yeah, I pulled it out and was holding the damn thing to my face when it blew."

I dump a gram in one of the pipes and hand it to Griffin. Getting high seems like the right plan before the burn, like a fresh cup of Joe before you go to work. Probably not the best idea with Griffin, I know. He gets too-high too easily, gets lost in the weirdest things. He can't help it—he was born with a rabid-ass mind.

"Got hot phosphorus in my eye, on my neck, all over the garage," I continue. "Scared the shit out of all of us."

"Damn." He hovers the bulb of meth over the propane. The white powder instantly turns into liquid, slightly discolored but clean. I am good at what I do.

"That's an expensive lesson to learn." Griffin takes a long, steady hit from the pipe, rocking it back and forth as the stem clouds up and clears a half dozen times.

"No, dude. I mopped it up with coffee filters. Off the floor, the ceiling, my neck, and then ran it through a lye bed."

He hands me the pipe; I take a hit, exhale, fill the room with smoke. Wait to transform.

"That's what I like about you, man. Whoever taught you, taught you good."

"Yeah, he was a good guy," I tell him. "Before the fucking needles." I say that, and wonder if any of this could be different. If it wasn't me who stumbled through the process, but someone who actually took me under their wing, could they have taught me the ropes, taught me respect, taught me control? Yet one more thing the world will never know.

Griffin averts his eyes, wiping his palms on his jeans. "Well, it ain't for everybody," he says with no conviction, then laughs nervously.

"Sooner or later, Griffin. Just watch yourself." Out of habit, I pump my fist, tighten my arm. Decide not to look to see if any veins show. That will have to wait.

Griffin says, "Yeah, my guy told me about an actual explosion. P2P recipe. Mutilated someone's face."

"That's what scares me, man. Pyrex is not indestructible."

"But this one is!" he says proudly as he reaches in a box and pulls out a fresh, unused 12,000 ml Pyrex flask.

"Not sure man, but it sure is pretty."

I tell him we should hurry, to "take a couple more hits" as I measure up the ingredients. I have a station specifically for this. It is isolated and small with hues of purple, orange, and yellow staining the flat surface. He asks twice about the ratio I use between the three ingredients and I ignore him both times. I can tell he's getting high by how fast he's talking.

"Having a flask blow up in my face sounds shitty." Griffin tilts his head, thinking now. "Or the coolest thing ever."

I tell him to shut up, to help me hold the flask so we can get started. For three days, he's been philosophizing about how the round-bottom flask is built for an open flame, how that's the "way it works in the world of science", although he couldn't explain why. Still, we figured out a way to keep the flame flat and wide and suspend the flask from the ceiling like an acrobat high above the circus looking down on the crowd. The flask is substantial and thick, with purpose and power and will, which for some reason makes me proud. The tube that filters the smell, the one that runs into a bucket of charcoal and kitty litter, is industrial and stiff and oversized like a misguided HVAC system of some dated institution. And I have to admit I'm kind of crapping my pants over the size of the flask, the open flame, and the absence of a Plan B.

But, no guts no glory; and like I said, Griffin knows what he's doing. I think.

I dump the ephedrine in with the iodine. The mixture slowly turns purple as I careen the flask side to side. "Why do you do that?" Griffin asks.

"This ain't a lesson, Griffin. Just do what I tell you."

And he backs up but I can tell he's biting his lip.

"Hand me the phosphorus and let's get some ice to keep the smoke in the flask." I wave at the table. "Once I pour it in, there's no turning back."

"I'm with you, dude. This is going to be awesome."

Initial reactions are impossible to predict. There are too many variables like the freshness of the phosphorus, the restriction on the neck of the flask, and the size of the burn. The name of the game is to contain the smoke. I use ice, I use condensers, and I try to keep it all in the flask and out of the tube so I can maximize the yield.

"Griffin," I yell loudly, "Get ready, you crazy bastard. You're tightening the seal. There won't be much time." The rubber seal that fits over the neck of the flask has a stainless-steel adjustable clamp. Griffin's only job is to tighten the screw on the clamp as quickly as possible. A task we've gone over hundreds of times.

"Roger," he says, his eyes red-rimmed and large.

"Griffin!"

"Roger, Dude," he assures me.

"Just pay attention."

I wipe my palms across my back pocket and look around the room—flammable liquids away from the flame, finished product away from the raw material and the fire extinguisher is tipped over at my feet.

I hold my breath and dump the phosphorus in. We fumble with the rubber seal. Griffin takes his time tightening it as I yell derogatory names. He seems unphased. The son of bitch is in his own world now.

"That oughta do it," he tells me and hands me the flask. The round bottom seems twice the size of my head as I stiff-arm the neck away from my body like I'm choking someone but scared I might actually kill them.

Suddenly, the ball turns black. Two and a half feet from my face, this huge glass ball goes from a clear see-through globe to pitch black in seconds.

I can feel the vibration of the chemicals reacting inside the flask, like pop rocks in your mouth. The darker it gets, the deeper my fear that this is how people like me make the evening news.

"Holy fucking shit! Tell me what to do! Tell me what to do!" I yell. Not the best time to reconsider my position. Its no different than the smaller burns, I told myself. Just more ingredients, more smoke to contain and more dope at the end of the rainbow. Yet here I am, seemingly holding a ticking time bomb, with the stark realization that with all the "mores" I can get with a bigger burn, the one I failed to consider was more danger. I'm in over my head. Punctuated by the fact that I'm asking Griffin for advice.

"Ride it out. More fire!" And that's his solution. Turn up the fire, accelerate the reaction and all I want to do is figure out how to stop it.

"Don't give me your crazy shit, motherfucker. We have to throw it."

"Throw it?"

"Throw it! In some water! Away from me!"

The flask, still suspended from the ceiling, seems as big as a planet as I stretch my arms as far as they will go. The image of an explosion, the thought of glass in my face is real to me. If I'll even still have a face. And if I had another hand, I would punch Griffin in the throat because I'm scared, because I have no idea what to do, because he continues to scream, "Turn the fire up, man!"

It's clear to me I'm on my own.

"Give it here," Griffin says and strangely reminds me of the *Dukes of Hazzard* when they get behind the wheel.

"Take it, motherfucker. It's yours."

"Fuckin' A, dude!" he screams followed by an extended "woo" and "holy shit" as I hand the flask over. He's smiling now like a child with a fish pulling on the line.

"What do I do, Griffin? How do we stop it?"

"Stop it? Why would you want to do that?" he asks as he swirls the formulating substance inside the glass. "Pray, I guess. If you believe in that kind of shit!"

"Oh yeah," I say as I envision the worst. I envision this thick Pyrex glass giving way and exploding with the force of dynamite with the soundtrack of my death being Third Eye Blind and his stupid fucking laughter.

"Turn it up. It will make the meth better," he promises as he holds the flask back over the flame.

"You're a fucking idiot!" I tell him and he leans his head back and laughs like a child on a swing set. And stays right there, over the flame, freaking me out. "Dude, why aren't you scared?"

"I am, brother," he tells me as he looks over with a half-grin, like Luke Duke gripping the wheel of the General Lee.

"Then why are you laughing?!"

"Because I can't think of a better way to go."

I stand there looking at him and, for the first time, in a long time, I see the depths of the allure, the strength of its grip, and what I will become in the not so distant future. It's prophetic, this moment as we try to contain the largest burn of our lives.

He is me and I am him with one slight difference—he was born with his rabid-ass mind. And, well…I guess I picked mine up along the way.

23

Now we have to leave the farm. Not because of an explosion in the garage. No, as it turns out, Griffin's dreams of dying in the line of duty would have to wait for another day; but because a few days later, the shit really hit the fan. And the only thing I can be sure of is the police will be at the door soon.

I'm not sure what I was thinking. I mean, what a cliché, right? The minute I knew Perry was using needles I should have packed up and left without saying a word. For his sake more than mine.

I knew how our relationship would play out. I'd seen it time and time again. How naïve the three of us were to think it would all remain normal in spite of the fact that they had a notorious meth cook performing life-threatening chemistry just fifty yards from where they ate their TV dinners or from where Perry cleaned his guns after hunting on the vast acreage of their land; a stone's throw from where Abby's teenage daughters slept every other weekend.

This was my favorite meth lab, even more than the warehouse on the Avenue in Northeast Kansas City. This place felt out of reach, felt like sacred ground, and I would irresponsibly bring companionship and hang out for days and do the maniacal things that drug-riddled people do to one another.

I would equally come out alone, enjoy the solitude, the lack of demands, and listen to college radio stations, forever pretending it had only been a short while since this addiction began. This was the promise of staying high, the lie that ricocheted within our better judgment. The lie that not only would we walk away someday, but that we would discover we still had full lives to live when we finally did.

But Perry wasn't walking away. Not after the stunt he pulled. Definitely not after he made the ill-fated decision to start shooting dope.

Trisha, the girl I know who seems to know everybody and introduced me to Abby and Perry, told me he was spun out. "Going off the deep end," she said, but I had my fingers crossed on this one. Like we're in some parallel universe where Perry could become the first dude in the history of methamphetamine to have access to copious amounts of dope and an endless supply of free needles from EMT kits, but somehow not become a crazy-eyed lunatic who creates an elaborate story of people who are coming to get him. Nobody's impervious to that. I've heard every story—from aliens to the secret service to circus clowns, and I allowed myself, for reasons unclear to me now, to believe this poor bastard was different. I even bought that story that I was protective of these two.

And as drug-Karma would have it, Perry ends up storming into his Fire Chief's office demanding to know why he, a fireman with a good track record, was being followed. "What are you fuckers trying to find?" he demanded.

Long story short, he got caught with a gram at work, went out kicking and screaming when the cops read him his Miranda rights and is now sitting in a Jackson County Jail cell, detoxing the old-fashioned way.

So, what choice do I have? Now we have to leave the farm.

Shame is always with me—unspoken, ignored, but always there behind the veil I never dare pierce. In this underground, in the dark, I can atrophy; I can crumble and not give a shit how it looks. Cigarettes are always burning in my fingers, hanging from my lips with squinted eyes that are sunken in and dark and lifeless. The taste in my mouth is awful: smoky, dry and stale. My jaws are clenched, muscles pulsating as I grind my teeth. I'm sick of hearing that I look like Jason Priestley but it's probably true. If he were a corpse. Kissing is now difficult, but sex is easy as long as they are like me, one of us. I am now self-conscious amongst the living and it causes me to burrow deeper into the fray. And Abby, as she slips into the garage, clutching a sweater to her frail body, is but a painful reminder of how far I've anchored in.

"How have you been, Kyle?" she asks tenderly. I'm amazed at how easy, how natural the niceness seems falling from her lips. Instantly, I wonder what she wants.

"Why are you here?" My question carries little conviction. She makes me softer in a way that I can't help but don't like.

"I don't know. Lonely, I guess." She looks into my face. "Is that crazy?"

I can't meet her gaze. "Naw, Abby, lonely's not crazy. Not in here."

The guys look nervous with her there but continue to work. We have a mission to save our asses, to destroy the evidence. It's cool, I guess; nobody reaches for a gun.

I watch her walk around like a florist inside the garden, smelling the bouquet and admiring the colors, but knowing that it all must go. "Abby."

"Mm-hmm?"

"You can't be here," I tell her as I thump my cigarette to the gravel floor, swipe my shoe across the cherry.

"I know. I'm not sure why I thought this was okay." She thinks for a moment. "I'm scared."

I say nothing.

"I just thought that once I saw this, I could, I don't know...see things differently." She hesitates. "Do you have to leave?"

The guys aren't working now, unsure what to do, so I motion her back to the door. "We have an agreement," I remind her, quietly so the fellas can't hear me, so I don't have to be harsh. "I need you back in your house now. Not out here."

And she looks at me, her eyes glistening and sad, and replies, "What will happen to him?"

"Smack on the wrist, first offense," I tell her, but I look away and she knows it's a lie.

The guys all tell me she's looking for sex. Now that she's gone, now that the discomfort of her presence has faded like the smell of her perfume, they tell me, "She wants it, dude," but it doesn't feel right. Their words sound ugly, insensitive because it's her. Abby is maternal and pretty and probably plain in the real world. A reminder of something divine, impervious to the darkness, and it just feels like an unforgivable sin to talk this way about something perfect and virtuous. Even if it is, in fact, her that provides me access to commit my crimes.

Yet they present a compelling case—meth moves everyone toward sex. Because I want to protect her, because I want to please this person who reminds me of life, I believe these people. I believe she wants to have sex and I see it as my solemn duty to help her with her loneliness.

Now outside her door, I watch her through the curtains, like a memory of my old life. She is cooking a meal, wiping the counter, experiencing something thoughtful and on purpose. The air outside the farmhouse is cold and frozen breath floats from my mouth. I debate whether to stand here and watch her moving or enter her house and drag it all down with me. The consequence of the bottomless bag.

I wrap my knuckle softly on the glass. Maybe she won't hear, maybe she won't answer. But she does and walks towards the door. I'm nervous, but I'm not sure why.

"Hey," she says softly as she opens the door. "How are you?"

"Not sure. Can I come in?"

"Of course." She opens the door wider and makes room for me to enter.

Once I'm in, I can see the room—TV dinner trays folded and stuffed in the corner, images of the last supper, boots by the door. My cheeks feel red as the warmth fills my face and I don't know what to say, I feel silly and self-conscious.

"I shouldn't have come out there," she tells me and asks if I want to sit down or something to drink. She comes back with water and hands me the glass. It is ornate and clean, engraved with flowers. I know it belongs to a set and has never been used for an ashtray.

"Did I do something wrong? Do you want to tell me now that we are alone?"

"No. Just—" I hesitate, uncertain what to say. "Why did you come out there?"

"Loneliness. I'm sure you understand, Kyle."

"Honestly, Abby, guys like me are never alone."

"But you know what I mean." She looks at me for a while and finally says, "You don't seem like a meth cook. At least not what I thought you would be like."

"Trust me. I'm what you thought I was." Pigs don't know pigs stink—an age-old adage, real country wisdom from the world that shaped who I used to be. Like scripture when you're ready to receive, the truth is always there when you take the time to read between the lines. So, it's not like I can't see how fucked up I really am. It's no secret that I'm a pig, no mystery that I stink. But when everybody wallows inside the same pile of shit, no one can tell the pigs from the mud. I avert my eyes, as I fish inside my coat pocket. "Do you care if I smoke this pipe?"

"Oh," she says, surprised, off guard, "I…I guess it's okay."

"I don't have to. I just thought—"

"It's fine. Perry was smoking all the time before—" she stops, stares at the floor, then shakes her head.

"I thought that's what you wanted. To get high." I jam the pipe back in my pocket. "Most people…" I trail off, forgetting that I'm even talking.

"You're a good person, Kyle. I can tell." She smiles at me and I hate myself even more because she thinks this.

"Abby, why did you really come out there?"

"I don't know. I apologize."

"You don't have to. I just feel compelled to get you what you want. I'm built like that. Especially with people I care about." I hate myself. I hate everything I know and everything I don't. Why would anyone ever believe in me? Why would anyone ever trust me? I am evil, I am lost, I am no more.

I am a runaway train consuming coal, stoking a flame, traveling through the darkness across a vast and lonely night.

I see it now, thanks to Abby. The ghost of me still lingers, still projected like a movie we will never get to see. She sees that ghost and believes it's me somehow. I see the same ghost and know it's never coming back.

She smiles again. "I like hearing that. I'm glad you're here."

It's silent now. Longer than I'm used to, at least when nobody's high. I struggle with this exchange; I have no position of power and feel exposed or naked or vulnerable in this moment. "What should we do?" I ask to break the silence.

"Do you want to watch TV?"

"Abby, I have a very illegal operation being cleaned up fifty yards from where we sit right now. I'm here 'cause I thought you wanted something."

"I still have the meth you gave me last week."

She's playing with me, wants me to ask. I know her type. They make things so complicated. But I can't do that. Not with her. "Abby, I need you to make the first move."

"For what?" she asks and her confusion seems genuine.

"For what?" I repeat.

"I'm so sorry," she tells me. "I think I made a mistake."

And I instantly realize that I have gotten it all wrong. Like everything in this world bent on lower desires, how do I possibly recognize kindness or compassion or love for that matter? I can't, there is only the drug.

"No. It's my fault."

I can see her face, it's red. She's blushing. "I'm so sorry," she repeats. "I never meant to…"

"No. It's okay." We sit in silence and she flashes an occasional uncomfortable smile. It's obvious we both want to part ways now. Soon we will be gone —everything in the shed, everything that ties me to this farm. Gone. Burned. Vanished. Nothing left but this uncomfortable memory and the addiction she has for this drug.

I'm sorry, Abby. In another life, I could've been a gentleman and you could've been a lady. I could've held your hand, brushed your cheek and felt those things that boil up from within. But in this life, I am a meth cook, as bad as anything you can imagine, and every road leads to three-day benders and one-night stands and emptiness in its wake. In your life, there are engraved flowers on dishes, pictures of Jesus and pleasant exchanges between strangers. In my life, there are men who want to have sex with you right outside your door while your boyfriend is on his way to prison.

And as long as we never meet again, I won't see how bad I've become, won't know how much to hate as I go straight to hell with the rest of 'em.

Because although it's no ancient proverb, it still holds true for me—if I root in deep, stay close to the pile, pigs will never know pigs stink.

I get to my feet, cross to the door, then pause to reach into my inside pocket, pull out my cigarettes, and tap the top on my forearm. "Do you still think I'm a good guy?" I ask her and put one in my mouth.

She gets to her feet. "Of course, I do," she tells me, but something's missing; something's gone.

I light the cigarette, take a deep drag and exhale into the room. I am confident again, in control, as I look her in the eyes. This will be the last time I see her, the last time I speak her name. It is the way it has to be if I want to be safe, if I'm going to remain the person she thinks I am.

"Still?" I ask. "After everything you know?"

"I do, Kyle." And it sounds honest and it sounds genuine.

So I check my pockets and confirm I'm leaving with everything I brought with me. I look at her and she at me. "That's too bad," I tell her and walk out the door.

24

THE SPOON IS miniature and tarnished—an antique collectible, an artefact from someone's past. It is the kind you feed babies with that gets grouped together with black-and-white photos of hard-looking people and tiny baby booties tethered by their laces. To someone somewhere, this represents innocence and love and precious moments. To me, it is the thing I use to mix the syrup I shoot into my veins.

It is now bent and shaped to sit propped up, bent and shaped to submit to someone else's will. And whatever innocence it once held for a faceless, nameless person is now violated with every puncture of my skin, every stab at my soul.

I've learned new words—the indigenous language of the junkie; like "point" and "rig", but I still just call it a needle and I don't care how uncomfortable these tweakers get that I'm not using their fucking lingo. The needle is winning, slowly killing me more and more every day. It is sharp, my senses are dull. The pain and the prick on my skin are now muted, my eyes slightly blurry all the time, even during the day. Night and day are now one. I have given in to the hopelessness that this is my fate; it is my life, and someday will be my death. As I hunch over this spoon that sits on the dresser full of pictures, moments of an untarnished life secretly bearing witness to me, I spiral to the depths of hell.

And other addicts can all pretend they're better than this; I'm so far past any of that. Because I know myself, even this version, and although I haven't yet, I know I would shoot up on a public street if necessary. Although I haven't yet, I would push the plunger hard and fast no matter who could see—a child, my mother, it wouldn't matter. And knowing that makes me sad. And knowing that makes me honest. And knowing that makes me someone you should lock up and throw away the key, I guess.

And so, I hate myself. This person I've become. Thank God for that. Because without that contempt there would be no sign of myself left in me. And once the hate is gone, I am lost forever. That is how it works. Even I know that. It's not something that is talked about, just something that is known.

God, if you're listening, let's make this the one that ends it all. In his name, I pray.

Amen.

The tiny round scabs up my arm are there now and undeniable, even to me. A consequence of puncturing the big vein on my bicep multiple times a day. A consequence of being able to do it myself. Hard to believe it's only been four months. Back when the dots were one, maybe two, I could pretend that maybe people didn't notice, or maybe it looked like a bug bite that had been itched too much. But now that there are so many and they run single file in line with the harder and harder to find green-blue track running up the center of my arm, everyone knows. The people at the pharmacies where I purchase my U-100 disposable needles, the curious and disapproving clerks at the hardware stores where I buy my chemicals, the young ladies with the pretty smiles who quickly change their expressions and avert their eyes as I stretch out my bare arm to give them money.

I have no doubt there is a name for me. No longer a question or secret but unspoken just the same. Most of my needles are new and unused, therefore, most of the scabs don't show a bruise. But I am no nurse, and shooting methamphetamine is no joke, so I slowly became the poster child for exactly what a junkie looks like. A junkie. There. I said it.

By far the most surreal and telling part of my day has been sitting alone in some dim and messy back room staring down at my thin, pale, pockmarked arm, dealing with the circumstances of my life. Frightened by the sight of all the puncture wounds not even a half-inch from one another, shaded with hues of yellow-green, wondering how I got this far. I was doing it again after I promised only two times a day, then just four times a day, and now I'm not sure how many I was doing. How could it happen so quickly and how could anything imprison me this strongly?

By this point I was tying off, the elastic rubber tube now always tucked in the inside pocket of my coat. I have also started exploring veins beyond the large conspicuous ones. There is the top of my hand but those scabs itch the most. And the ones in my forearm, where I can hide the pockmarks the easiest in the furrows of dark hair but for some reason I always feel the slow, sweet pain of the drug working its way up the canals of my inner arm. And although I use this spot often, it always makes me feel weird and like a machine more than any other way.

That is, until the cough comes.

Suicide is on my mind all the time now. Cooking meth, shooting dope, and being dead are the thoughts that I can't control. This thing has taken me over, completely, wholly, and in some strange twisted way, all three are about survival.

And I am convinced that the only way for Kyle Houston to ever survive is going to have to be through the fond memories of the people who once loved me. I could never let them see me now, so thin, so lifeless, so…someone else. That would be best for everyone, the responsible thing to do, but staying high just continues to kick the can down the road.

I wish I could be clean for one one day—by some miracle, fatten up, regain color in my face, so I could tell my dad I'm sorry to his face; tell my mom goodbye.

But there is no right way for any of this, no system of rules to follow. There is only death that seems easy and death that seems hard, and they both occupy my mind at the exact same time. It feels like a decade ago when I was that kid who wanted to, and maybe could have, taken on the world, but it hasn't even been two years.

And now it's all gone—my ambition, my smile, my will to live. Just me, dangling from the unraveled fabric of lost hope.

Now finish the job, God, and let me go.

25

It's strange what I still remember about that night. Like how the world was brisk and starless as we barreled down I-70 at the wrong hour of the night. My energy level was low, lower than it had ever been, and I remember describing the way I felt as if death was slowly creeping in. All night, I'd been dragging myself all over Kansas City searching for a single missing ingredient to an epic and final batch of meth. This was it, my last burn; the elusive "one more time" that would satisfy the deepest hunger.

Yeah, right.

And making matters worse, the virus my body was fighting, that I had hoped was only cotton fever, made me heavy and weak, and unable to make sound decisions.

Cotton fever is a real son of a bitch—high fever, joint pain, you name it. Whether it's from bacteria or a fiber from cotton doesn't really matter. What matters is it's a fate worse than death, or so I'd been told. In our world, everybody used cotton from cigarette butts to filter the syrup into the needle. It was Russian roulette because nobody knew who might get it, but that wouldn't stop us. If AIDS, hepatitis, and death weren't enough to turn us away from the needle, then cotton fever was just another landmine we skipped around, like children playing hopscotch, blindfolded on the ledge of a twenty-story building. This constant disregard for health and safety is something we all understand, yet I could never explain. It's a junkie thing.

"Are you all right?" Valarie replies, as I ask her to turn up the heater for the umpteenth time. I grimace as I shift toward the vent in the passenger side of her brother's car.

"Uh-huh," I say and cinch up the collar on my leather jacket and stare out the window. The thirty thousand dollars in my pocket is bulky and uncomfortable. The gun tucked in my pants, stolen and out of place, reminds me of the danger I have created in my life. As if I needed another reminder.

"Cigarette?" Robbie asks and I pull out my pack of Camels to let him know I'm fine.

Robbie and Valarie are odd. I met them in Northeast a couple of days ago, among the tweakers hanging out at Ruby's house. Wide-eyed and a little nervous, they were out of their element, but had a reliable car and I needed a ride. Although I can't put my finger on it, something about them makes me uneasy. One, they're brother and sister; two, they use words like "please" and "sorry"; and three, they actually have fucking manners. They're either new to the game or just visiting, but either way, they make me nervous. Still, here we are, the three of us, at two in the morning on God only knows what night, in a 1980 Impala that is probably stolen.

"What do you think is wrong with you?" Valarie leans in and reaches for my pack of Camels.

"I'm sorry," I whisper because I don't know and hand her my lighter. Valarie's face lights up as she cups her hand around the tip of the cigarette.

Her body is supple, tight. Her face is different than everyone else's—not furrowed, clean. I can see the curves of her chest under the flannel jacket and remember kissing her in the basement earlier that night.

"Me too," she says and blows a cloud of shadowy smoke up into the car's ceiling. "Sorry, that is." Her eyes stare straight ahead.

Robbie asks what we're talking about and cracks the window.

"The rest of the night," Valarie answers, glancing over at me, smiling.

I wish I could touch her. No, I wish I had the *desire* to touch her. I don't know what's wrong, only that I feel like shit and I'm on a mission. So, I ignore her advances, apologize, and concentrate on the reason I left the house.

Valarie seems kind, but I know there's a catch. She uses; therefore, chances are there's something fucked up about her, right? Still, her body is warm and her voice is soft and I don't have a lot of give-a-shit left in me as we head up the off-ramp to Bates City.

Valarie sits a little taller in her seat as we quietly pull into a trailer park. Everything's vacant, like a modern-day ghost town, but mainly because it is two in the morning. Filthy unkempt trailers with dilapidated stairs leading to dented, discolored doors lay in rows in front of an orchard, like graves of people not meant to be there permanently. Inoperative cars parked beside each trailer, dated and dying, as gravel ricochets from underneath our slow-moving vessel.

As we amble through the trailer court, I realize for the first time that everything I have cobbled together over the last three months, everything I have sacrificed for, is now in one place. Here. Every chemical, every stolen vehicle I store them in, every piece of lab equipment I have garnered over months by sending low-level users into science stores to buy, is here. And now a fifty-dollar throwaway .45-caliber pistol, the money I have remaining after buying all the chemicals, and two newbies who thought they were going to get some free dope.

Oh, and me. The dumb-ass tweaker who unwittingly grouped everything together. What. The. Fuck.

Suddenly, headlights beam from across the lot.

"Shit," Robbie says and his hands clamp onto the steering wheel. "Shit, shit, shit." I tell him to settle down.

Valarie leans into me and asks for the gun.

I tell them to be cool as the silhouetted outline of the emergency lights on the roof slowly register. It's a fucking cop. The cruiser creeps out and follows us. I remind everyone we've done nothing wrong, but something tells me this is no surprise. Something tells me we are minutes away from having the entire county and state patrol out here in this tiny rundown trailer court.

At this point, I have to remind myself to care. The sickness, whatever it is, is deep. I'm almost too weak to open my eyes, let alone move my limbs. The last thing I want to do is try to run but I have to try something. The leather jacket feels stiff and heavy. Valarie whispers, "Give me the gun, I'm a girl," and I'm honestly not sure what that means, but I'm cold and I'm tired and I don't even have the strength to listen to her.

A stone's throw, maybe twenty feet from this beat-up vehicle, in this shitty trailer park, in rural Missouri, in the middle of the night, are the vehicles that hold my life's work. In this moment, I am an embarrassing cliché.

You can't make this shit up any better, folks.

"I'm bailing."

"No, Kyle! Slide me the gun."

Sure thing, Valarie, so you can drop the gun, shoot my leg and I limp into the woods like some one-person three-legged race. "I'm not asking for approval or help. Just stay here."

My plan is simple: unload the evidence, stash the money, and maybe—if I'm lucky—get to the woods without anyone following me. I'm not hiding, I'm not praying, I'm not kidding myself. I don't have it in me.

I check my pockets, my pants—it's all here—then I pop the door and run. The cop yells, "Halt!" but that only makes me run faster as the two of us engage in a race.

And once again, I'm running from the cops.

The lights from the cruiser are bright and alarming as I dart into the dark field. Not sure how far back the officer is, I semi-count the strides from the initial tree line and then toss the brown paper bag full of cash. I minimize the movement of my arm as not to draw attention and ensure that I never break stride.

It's disturbing how comfortable I am running into dark, moonlit fields chased by cops. I'm amazed at how commonplace this is now, how I don't give it a second thought, how it almost feels like I'm supposed to be here, in this act, on this night. And as I drop the pistol just to my right, like a blackjack dealer hitting the table, I think about how much easier it would be to get caught. This heavy, out-of-shape person is keeping up with me, stride for stride it seems, and I know that's not possible if I really wanted to escape.

"Halt!" he screams again. "Or I'll shoot!"

And I'm sure that can't be true, but I don't care. *Please shoot me officer, hit me in the head.* Because I'm tired of running. I can't do it anymore; the fear, the shame, living life looking over my shoulder, always avoiding the mirror with knowledge I am only prolonging the inevitable. Like a patient with a terminal illness who knows it won't be long, I know I'm on borrowed time. I don't know if it will be the criminals in Northeast, the authorities in multiple counties, or this insidious drug that will take me down, but it won't be long. And I don't care because I'm tired. And I don't care because it was over long ago. And the weakness in my body is finally catching up to the weakness in my soul.

So, I stop and I fall to the ground, and I submit to the chase that is nothing but a formality at this point.

The ground is cold and wet. I lie face down as the weight of my life starts to lift. The officer is kicking me now, screaming out of fear and somehow, I feel safe. I pretend the blows hurt so he doesn't kick harder, cover my head, and wait for him to run out of steam.

And the punchline is that sometimes epiphanies are a swift and thorough ass whoopin'. Because every kick, every stomp, feels like answers to so many questions.

In a way even I can understand.

Surrounded by strobing lights, I am reminded of the nights on the Avenue when the lights would whisk beneath the windows, in search of something dangerous, possibly deadly, to catch and lock away. Tonight, that thing is me. Teams of law-enforcement rummage through the back of the dilapidated pickup trucks, pulling off tarps, carrying flasks and tubes and chemicals that will build this case, build their careers. Let's not kid ourselves, this isn't some beginner's crime scene.

And I'm somewhat sure they have no right to touch the trucks that we weren't driving or sitting in, not even when Robbie told them "We came to pick it up," but, as they catalogue it all, I know it's what will keep me away for a very long time.

I sit here, hands behind me, back against the bumper of the running squad car, my breath visible in the headlights. I've been positioned strategically, so that I can watch them itemize the contents of the trucks. They might as well be rubbing their hands together, like they just won the lottery, with the way they high-five and whistle and laugh at the tragedy my life has become.

A deputy sheriff stares at the driver's license he pulled from my wallet and shakes his head in disbelief. I hear him mention my name to a cop in dark fatigues and ask if I'm the one "'who ran the ball for Higginsville," and instantly, I know what county I'm in. Only this ain't no homecoming as I sit handcuffed on the outskirts of a world I knew as a boy, while a giant German Shepherd strains against his chain until he's two feet from me and barking in my face. And the viciousness and the saliva and the booming woof of the dog's bark vibrates through my body, and it feels like my conscience yelling I should've died.

No officer, I'm not the one who ran the ball for Higginsville once, but I know that guy and he was something to watch. I am just what's left of him, a defeated soul, someone he would never have anything to do with.

So I wait for whatever comes next because this part is new, although I've obsessed over it a thousand times. And my twenty-eight-inch waistband is loose on my hips and these shoes belong to somebody else. I am a skeleton of a man, a withered shell of the boy who once ran the ball. The officers crack jokes about the time that I will do, laughing and pointing and reminding me that a single cop who is out of shape caught me on foot, alone. And I contemplate this moment, how surreal it all truly is, to be here in the night, notorious and caged. When did my sins become so reckless, so permanent? Is God Himself laughing at the irony of how His little life lesson played out? Because fate, for me, is a dark and lonely highway with no road signs, no U-turns, just the realization of detours once the sun finally comes up.

But, in this moment, I have respite from the stress, release from the meth nightmare, and I'm not sure if I'm grateful or mad as hell. Because the good news is that I got what I wanted, I'm out of the game; but the bad news is it looks like I'm going to have to live. And now there is no stopping what's chased me for as long as I can remember, that thing that has been kept silent in some dark corner of my mind, waiting for the drug to step out of the way. Because not even death itself is as patient as the conscience of a junkie.

I'm sorry, Mom, I never meant to make it out alive.

PART TWO

CRASH

26

THE EXPERIENCE OF the first forty-eight hours in county jail is all just a blur. I was packed inside a tiny cell by myself next door to a holding cell for the ebb and flow of inmates. For many reasons, my mind and body rejected consciousness, so the only real memories I have of those two days are the haunting sounds of keys jingling just before they entered the lock, the annoyingly loud sound of the chuck hole opening for my three squares per day, and a very frightening spot of blood on my pillow. Oh yeah, and the lifelessness of everything because I didn't have meth.

I had no fear of how much trouble I was in for those first two days. Maybe it hadn't occurred to my drug-addled, angry brain, or didn't matter, but in those brief moments when I was awake in that detox cell, I felt like a feral animal who had been brought to captivity, put in a cage and was being viewed for all to see. Medical professionals took my vital signs. I know because I vaguely remember a conversation about my ear, specifically, the dry red-yellow crust flaking from the ear canal, and then quickly plopping back into bed because maintaining balance was impossible. Sleep was my salvation in those first forty-eight because without it I was forced to ache, I was left to yearn, and worst of all, my mind would circle back to the frightening realization that tiny rooms just like this, with the antiseptic stench of institution, the constant clanging and shouting, and a toilet just inches from my head, were what the future had in store for a guy like me.

I'm not sure anyone can feel more 'by themselves' than being in one of those detox cells. All human contact is mechanical and routine, and in my case nobody—no friends or addicts or family—had any idea where the hell I was anyway. As alone and forgotten as I felt in those first few days, I would soon realize that it was in fact possible to feel much more alone and empty.

Those are the thoughts that haunt the edges of every second I am awake and in an agony that reaches every cell of my body. When I'm not in pain,

I'm relishing sleep and consciously bracing myself for the withdrawal of two things—freedom and, more importantly, methamphetamine.

Two really good reasons to be pissed at God and that fucking drug for letting me live.

So, in the beginning, wakeless and alone, I wasn't sad, I wasn't hurt, and I wasn't scared. But deep down inside, I knew the fog would lift soon; and when it did, I was going to assess the overwhelming amount of damage I had inflicted upon my life and a world better off without me.

And out of all the shithole jails in this drug-riddled part of the country, how in the hell did I end up in Lafayette County, Missouri? Home sweet home.

Fate, as it seems, has a nasty sense of humor.

"Get up."

A deep, muffled voice cuts into my unconsciousness. And as I struggle to wake up, I realize it's day three. Fuck.

"Houston, get your ass out of bed! Someone's here to see you." The guard orders me to back into the door with my wrists held together down toward the chuck hole. I kind of listen, kind of open one eye, as I hear something about handcuffs and standard procedure and shit I've already heard from this power-hungry son of a bitch.

It takes more than a minute, but I eventually muster the strength to get out of bed and relieve myself. Pissing seems to take forever and I can hear the impatience in his muttering, but why should I care? Finally, I comply and fat-fingered hands that smell like cigarettes come through the chuck hole and grab my wrists. The steel handcuffs, which quickly clamp and secure, are cold and tight, a painful awakening to the reality of my new life.

"Still got blood coming out of my ear." My voice is gravelly, weak. And the spot on the pillow is fresh, not yet brown. Is this how your brain fries like that egg in the 'Just say no' commercials? I'm starting to worry.

"We'll swap out the pillowcase, Houston," a woman's voice says in the distance, her tone annoyed and put out. "Again."

"Turn around and back away from the door," the guard orders and I comply as my feet struggle to find the floor.

"What's going on?" I hear myself ask. Everyone remains silent. I wonder how many times "again" implies. And why aren't I more concerned about blood oozing out of me from…what? My brain? Is it to be expected? Is this what happens to people who shoot up to the degree I do? Is this my body's way of saying, "Fuck you, Kyle"? Can any of this be fixed? Do I really give a shit either way?

But I'll have to circle back around to all this. For now, I wish they would just let me sleep and not drag me down the hall.

The concrete floor seems unstable and hard beneath the too-thin soles of my county slip-on shoes as I stumble towards the door like I'm trying to walk on the deck of a careening boat. Yet another exclamation point on how bad the drug abuse has been. My legs, my body, even my head feel heavy. Although my frame is holding fifty pounds less weight, it feels like gravity pulls a hell of a lot harder in county jail. And as I step out of the cell, arms locked behind my back, the guard steadies me to clamp another set of cuffs around my ankles and I wonder how normal this will all become—disheveled hair, eyes trying painfully to adjust to the light, the thick canvas-like material of my orange jumpsuit twisted around my legs and crotch from too much sleeping.

In front of me there is a small team of deputies and some type of medical professional who couldn't care less about a human in this condition. Don't they know I played football against their high school team and that I was a threat to their defense? Don't they know I have a family who loves me? At least, they used to. Or that I once had a business and employees and responsibility and hope? I mean something to somebody, folks. If no one else, I mean something to Dylan, my young child who misses his daddy.

No. To them, I am a pathetic, skeletal shadow of a human, one of a thousand who will funnel through this county over the years, one who is now seen simply as a threat to society. The details of my former self have been erased by the mounting headlines of the destruction of methamphetamine. The world has been desensitized to my kind and the sooner I come to grips with that, the less painful this will all become. Or at least that's what I tell myself.

As the deputies usher me down the hall, the whole episode is a callous and detached experience. They talk between themselves like I'm not here, referring to me as 'this one' while I struggle to understand what's going on and where I'm going. Who the hell is here to see me? I haven't had the energy or motivation to make any calls.

They lead me into an interrogation room. Gray and cramped, with a metal table and two tall, heavyset men in sports jackets and badges stand on one side. I sit down in a chair across from them and they toss a manilla folder on the table and sit down.

"Mr. Houston," the taller one says as he opens the file and thumbs through the contents, "my partner and I are U.S. Marshals." He looks up from the file. "You're in a lot of trouble."

"For what?" I pretend not to know.

"Really?" The second one stands up and begins to pace.

The room is confined to just the three of us and our words bounce off the concrete walls.

"Let's see, you were found with…" the taller one continues, reading from the file now, "…with five pounds of red phosphorus and eight pounds of iodine. The list goes on." His face is expressionless, almost robotic.

"I was found with it?" I'm good at this playing dumb thing.

"I told you," the officer pacing the floor tells the tall one. He's young, possibly my age, possibly what I could have been if I stayed in college and became something Mom could be proud of. His hair is short, neatly combed above a furrowed brow. I get the impression he'd rather be doing anything else. Like in some choreographed play, the pacing man steps behind me where I can't see him but I hear his shoes on the concrete floor. He sounds close.

"Look, Mr. Houston, I'm going to give you some advice and you can take it or leave it." The man holding the file tells me.

I straighten a little. "Let's hear it."

"You're in a lot of trouble."

"Uh-huh."

He hesitates as if trying to determine whether to continue or not. He does. "Right now, the State of Missouri is deciding what they want to prosecute you for. They have a lot of choices."

Another pause, maybe to gauge my reaction or check that I'm listening or to add drama, I can't really tell.

"I hope you hear this," says the man behind me.

The big guy leans in. "Tell us where you got these chemicals and we can make this a lot easier on you."

I posture up, take a deep breath and ask, "How would I know? They aren't mine."

The tall man scoots his chair out and slowly gets to his feet. "No problem. You want to stay loyal to people who aren't your friends. We see it all the time. You're not special."

I'm clearly out of my league here. It's the fucking Feds standing there with truth inside that manila folder. "What's that supposed to mean?"

The man behind me interjects, "It means, it all turns out the same. Somebody will give us what we need." He pounds on the door to alert the officers. "The people who don't, end up losing." He hesitates and then adds, "What's it matter? You don't give a shit."

I hear the keys jingle like haunted chains on a ghost as they twist in the heavy door. The taller man sighs as he gathers his things. "Do yourself a favor. Think about it. The federal government has a file with your name on it. Here's how it works: it might be next week, might be a year from now, maybe two, but we are going to come get you. Make life easy, Mr. Houston, and tell us what we need to know now. The prosecutors don't give two shits, but I do. Let me help you."

The two marshals make their way to the door. Just before they walk out, the taller one turns and says, "You have forty-eight hours to decide. After that, it'll be too late."

And they leave, the door closing behind them.

I sit there alone as sounds of low, muffled voices reverberate from the other side of the wall. Something about this moment is both fitting and surreal for me. Fitting because I strangely feel prepared for this outcome, for this exchange with the U.S. Marshals, and surreal for the exact same reason. Something inside me weeps for the loss of who I used to be, which is exactly what this is, I think. And something more demanding inside me just wants to lie back down on a metal rack and sleep and heal or die and go away.

The voices stop for a moment and I hear laughter and I wonder what the hell is so funny. I think to myself how little my situation means to any of these people. How I am officially a statistic, a tragedy that replays over and over in front of these people's eyes until they are desensitized to any of it. I am on the other side now, the enemy, and my worth will now be measured in things I can't quite comprehend. I will learn new rules and I will figure out life differently than I have been taught up to this point, and I will see sides of human beings that I'm not sure I'm prepared to witness.

Is this the path I travel and never make it back? Who knows?

The door swings open and the guard says my name and cuffs my hands in front of my body this time. He grins. "You belong to us now, Houston."

I say nothing but look at him like he's messing with the wrong person. Maybe tomorrow I'll have the energy to be nice, maybe next week I'll realize how I must appear in his jaded, judgmental eyes; but for now, he's on the other side.

"You'll remember this decision someday," he tells me and I want him to shut up.

"You don't know me," I say. "I don't give a fuck."

"Is that right?" He shakes his head. "Somebody told me you ran the ball for Higginsville," he says and then adds, "What a waste."

He follows me down the hall, the sounds of the chains around my ankles seem louder than they were heading away from my cell. And, moments later as he's slowly closing the door to my tiny, metal cage, he smirks as I avert my eyes because it's clear his words are stronger than mine.

And I keep my mouth shut. And he whistles. And he wins.

My pillowcase has been swapped out. The new one is clean and it is white and it is free of whatever is leaking from my head. And I pretend that someone cares for my life and I pretend that I'm worth something in their eyes.

Even though I don't hold myself in the same regard.

The guard shuffles down the hall.

So I close my eyes and prepare to sleep for as long as they will let me.

27

Withdrawals are different this time. Not that I'm an expert, but I've tried to quit enough times that I have a baseline for how my body and spirit crave the high-octane I've been running on. I have weathered the instability of emotions, suffered through the deep sadness and the manic explosions. I have pushed through the itch and the aches that vacillate from just beneath the surface of my skin to deep within my bones. I have lived through the mouth sores and the annoying feeling that seems to reside between your teeth below the gums, maybe from dehydration, maybe from the cocktail of poisons swimming in my lungs, surging through my body, resting in my bowels.

I've dealt with the diarrhea and the pain in my stomach because food and water are foreign to my body, yet it still craves anything that will fill the void. In the past, I have had my share of shoveling chocolate and fast food and Xanax and alcohol into my system, praying it would somehow fill my soul while suicide frequented my thoughts as possibly the better option.

With every detox, I have pinballed between complete tranquility and a volatile temper as I rode out the residual insanity that circulated through my veins, but never have I braced myself for the withdrawals from this kind of a habit. The kind where I punched holes in my veins seven to eight times a day, each shot bigger than the last. What's it going to take to starve that shit out of my system? How much resolve will it take me to go another hour, never mind another day?

It's been just over two weeks since I was on the streets and I'm sure I haven't been conscious more than a couple hours total.

But that's starting to change. My body, which has been screaming to hibernate, to power down, is now staying up late at night when it is quiet and I let the fact that I am incarcerated and in need of new survival skills sink in. They've moved me from the single cell to the second floor and I have somehow found the courage to close my eyes in a cell with seven other criminals and slip into unconsciousness. Deep down, I know I am vulnerable, but the fact that I still look like a feral beast ready to attack anything that tries to back me into a corner helps my cause.

And what little dignity I had salvaged coming in here has been lost in the common area where I, like everyone else in the cellblock, shit in the open only a few feet from where twenty-four men watch TV. Maybe this shouldn't matter, but it does. I mean the reality of my life is that I was prepared, no determined, to die only a few weeks ago, so why care about this…right? But I guess having strangers carry on around me while I'm crouched down in a too-small toilet stall hidden only from the chest down, just seems to punctuate how utterly fucked up my life is going to be.

This impossibly noisy room is a cacophony of conversations on the pay phone and aggressive slams of the dominoes on the steel table and people eating or showering or enjoying loudly what is on the TV. I bury my head in my hands and try, unsuccessfully, to pretend no one can see me as I quickly and uncomfortably take a shit, looking like some misguided jack-in-the-box whose spring has lost its bounce. I wonder if I will ever get used to this and hold tightly to the necessary lie that this is only temporary.

And I try to forget about the amount of time that now hangs over my head; I try to ignore the fact that, just outside these walls, there are people who I grew up with, people who know my parents and my name and what I was like as a teenager, even as a child. I try to forget that there are newspapers that have my name in them. The same newspapers that not so long ago printed images of me in a football uniform or wrestling singlet and wrote about my stats. My stats are now destined to be nothing more than rumors swirling about crimes I'm charged with without any understanding of the entrapment of addiction, without any understanding of how this drug hides the consequences from my brain or who this story would reach if, God forbid, I didn't die. No one will know that the plan was to secretly disappear in some lonely, seedy backroom where it would be quiet and uneventful; and no one would know me or miss me because I hadn't been in their circle very long.

But now the consequences hit too close to home. There is no ignoring what's been done to my family or their reputation.

And again, I have to ask—why here? *Out of all the jails in the world, God, out of all the many places I've been hiding, doing drugs, cooking drugs, shooting drugs, did You have to pick here?* Where the next day after my arrest the people in my home town would have started saying things like, "Hey did you hear about Tom Runge's boy? He got arrested for meth." And I imagine they talked about how they always "knew there was something wrong with Tom Runge's boy" or how "Tom Runge's boy always had something missing" and "that's what you get when your family has money." Or the pièce de résistance, "That's what you get when you spoil your kids."

But the people who really knew me would feel sorry for my mother and shake their heads and say, "What a shame. Bless his heart." Which we all know is a horseshit way to say my mother didn't deserve what I put her through. And they'd be right.

But either way, I know they all know by now and I can't imagine how I will ever show my face in Higginsville again. It's a small town, a world unto itself. Until you've walked into a gas station or a diner or even church and the resounding conversation is how the football team is doing or how the basketball team should look this year, you won't get it. Until you've traveled in packs for hours just to support the wrestlers who made it to state, not *the* state wrestlers but *your* state wrestlers, you don't know what it's like to belong to a small town. The passion, the emotion, the love for what might get overlooked somewhere else is majestic and important to the development of the most authentic person you will ever become.

And I loved the years when it was my turn, the times when all the attention was positive and uplifting and the team felt four thousand people strong. In my hometown, Saturday was for drinking, Sunday was for church, but Friday belonged to Husker football. And I was good. Above par for our small town. I was exceptionally strong for my size. I was quick off the ball and loved to run through walls. The boys I played with meant the world to me, and hearing my name over the loudspeaker was so motivating and never got old. I'm not sure when I felt more alive—Thursday night dreaming of the perfect hit, watching Lawrence Taylor highlight films, or actually feeling that leather ball tucked into my side as I ran a sweep around the outside.

Right now, that world might as well be on Mars because it's too far in my past and out of my reach. Yet I crave it, miss it, and want to see it again.

That is, if I ever get another chance to walk those streets.

And so, the withdrawals are very different this time. I guess I deserve that. What I, the junkie, am forced to slowly, unrelentingly think about as my body heals, and I marinate in regret and regain consciousness and my missing equilibrium. And I don't have the need to cry, although my conscience is screaming that maybe I should. That even though I have somehow developed a mechanism within me that allows me to ignore the severity of my situation, I will soon have to come to grips with where I am, that the amount of evidence in my case is enough to keep me in these unfathomable environments for the rest of my life.

Although there are no tears in my worn, bloodshot eyes, there is an unfriendly voice inside that whispers, "You really fucked up this time. This one's going to hurt, going to last, going to be more permanent than you can possibly imagine."

And, somewhere during the first two weeks of being here, I gained enough clarity to miss my mom. My poor, confused mother. I wonder which emotion will be stronger for her, the heartache of seeing her baby boy shackled and dressed in orange or the relief of knowing that at least I'm alive and in one place for a while. I don't know much of anything else about what's coming next, but I know I miss my mom and the life I had before.

Holy shit, what I wouldn't give for a bump of meth right now.

28

"HERE MAN, YOU look like shit," a white inmate tells me as he hands me a plastic container of instant coffee granules. His hair is long and straight, his build thin but scrappy and covered with lots of tattoos. I can tell just by the way he carries himself that he's far up the food chain in this shithole jail.

"Instant," I say, more as confirmation than a question.

"Just like your karma, motherfucker," and he laughs and I see that he is missing a front tooth but he wears it well. More like a battle scar than a dental hygiene problem.

I stare at him. He stares back. And I'm sure I don't have it in me to finish a fight. I don't know if this is some pissing match or if this is some weird pre-duel-at-dawn dance over a cup of Nescafe, but if it is, I just want to go back to bed.

"Don't get sensitive this early in the game, dude. You never know who's the killer among us." He brushes past me toward the shower and turns on the hot water. Like the toilets, it's all part of the common area. "Consider that free advice. But the next one will cost you." He hesitates. "Motherfucker." No smile.

He offers me a cigarette. I scramble for it, my hand shaking. He flicks his lighter and I inhale as deeply as I can, the smoke hitting my throat and lungs with a hot, deep burst. I exhale and feel the nicotine enter my bloodstream.

"You'll be all right," he tells me.

"That's what I'm worried about."

He laughs and points over his shoulder. "The shower is hot enough. Make your coffee."

I fill my cup, watch the granules semi-dissolve in the water, and walk back to the bench to thank him and smoke some more. The other men notice us talking but nobody says anything.

"I can tell you're a tweaker," he says. "What are you in here for?"

I take a sip of the coffee, a drag off the cigarette and stare down at my pale, cadaver-like arms, the track marks no longer visible unless you know where to look. The chemical burns on the tips of my fingers now just dry peeling skin. "For breaking my mother's heart," I tell him and look away to the sunlight peeking through the crisscross lines of the steel-inlaid window.

"We're all in here for that. You ain't no different, motherfucker." He shakes his head. "No fucking different."

I feel the urge to tell him I'm different, that he doesn't understand, but what do I know? "My name is Houston."

"I know your name."

"I don't know yours."

He reaches into the waistline of his pants and pulls out a pouch of Tops rolling tobacco. "It's Tuck," he tells me. "Short for Tucker."

"Thanks." I tell him, unsure if that makes me look weak or grateful to a guy who could be a murderer, could be a thief. Or maybe he's just an asshole.

"Number one rule in jail," he says, "especially in prison, is 'Be careful of people who give you things. There are always strings attached.'"

"No shit?" I hold up the cigarette. "What about this? What about you?"

"*Always* strings attached." There's silence as he lights a cigarette and takes a drag. He exhales and looks at me and says, "But you've got to find a white boy you can trust."

Trust? In here? What does that really mean? I hear the keys outside the cellblock as a guard shows up to serve breakfast. The two of us shuffle toward the line forming by the chuck hole.

"Do your people have money?" As he asks the question, he takes his position in front of everyone in line. I watch as no one says a word.

"Maybe," I tell him. "But I'm not sure I know who my people are."

"Well, Houston," he grabs the first two trays of food that are passed through the square hole, "sounds like you and I have the same people."

I take the tray of instant eggs and runny grits, and I do my best to read between the lines.

"But you still owe me for the coffee and cigarettes…" he narrows his eyes and punctuates his sentence with, "motherfucker."

Then he grins and the missing tooth makes him look like a formidable hockey player. And I know he's dangerous but so are most of the men in this cell block. So we eat in silence as I ponder deeply what he did to break his mother's heart. Because wondering about his issues and all the unforgivable things he committed is a hell of a lot easier than thinking about mine.

29

I LIE HERE in my rack replaying the heartbreaks over in my head. Unable to sleep, the guilt and shame bubble to the surface as I remember the time my mother came to my house after not hearing from me for weeks on end.

Would it make a difference if she knew I was crying? Like a sniveling child, I had tears streaming down my red distorted face as I tried not to gasp, afraid I would give away the secret that I was just up the steps and around the corner. It was at my home on Sala Lane, where grass was overgrown and windows covered with overlapping bedsheets and the neighbors had all counted me out. But she knew I was there, she had to have, because mothers sense these things in ways only they can; in the same way she always knew if I was being ornery in the backseat when I was a child, even though her eyes were always looking straight ahead.

I was so sorry in that moment at the house, listening to that strange girl tell her I was nowhere to be found, listening as I lied to my mother through this person she did not know, listening to what it said about what I was willing to do to remain an addict. It broke my heart to break hers, because I heard it in her voice—the way she hesitated, the way her sentence trailed off when she acceded, when she finally gave up.

What does a mother do when her son sends a disheveled meth whore to answer her knock? This person neither one of us knew, now the gatekeeper of her child—the child she sheltered, the child she held, the child she fought for her entire life—until there was no fight left. Until this stupid person stood between us, stood between a mother and her baby boy, stood only six simple steps away from me as I silently cried for all that this meant.

And what does your mother do after she's cried, after she's swung with open hands at the dash, at the rear-view mirror, now slanted and off kilter? What does she do after she's gripped the steering wheel with white knuckles, screaming with her mouth wide open until her voice is hoarse and her body's numb, and the artery in her neck bulging with her fury?

She gives up.

And I'm sure as she wrote that note, the one on the back of a Wendy's napkin, she struggled with what to say. But I felt every word that was said and every word that was unsaid. How I hadn't spoken to Ana, the girl in Chicago; how mom and her had talked and compared notes; how this whole thing had gone far enough. To please call, please come home—she didn't care how bad it was, she just wanted me and whatever disease I carried.

Dear God, I beg you, don't let her give up now.

30

A COUPLE OF days later, they move us to appear in court. A restrained, staggering mob of orange jumpsuits punctuated by the loud jangle of our shackled ankles. I move my feet deliberately, trying to accommodate the chain between them, but am limited by a sharp pain in my Achilles. They herd us like ducks in a row, down the street of Lexington, in broad daylight, where I hope nobody recognizes who I am.

"What are you doing here, Hollywood?" I turn and see the familiar face of an old friend just before I pass him. It's a nickname he gave me during my freshman year of high school when he was an upper classman and I looked up to the bigger guys. Only now he's a deputy sheriff. Wouldn't you know it? Working this county, in this jail, where I am a criminal in chains.

And how do you answer that question from a man who drank beer on the same gravel roads, who sang your school fight song, whose mom knows your first, middle, and last name? I had no answer. Just shame in my eyes when I smiled nervously, looked away, and hoped that the other inmates didn't notice that I knew a cop.

I am paraded up to a courthouse that still has a cannonball lodged in one of its pillars from the Civil War, something I learned on a field trip as a child where I held hands with little friends and walked daisy-chain style up this exact same sidewalk. And, like salt on the wound, this is the year of my ten-year class reunion. Where all those kids I held hands with years ago will be hyper-curious as to what became of Kyle Houston.

The guard leading us inside is cool—grey hair, fat belly, and a leathery tan face, most likely from working on a farm off duty. I know his type—dry humor, horse sense, and the kind of man who wears cowboy boots with his Sunday clothes. And I'm reminded of Mayberry and Andy Griffith, and I feel oddly at ease as we all hotbox our cigarettes in our orange jumpsuits just before we go inside to declare we're "not guilty" to the state of Missouri.

The courtroom is full as all eyes follow our criminal parade, minus the ticker tape, minus the candy, minus the cheering crowd. Except for the creaks and groans of the hallowed and ancient benches, the room is silent.

I see my parents in the third row, emotionless and confused. I wasn't sure I'd see them here. Our conversation on the phone the other day was brief, my paranoia of tapped phones was difficult to work around, so we stuck to the pertinent facts—the court date, the charges, and if they were feeding me well or not. But it wasn't clear what registered and what went in one ear and out the other because all Mom kept repeating was, "At least you're alive."

Dad sits tall, arms crossed above his belly, stoic and pensive, taking it all in as he slowly chews on a piece of gum. Mom sits primly, so tiny next to him with her makeup and business suit, but I know this woman well. On the inside, she blames herself.

I raise my handcuffs and try to wave with one finger, and Mom smiles. It is fake and I return the favor. Dad doesn't move. It's not his role to make me feel better; it never was. He gets the same smile anyway.

Two rows away this fucking girl named Amber, who I'm pretty sure was the last person I had sex with before the cotton fever scare, is in here waving and pointing like I've known her my whole life. And in this light, being kind of clear-headed, I can see now why we had sex. At nineteen or maybe twenty, she has the advantages of youth—smooth, porcelain skin and a pristine aura of innocence. She is pretty enough with soft, shiny, long, dark hair—but she's definitely no angel.

She waves at my parents. My mom doesn't know what to do.

And I wonder how long it is going to be before I touch another girl, get intimate, whisper in the dark. I nod my head, produce a smile for this girl but feel ambivalent. On one hand, she is a link to the underground world, where I could find money and make bail, then find freedom. On the other hand, she is a link to the underground world, the reason I am here, the thing I shouldn't want.

I wonder how deep the depths of despair are, the furthest reaches of loneliness. Because out there I was alone, but I had meth, I had speed, which camouflaged the hollow center in my life.

And in here I have loneliness but it's never alone. It comes with epiphanies and pain and the vivid reminder of what's been severed from my life. And there will be no softness, no maternal presence, no feminine energy. There will just be bricks and bars, and callous hearts, and me, surrounded by the slow burning fuse of clarity. A real motherfucker; Karma's closest friend.

After we've all individually stood next to interchangeable, apathetic public defenders and pled 'Not guilty', even though not a single person is innocent, the judge stands up and dismisses the court. The people file out slowly. Family members approach their loved ones, showing support and letting them know they'll always be there for them. I wonder how many times they've shared this exchange.

Amber sidles up to me, impatient, happy. "I made it, Sweetie," she tells me and I'm annoyed by her choice of words but don't show it.

"How did you find out?"

"Called the sheriff's department." She beams. "I'm here for you. We are special."

We? I need to hurry and get rid of her, and then talk to my mother. "Thanks," I say, "but I don't want you to get in trouble. We need to limit our contact—"

"But I love you," she tells me. Fuck. *Love?* This is worse than I thought.

"Cool. I'll call you later." I glance over her head at the sea of people. Mom and Dad are weaving through the crowd. "I need to talk to my mom."

"I thought that's who she was. I said hello."

"Cool. I'll call you later, Amber."

She looks sad and disappointed, but I don't care. Her words are empty; because if I don't get out, she'll use my name to get new connections and love the next meth cook. And if I do get out, I'll never talk to her again for pulling this bullshit. But for now, she can be a conduit to the outside.

"I'll call you later."

She kisses me on the lips, the gesture clumsy and out of place. The inmates make comments like construction workers on a busy street.

The inmates file out of the first two rows and shuffle toward the door like cows into a stockade. Amber watches me as I move with the herd, her face wide and hopeful and naïve. Mom and Dad are waiting by the door. My mother's eyes are watery and she is shaking, unsure what to do. I feel like an asshole.

"Can I hug you?" Mom asks.

"Not sure. Never been in this situation." I look to the guard and shrug.

"You can hug your mama, boy. I won't say nothin.'"

I lean in with my shoulder, hands cuffed in front of me. Mom's embrace is meaningful, strong, and I hear her sob. "At least you're alive, Kyle," she whispers in my ear.

Some consolation, huh, Mom? At least I'm alive to witness all the pain in your red-rimmed eyes. We separate and I nod my head affirming that it's true. I look at Dad. The passing years have taught us a way of communicating without words, in spite of the complicated history between us.

"How are you doing, kiddo?" he asks. I feel a lump in my throat.

"I'm sorry for—"

"I know you are," he interrupts. "We need to figure out the next steps." He's looking at me, waiting for something enlightening, as if I have an answer.

"They don't say much, Dad. I'm really sorry."

"Come on, Houston," the guard says and puts his hand on my shoulder. "They're going to think you escaped." I back away from my parents.

"I need to make bail," I tell them. "I can get the money for a good lawyer if I can just get out."

"Where do you expect—"

"At least you're alive," Mom repeats, interrupting Dad. "And now we know where you are." She's struggling now, fighting not to cry, but the tears are winning.

"Yeah, Mom, that's right, at least you know where I am," I agree, an edge of sarcasm in my voice.

"We'll talk to your lawyer," Dad says.

"I love you guys," I tell them but it sounds wooden, rehearsed. They look at each other, unsure what to say. The guard clears his throat, tugs at the back of my shirt. "Dad?" I say. "I need to get out."

He says nothing, just looks at his feet.

"Dad?"

"Houston. Now!" the guard demands.

"Get me out," I say again, looking to Mom, hoping for sympathy, understanding.

Instead she wipes her eyes, stands taller, and straightens her skirt. Her chin out now, she says, "Give us time to be grateful before you remind us what a selfish asshole you can truly be." No more tears. "Now that we know where you are."

I turn away, find my place in the line where we all walk with our heads down, like sad, orange penguins. One of the inmates says, "Damn, Houston, that yo mama saying that?"

"Fuck you. Mind your own goddamn business," I tell him. "We won't be in these cuffs all day." Daring him to say something, staring menacingly, furiously.

"All right, boys, let's play nice," the guard tells us.

"My bad, Houston. That yo mama," the inmate says. A pause, then a glint in his eyes. "But if you talk to me like that again, that's yo ass."

I don't care. I have no strength, only anger. I have no fight in me, only pride. My mind keeps going back to my tired and broken mother, and no matter how far the drug has pulled me away from my feelings, from my heart, there is one thing it can't erase—how sorry I am for who I've become.

You're right about one thing, Mom. At least I'm alive. But I don't know this version of me. How I use everybody, how I lie and cheat to achieve my end goal.

A mother's love is incurable even when her baby boy is the disease. So please don't be fooled, don't hold hope, don't keep looking for the boy you have raised.

Because I am nowhere to be found.

This sidewalk, this courthouse, this town…they are all a part of my past and now a part of my future. I stare at the feet of the convict in front of me and do the only thing I can—continue shuffling forward. My life now is these people; three hots and a cot, as they call it. And I'm slowly starting to realize that the punishment of incarceration isn't the fear, isn't the lack of freedom, isn't even the shitty, vile people you rub elbows with every waking moment. The true consequence of my crime is being locked away with myself 24/7.

31

I'm seven now and playing with the older boys from the neighborhood. Our house is two stories, on the corner lot, and 'huge and beautiful'. I know this because everybody says so. We have this fantastic wraparound front porch that is built with bricks and mortar, not see-through wooden railing, which is perfect for little boys like me to play war. It is a wall that I often hide behind, pretending it is the dug-out trenches of a war-torn landscape; where I sit with my back against the cool, red bricks, holding a long stick as if it were a rifle, and then leap out and start shooting. This is my go-to spot for a surprise attack on the other boys.

School is out for the summer and although it is hot and dry, everybody is laughing and running and diving behind trees. Tom is working in the yard but well out of range of our games and I know he's pretty hot too…I've been getting him beers all morning. Shirtless tan boys in jean shorts and striped gym socks that come up past the knees, have been circling the house for hours. Some of the older boys have squirt guns and Bradley, the boy whose mother gives me his outgrown winter coats, has taken control of the garden hose and is spraying anyone who turns the corner on our backyard. I scrambled down the porch and sprint around the side of the house.

"Gotcha, Houston!" Bradley yells as he nails me with a sharp, steady stream. "Lay down. You're dead."

The water is cold and focused and catches me off guard. "God dang!" I say without thinking.

"Watch your mouth, kiddo!" Tom yells at me.

"Sorry," I holler back and mean it sincerely as I count to a hundred before leaping back into action and darting behind a tree. As I sit there catching my breath, I hear Bradley's voice yelling the same thing to other boys. They are older and more experienced so they leap behind the tree before they start counting.

And my emotions are electric as I realize how unthinkable it is to have the older kids at my house playing with me, not just here to see my pretty, popular sister, and I can't contain the energy and excitement because I feel, for lack of any better word, 'cool'. To be somewhat an equal with these fellas is as awesome as it is unexpected. I mean me, Kyle Houston, up close and studying what seems like an entirely different world. But it's the summer of 1978 and school's out, and I'm basking in the sunshine of freedom and acceptance and all the emotions of boys in June.

From behind the tree, I jump up and square off with my makeshift rifle. Almost as if he was waiting for me, Bradley soaks me again.

"Whoa!" I scream. "God dang it." And I run back behind the tree again.

"Bradley," I hear Tom's voice. "Put the hose down," he tells him and I remember that I was just told to watch my mouth.

"I'm sorry," I say as I come out from behind the tree. "It was an accident."

Slowly, I see the other boys appear out of hiding as Tom continues to walk my way. The boys are expressionless, slow moving, but fixed on me. I tell myself that it's not that bad, I just made a mistake, but I see his temples pulsing, his jaw clinched, and I wish I could scream maybe 'time out' or 'red light'—anything that could pause this thing that is unraveling in front of all these boys I've wanted to play with for so long.

Tom becomes more deliberate and takes longer strides, more frightening with each step, closing the space between us. I know better than to run; I know better than to resist as I pray that I take my lumps with dignity. I'm terrified. Because of the lessons I have been taught, mostly in private, almost never in front of others, my heart is pounding and fear scrambles my thoughts as I close my eyes and prepare for what comes next.

He's here, and the pain is sudden, overwhelming, like being attacked by a crazed and powerful beast from out of nowhere—a bear or a mountain lion, maybe. He's just so big to me. I know now I should have seen this coming, but I didn't. I should have paid more attention to his words, but I was lost in the moment with the boys from my neighborhood. And I'm pretty sure the boys can see my eyes are wide and frightened, like a field mouse caught in the sharp talons of its predator, as I'm suspended by a single arm, dangling and screaming.

And I hate the sounds I'm making, the sounds of horror, the sounds of shock and excruciating pain like someone is being killed, but what am I supposed to do? Although I desperately wish no one could see this, I'm too busy just trying to escape, trying to survive. His hand is so big, so powerful as he beats me—my butt, my back, my legs—viciously and with speed as I realize how futile it is to try to deflect the blows with my other hand. I raise my legs in hopes that I'm too heavy for him to keep holding in one hand. Maybe I can hit the ground and somehow roll away, but he's so strong. The power behind his anger feels worse than before; this feels personal, and I'm scared that this won't stop, and I feel weak and at the mercy of something possibly out of control. Why do I always make him this way? Why am I so stupid?

Then I feel it, he lets go of my arm and I land on the ground, on my butt that will be sore in a few hours. I have learned the bruising doesn't take long to show up. He stands over me now, his shadow looming, his finger pointing straight at me, "The next time you think you can do whatever you want, think about that."

I say nothing. I can't, I'm crying too hard. But if I could, I would tell him I'm sorry; I'm always sorry. That I never meant to hurt his feelings like this or disobey anyone. I am just a dumb kid who forgets things when he's having fun. If I could stop sobbing for one second, I would beg him to please tell me I wasn't all bad. Please. Because I don't remember feeling this ashamed, which proves that I love him, right? He doesn't know it, but this hurts my heart worse than the spankings.

Haven't I been trying? Haven't I been doing better? I don't care how much he hits me, I love him and I want to make him happy. I want him and Mom to get along and to not fight over me and my presence in this family. I want to belong and be special like I seem to be able to do with the kids at school. He has no idea how badly I want to wrap my arms around his ankles and cling to him tightly and not let him walk away mad at me. I don't care if the older boys see me, I want to scream with all my strength, "Please, don't hate me. I will never do it again."

But that's a lie. I know I will piss him off again because there's something wrong with boys like me.

It's over. He has walked away and so have the other kids as I wipe the tears from my face. I lie on the ground, embarrassed that the kids had to see this, embarrassed that I wasn't tough enough to take it. What will they think of me? What will their parents think of me when they all tell them about what happened today? Does this mean they won't be back?

Because everyone now knows I am a bad kid and I have disappointed Tom. Again.

The world is now a place where bad things are obvious to everyone but me. I don't know why I never see the cost of my mistakes before I make them. I just want to be forgiven.

Please, God, let Tom forgive me.

32

Sure, I plead 'Not Guilty' to the shitload of charges against me, but deep down I take full responsibility. Sort of. But what do I know? I'm new to all this incarceration crap. There's no doubt in my mind I was a junkie, or am a junkie—whatever, but when you're trying to wrap your head around doing an undetermined amount of time, what's it fucking matter what you call it when you crossed that line? Who gives a shit whether you became a junkie three months ago or twelve months ago or last week; because here you are kid, and not a single label can make me feel better or worse about this situation. Trust me, I've tried.

In my predicament, labels are like trying to explain abstract emotions with sketches of stick figures.

The truth is I was that runaway stagecoach headed toward the cliff and now that it's slowed down, I have nothing to hitch my wagon to except daily realizations of the unthinkable acts I committed. Because now, as my body starts to change—my frame packs on weight and color comes back into my face and I get some fat on my belly, and the ache and that goddamn itch starts to subside…it's all worse.

And I tell myself I'll never use again, but that's just to make a deal with God, or the universe, or whoever listens to the sorry sacks of shit lying on their backs in broken, rusty county jails. I can't deny this disconnect between what I think and what I feel. I think I'll never do that drug again but feel like that is probably a lie. I think I'm a human being responsible for my actions but feel like that doesn't make sense. And I think I could find a way to navigate my rocky future but feel that I don't know what the fuck I'm talking about. This shit is as bleak as a terminal illness. And maybe it is a terminal illness…one with a slow, painful death.

And I see the physical action, no issue there, but where's the spiritual conflict that rears its head in all our bad mistakes, the moral ping-pong, the two sides? That's normally where I appear in those moments, but I don't recollect any of that now. And look, clearly there are stages of addiction. Clearly, some addicts have a choice. But every choice a junkie made is in his past—snorting, smoking, shooting—all decided back when he could see both sides of the argument. Back when there still *was* an argument.

And it's not a line of crap. I don't feel this way because I'm in a bunch of trouble, although I'm in a bunch of trouble. This isn't driven by getting back into the good graces of God or the courts or my family or even myself. Like that could ever happen.

I am Kyle Houston, kind of, and sorry for what I've done. But if I'm being honest, the most accepting thing I can possibly admit is that I don't understand. Ask me how I could do this to my mother. I don't understand. Ask me how I could do this to Dylan. I don't understand. Ask me how I can be honorable, honest, caring and still shit on my life, shit on the friendships, shit on the people who believed in me. And still the answer is *I don't understand.* That's not a cop out, it's the truth. Not a plea for everybody to overlook my actions. Just simply the only answer that comes when I'm brave enough to travel into the dark parts of my soul, when I'm alone and hurting and honest with myself. The only answer that surfaces is: *I don't understand.*

Addiction is a complex and primal thing, as individual as a snowflake. So here is where my head's at—the need for the drug can become ingrained in someone's survival instincts so deeply that there's no separation between being spun up and needing to breath. And in a world where tiny, crystalline flakes are as critical as oxygen to your mere survival, what are the limits to what you'll do to get it? That's the questions to ask. That's the consciousness I don't comprehend. That ever-moving substance of being a junkie that you can never quite look at head on, the thing inside itself that shifts once it's under the microscope. And to truly understand the complexity of this would be to somehow catch a glimpse of how God forgives us all. Yeah, it's that serious.

And my journey, my salvation, is now galvanized by the mystery of how the fuck something like this happens. And all I want to do is hold somebody, bury my head on their shoulder and cry.

The one thing I'm not going to get to do for a very long time.

33

TUCK NEVER SAID what her name was, just that she was "his Ana". He did say that she liked Harleys and that she was the girl who invariably "tattooed everything"—words he borrowed from the lyrics to a song by Pearl Jam and passed off as his own. "His Ana" didn't sound anything like my Ana, the girl in Chicago, the one who hung in the back of my mind like a smoky mirror of all that could have been. I didn't tell Tuck that. Because no matter how different the two girls are, they both harbored lost innocence, broken trust, and a lifetime of regrets because of each of us. And that's all that really mattered in our sad stories.

Higginsville, instant Karma, Eddie Vedder, and facing a shitload of time, were the common ground of our relationship in the beginning. Well, that and the shame we brought to our family's name. It was odd that people with such hardened interiors would connect on such an open and vulnerable level, but we did. Many late nights in an otherwise quiet eight-man cell, with the light from the walkway shining through rusty metal bars, we would smoke cigarettes and talk about the lyrics and talk about the streets and talk about the girls who etched their names across our hearts.

And then we would go quiet, with only the sounds of the other men snoring like bullfrogs across a swampy marsh, as Tuck and I lay on our hard bunks contemplating the price these girls paid for believing they could make us change. And in those moments, it became clear to me that the cost of loving a boy like me was just as expensive as the cost of loving a boy like him. And through our stories of the one who got away, I felt the brotherhood of a broken heart; and that is how two dudes from separate walks of life bonded. At least, in the beginning.

Many saw Tuck as some jailhouse guru—the guy who had "been in" before and had all the answers, sharing his anecdotal philosophies of how to do your time. And he runs the cellblock, not even the guards would argue with that. He enforces rules, controls the TV, and negotiates on our behalf with the guards. But his bit was murder. And although he had elaborate stories confessing his innocence, there was an element of empathy that always seemed to be missing. I saw our acquaintance as rare for him, something he would get over quickly, and for the first time it forced me to imagine these men and what they were like on the streets. This one was dangerous. Like a circus lion in the spotlight, he would go through the motions to gain the approval of a crowd. And no one should ever turn their backs on him because no matter how easy he was to admire—the claws, the teeth, the mighty roar; at the end of the show, he belonged in a cage because he would tear a person apart and devour him—bones and all. Not his fault… life made him a lion.

There was this one story Tuck told me that stuck out more than all the others, about some kid he met during his first three-year bit. I can't remember what for, but definitely not murder. This kid—overwhelmed with grief, or agony, or any of the hundreds of unbearable emotions that haunt a convict's conscience—hung himself at night in the cell he shared with Tuck. Just the two of them alone in the dark. The thing that stuck with Tuck was that the kid wrapped a towel around his neck, tied the ends to the bars so the makeshift noose criss-crossed behind his head, and then got down on both knees and leaned forward, just enough to cut off the air to his brain so he could quietly, painlessly slip into the dark.

Kind of genius, in a way. A convict's mind brims with ingenuity, if you really want the truth. And although convicts aren't inventing the light bulb or discovering plutonium, they forever reinvent the wheel because they are often brilliant people who are simply lost and hurting.

I could tell Tuck loved telling the story—the shock value, the uniqueness, the I-know-more-than-you-do-ness about it all. The next day, the cocky bastard started singing *Another One Bites the Dust* when the guard showed up. Tuck ended up under investigation and in the hole for months, even though he insisted he had nothing to do with it. I wasn't there, but I believe in Tuck's innocence on this one.

Having a heart didn't seem to serve Tuck well. But he and I were cool, sharing lots of sad stories about our families, about our lives, about our addictions as the days slowly unwound. And that's how it was for me, my future as a convict in a cage.

At least, in the beginning.

34

Okay, it's been three months and what do you know, I'm tired of these people. Not all of them and not completely, but I've heard the same comments so many times. Clearly, Tuck, has exhausted his depth and I'm tired of subscribing to this pecking order that lacks any real leadership.

And I yearn for just one original thought…or, holy shit, how about something resembling honesty? Or maybe I just really miss the way life used to be…I don't know, civilized? I'm tired of being around people who don't give a shit about anything other than getting money for the commissary, like being broke in jail is somehow an injustice they shouldn't have to endure. They whine about kids and girlfriends and mothers, but in the end, the only thing that really matters is whether they can afford fucking honey buns and oatmeal pies.

I listen to '80s music on some KC radio station that reminds me of better times, when Molly Ringwald or John Cusack starred in films with iconic moments and amazing soundtracks, where kids lived life like an MTV video. Not like these people who live like animals, with personalities that are black, grey at best…and what I wouldn't give to hang out with one single person who knows the words to a Violent Femmes song.

Third Verse, same as the first. / Just last night, I was reminded of / Just how bad it had gotten…

But nobody does.

I write poetry at night now, but have no idea what I'm doing so I keep it all to myself. I intertwine elaborate stories of Ana into recreations of the high school in *The Breakfast Club*, and although those stories are all made up, for brief moments I feel like…me. I think of Kennedy, the VJ, from MTV's *120 Minutes* and how sexy she always was to me. And that night I tripped ecstasy in the bars at MU and I wished I went to school there instead of just crashing on friends' couches.

And how did I ever end up here?

The stark reality of my future is a loud, unintelligible freak show set on a stage of cinder blocks and paint-chipped iron bars. I bounce between the five stages of grief, slamming up against anger more than any other. But day by day, I feel different. Sane, more or less, maybe familiar or awake, I'm not sure. Whatever it is, after three months in, I'm recognizing the thoughts in my own head as, well, mine. Finally.

I'm beginning to see how deep this rabbit hole might go. I tell myself I made this bed so I have to lie in it, but the words feel so contrived. Like bullshit I tell myself to feel better. Only, who feels better after saying that? No matter what life affirming cliché I come up with, this fucking sucks.

I miss the simple landscape of my tiny hometown. I ache for the scent of freshly cut grass on a sweltering late afternoon. Where soon the crickets and cicadas will sing their songs as the green and yellow lightning bugs float through the night like tiny burning stars, and the air cools, and the streetlights blink awake as the sun sets on McCord's park.

And I'm tired of empty conversations with people who are nothing like me. I don't fit in this place, but lucky for me, we've got plenty of time to pretend I do.

"All I'm saying is, let's take a huge leap and assume there is someone in this jail that is actually guilty," I explain quietly one night in my cell to Reid, this large corn-fed kid in the bunk above Tuck. Tuck and I are in our bunks smoking cigarettes and sharing lies. The cell is dimly lit as I listen to the same old bullshit about how we're all fucking victims of the system. Everyone else is sleeping.

"I'm telling you, I didn't do a damn thing, fellas," Reid says, then punctuates his sentence with, "This time."

"These fuckers don't care." Tuck is lying on his back, one knee up, staring at the steel rails and thin mattress above his head.

"Right on," Reid says. "I feel ya, dog."

Tuck takes an extended drag from his cigarette. The glow from the tip lights up his face.

"Cool, you guys are innocent," I continue, my sarcasm obvious. "For the small percentage of us who actually committed a crime, I'm talking about choice versus action."

"Sounds like horse shit," Reid says and Tuck turns, silently looking at me.

For days now, I have felt Tuck getting territorial, becoming quieter, more irritable. Inmates have started to confide in me instead of him, but what am I supposed to do about it? Being in county jail is like people watching with a front row seat. It's not like you want to get involved but it's just so damn tempting. "OK, let's take oxygen, for example," I say. "If one of us was being held under twenty feet of water, we'd never give it a second thought about what we'd do to survive, to get to the surface and breathe oxygen." I glance sideways at Tuck, who just shrugs.

"The fuck's that got to do with me?" Reid asks. "Oxygen? Water?"

Tuck smirks and blows smoke in my direction. Asshole.

"It's simple—replace drugs for oxygen. It's a short circuit in our survival instincts. We are convinced we need—not want—to smoke, to snort, to stick needles in our arms. To breathe."

"Yeah?" Reid asks. He props himself on one elbow and watches me.

"We never 'choose' to drown, we never 'choose' to breathe," I explain to my audience of two. "Like the sorry bastard at the bottom of the pool, we just act on our survival instincts."

"Yeah," Reid says. "I'm with you, Houston."

"Our actions are compulsions, but the piece to the puzzle that doesn't seem to fit for me is the complexity of choice in all this." I pause for a moment to think. In the distant background, a door closes and keys rattle. The sounds of sleeping men fill the silence. "Don't get me wrong, I accept the blame, but that's a function of shame and morality. The responsible thing to do is to dig into this shit pile where my instincts, my free-will, my choice are all buried."

I stand and walk over to the door, lean my forearms on the bars and stare out into the hallway.

"Fuck that," Tuck interrupts. "Oxygen won't ruin your life, Einstein. Meth will. Your theory is flawed, dude."

"I thought about this, too. Take the same pool—you're twenty feet under, but this time handcuffed to the floor and given a hacksaw. You, Tuck?" I point at him directly, "Given that circumstance, you would saw your own hand off to get to the surface."

"So would you."

"Exactly." I walk over to the toilet, flick my cigarette in, and flush. "It's hard-wired into you, into me, into each of us to swim toward the shitty life rather than accept the shitty death every time." I sit on my bunk. "Where it gets really fucked up is, in our case, 'life' is the needles, the broken hearts, the prison sentences. And the shitty death is drowning in your overworked conscience by running out."

Tuck sits up and chuckles, "Fuck, Houston, you and all your big words and your theories don't fit in here. But don't worry; you leave tomorrow for Marshall, where all the soft motherfuckers go."

"Cool," I shrug, but I'm angry and stare out through the bars so I don't have to look at them. The light from the exit sign casts shadows on the floor.

"Cool," he mimics and I feel the weight of his stare. "Maybe you'll get that change of venue while you're there and I won't have to listen to your shit anymore."

It's never clear to me how Tuck always seems to know so much about people's transfers and cases, but he does. He was the first to suggest I transfer my case out of Lafayette County. "You'll never get a fair trial here," he told me. So, I brought it up to my lawyer, who decided it was a good idea. While I'm waiting for the courts to get around to it, I'm getting transferred to a newly built facility in Marshall, the next county over. It's an odd feeling, but the transfer makes me nervous. Kind of a 'devil you know versus the devil you don't' situation.

"Let's hope so, Tuck," I say loudly and turn to face him.

"Guys," Reid says, his voice sharp and anxious like he just beat his case. "We're saying the same thing, don't you see?"

"What are you talking about?" I ask.

Tuck still stares at me. "Oxygen. Dope. Survival," he says.

"Uh-huh," I say but my attention is on Tuck. He's pissed or jealous or threatened or something, I don't know. I'm so fucking sick of this place and of him.

Tuck takes a drag, flicks an ash on the floor and lies back down.

"But it's like I've been telling you," Reid continues, even though none of us are listening anymore. "It's not my fault. I didn't do a damn thing…" He pauses. "…this time."

I stare up at the ceiling and think about how fucked this whole thing is. Choices, chances stamped out like cigarettes on a prison floor. I could have been somebody, if I was willing to try. Just a little.

But goddamn it, I am not this. I am not forgotten and lonely, spending thirty years getting letters of loved one's deaths and once-a-month visits. I'm not that guy who never loves, who never lives; who walks out of prison at retirement age, institutionalized, and afraid, and dead behind his eyes because all he knows is this. Whatever this is.

Three months in and the irony is that, although I wasn't willing to find a way to want to live out there, I'm trying desperately to find a way to survive in here.

It is the saddest at night. When I can feel the death of my life, the death of my reputation, the death of hope and love and anything that resembles a future.

Reid and Tuck are quiet now, and although I am surrounded by dozens of men at all times, it is clear I am alone as I lie awake listening to my thoughts.

And in this moment, I just want to close my eyes and fast forward a million years. To that place in time where I find a way to laugh.

35

I'm eight now, and I'm tiny but strong. I've already broken one bone and gotten sewn up on two different occasions. I'm what they call 'all boy', and I hear them use words like scrappy and hustle when they talk about me. But really, I just want Dad to look at me the way other dads look at their boys.

The older boys like me because I do whatever I can to prove I want to be here. I carry the equipment, I show up early, I pay attention. I know that if I practice hard and show up, the coach will put me in and let me play. And it's summer, and it's hot, and I can't wait to show Mom and Dad what their little boy knows.

The uniforms are throwbacks, the kind with elastic at the bottom of the pant leg that is designed to hit just below the knee. But because I am a little fella, mine bunch up around my cleats. And our shirts have short sleeves that hit everybody at the elbow, except me—mine hang almost to my wrist. My belt is tight above my belly, keeping my pants from hanging too low; but even so, I'm thrilled at how everyone on the team looks so much like the Royals group photo on Grandma's favorite iced tea mug.

Some of the boys can hit over the fence, some can throw curveballs, some have fathers here all the time, helping with practice and cheering every hit. Then there's me, a quiet boy who is just trying to figure out where I fit. The other boys have grass stains on their knees and scuffs on their cleats, but my cap's new, and the white stripes on my uniform are bright and perfect. My mom wouldn't have it any other way.

In my town, baseball is important. Even though the town is small, we somehow fill the roster for seven complete Little League teams. People you have never met are in the stands, rooting for you because they know your last name so they know how well you'll play. And up there, in the middle of them all, is my mom, a woman who doesn't miss a single minute of any activity I do. Tom is sitting beside her, squinting in the sun.

But the person who gave me my last name is nowhere to be found.

All the boys seem so good, so polished with their movements as they swing the bat, two at a time, to make their arms stronger, their swings faster. Before practice, their dads stand on the field and coach them, smile at them, pat them on the back. All I can do is watch and shadow them. I am good at teaching myself. To every boy who steps up to bat, Coach hollers, "Keep your eye on the ball, Son" and when they hit the ball square with the bat, it seems to please him, so I know if I want to be good and want Coach's approval, I'll keep my eye on the ball.

But the pitcher is good, maybe better than ours. He's a farm boy from a small town close to ours, and because I am eight and he is twelve, he seems as big as a man out on that mound. His pitches are fast and I hear the ump yell, "Strike!" a lot, and I'm afraid I'm going to let people down; so I get nervous and I pray that I don't have to bat.

"Hey batter, batter, swing," the boys from the other team chant as I watch the pitch smack the catcher's glove and Johnny is standing on the plate, waiting for the throw.

"Look alive, fellas," someone hollers as the catcher throws the ball back to the mound and I swallow hard. My turn is coming up. My first time at bat. What if I miss?

I hear Tom shouting words of encouragement to the team and catch myself daydreaming that Jerry Sam can see me somehow. He might not be yelling but he's rooting for me, supporting me in spirit. I can feel it.

Then I'm on deck. I kind of watch, kind of swing a bat, trying to work some of the nerves out.

"Keep your eye on the ball, son," Coach yells and I hear the ump holler, "Ball three," and I know I'm up soon, so I look around for Jerry Sam. Although I haven't seen him yet, I know one day he'll be in the crowd.

"Ball four! Take your base," the umpire says. Johnny jogs to first base, and I'm moving now, trying to remember to breathe. Everyone in the stands is clapping and I know I'm expected to do something, so I repeat what I've been told. Keep your eye on the ball. Keep your eye on the ball.

As I step up to the plate, it suddenly feels like the entire world is watching. The older kids are standing in the dugout, fingers woven into the chain-link fence, faces serious and attentive. I'm somewhere between loving the attention and being scared to death, but I trust my coach, I trust his advice and so I squat low and put the bat on my little-boy shoulder.

"All right Kylie-bo, let's show 'em all what you're made of, little man!" Mom yells. A slow build of claps follows.

"Eye on the ball, young fella," Coach hollers and I feel like I belong.

The first pitch comes and I pick the bat up off my shoulder and step in and swing. And miss.

"Strike one!" the umpire yells in a deep baritone voice.

"Bring it in closer," the catcher calls as he tosses the ball back to the mound. Closer, I think; that should do the trick. That's exactly what I need to make contact and send this ball flying out to left field where everyone yells and cheers and chants my name. Where my mom is proud and Jerry Sam hears about it later at the coffee shop, or the truck stop out at the junction outside of town, but he'll hear nonetheless because the whole town will be talking about what little Kyle Houston did his first time up to bat.

And maybe my dad will want to spend time with me then because he'll know what I accomplished without his help; and he'll teach me secret tricks that he learned as a boy, like how to swing the bat like the others who aren't scared because they know all the things that I don't know yet. And I'll be better than them because of my dad. Because he knows things about me that not even I know yet; because he's my dad and I'm his son, and he was me once and I'll be him…and I just need to keep my eye on this ball.

At the very least, Tom will be impressed and he will change and like being around me. At the very least, that's what a hit your first time up to bat will get you.

The pitcher winds up. Eye on the ball. Eye on the ball. He releases the pitch. Eye on the ball. Eye on the ball. It's coming to the plate. Eye on the ball. Eye on the ball. This will change my life. High and inside.

Boom!

Sudden and without warning, like lightning, like a power surge, like a blackout, everything comes in short bursts now, brief images, freeze frames. Like a stack of pictures that you flip through to appear animated, the world moves around me. There is me, on the ground, spun around and facing the fence. Now blackness. There is Tom, I think. I feel arms helping me up, something warm and salty in my mouth; my mouth is numb, and maybe a rock or pebble in there as well. Still blackness. Now strong arms lift me—they're frightened, I can feel it. Carrying me, whispering, "You're okay."

I open my eyes, everything blurry and my stomach feels sick. I hear myself sob; I think I'm crying. There is a crowd. Did I hit the ball? Did I make it? But I can't seem to make words or to remember what happened.

"It's okay." A kind, masculine voice. My heart leaps. It's Jerry Sam. He came and now he's holding me, trying to wipe the blood, trying to wipe the tears away.

"I've got you, kid." His arms are strong, but hesitant.

"Dad?"

"Of course," he replies. "It's me." Then he covers my ears and yells for someone to get ice. The pebble in my mouth, I realize as my tongue skirts around it, is actually my front tooth.

He cradles me in his arms and shushes me as I cry. I feel a handkerchief wiping my face.

"Dad?" I repeat with a smile and wrap my arms around his neck. I squeeze tightly, but something feels different, smells different. Not like the aftershave a cowboy wears or the unfiltered cigarettes they smoke. Not like Jerry Sam.

Then he pulls me in and wraps his arms around me, so tight I'm crushed to his shirt. "You scared me, boy. You scared us all."

I begin to cry, harder and harder, as my brain realizes I've been hit in the mouth, realize this isn't Jerry Sam. It's Tom.

But he's holding me against his chest, and his voice isn't angry, and I realize he cares about me even though I didn't hit the ball. I didn't impress him. Even so, he picked me up, and he's hugging me, protecting me. Like a daddy. Like Jerry Sam would do. But Jerry Sam isn't here and Tom is.

I squeeze tighter; cry harder.

"I've got you, son." His voice is low and caring and warm. "It's all going to be okay now."

And for the first time, I think I believe him.

36

***Dear Ana** -*

I sit here in my very own cell with a pen and a thin, lined sheet of paper and start the letter I should have written a long time ago, the way you'd start a letter to your aunt or your pen pal. I agonize over the next words, wondering how she might take what I have to say, what my life has become. The worry is intense and scary, and I'm almost sick to my stomach. There are things I want her to know, *need* her to know, but the trouble is I'm on the verge of a breakdown that I'm not qualified to manage. And I gotta say, that makes overdue letter writing pretty fucking tricky.

> ***I know it's been a while, Ana, and I'm not really sure how to start, except to say that I'm sorry.***

The transfer here, to Marshall, Missouri, was uneventful and a welcome break from the depressing backdrop of Lafayette County. But now I'm alone for the very first time since the detox cell when my ear was bleeding—no cell mates, no noise, no philosophical conversations with other convicts. No excuses not to finish the letter I should have written before I got distracted by drugs and needles and the straw dogs of incarceration. The facility is clean and unused, and the food is good. And I'm sure I could enjoy all this goddamn silence if I didn't have to deal with my thoughts in this lonely-ass cell. I'm surrounded by myself and these cold and callous brick walls. The concrete is unkind as I sit here cross-legged on the bunk with my state-issued boxer shorts that slip every few seconds because the elastic is flat and useless, and the itchy wool blanket that I have stretched taut across the rack—a moment of control in a chaotic environment—and the stack of notebook papers that I borrowed from a dude who gives tattoos with a sharpened staple and the jerry-rigged motor of a Walkman.

And right now, I desperately want Ana to know, for someone to know. Someone to see me for who I am or was or whatever it is that will make my heart let go of all these feelings that have been waiting to ambush me alone.

I need you to know that in spite of what I've done, I've never stopped loving you.

Although she'll probably never get it, releasing these words somehow makes sense. She's been this light in my past for so long, an impossible destination to ever reach again; tonight, she's the only person who makes sense. I imagine myself slipping the letter into an envelope, sealing it shut, but then realize I have no idea where to address it. She is somewhere in Chicago and I'm in this shithole county jail in middle America.

> ***I'll probably never send this, Ana, but I need to write, I need to release, because what else do I have now?***

And then the letter shifts because maybe it was never really about her. Well, not only her. This letter is about the guilt that sits in my chest, so patient, so permanent, so immovable—like a huge stone carved over time silently waiting for me to stumble into it. This letter is about my son Dylan. It's about the unfathomable pain and confusion he must be suffering because I am his daddy. What a cosmic tragedy. I've been his father in name only for almost two years now and I wonder if he has forgotten me. If he pretends that I'm dead. If he's calling some other man Daddy, and that man is in a backyard somewhere in Kansas City, playing catch with my son while the day comes to a close.

This is the pain I have hidden from, that stalks me now because I have let down the one person I promised to always protect. I have let him feel the way I felt when Jerry Sam walked out the door.

Tonight, there is no escaping these haunting and unrelenting thoughts of the son I left behind.

> ***Little Dylan never asked for this, never deserved any of this. Neither did you.***

I close my eyes and I can see his big blue eyes, and hear the hopeful lilt in his voice when he says, "Daddy," and the way he opens his arms to me and giggles when I lift him high. When he was little, he would play so quietly with his toys by himself, and I would lean against the doorway watching him and marveling that I was a part of this little person's DNA.

But now I'm just so fucked. I am shitty, I am thoughtless, and I am still his daddy. That doesn't change because I'm locked away. Does it? There are no words to explain why I did what I did, or how much I hate the powerful self-centered spell of meth, but I'm still his daddy, right? I can see all the damage I have wreaked and everything inside me aches for a chance to repair it all. I'm ready for him. I'm ready to be the father he always needed, but he'll never know. Never.

In here, I pray, Anna, and hope it's not too late. But the sadness is deep, deeper than I think I can handle. This could be forever.

> ***Holy shit that can't be right. I can't do this, God. Don't let this happen to me. Not thirty years. Don't take away my life. That only happens to criminals who hurt people, who rob banks and shoot guns into innocent crowds and ruin lives. That only happens to the evil people of the world. And now me.***

And Dylan.

Does it help to know I can't breathe when I think of what I've done to you? To all the people I love? I'm not asking you to forgive me. I'm not even asking you to talk to me. But I'm scared and I'm alone and I would give anything to know that my life still matters…to someone.

It's selfish, I know, to even mention that I want my life to matter to her or anyone else. But I want redemption, I want a second chance, I want to hug my son and convince him I'm sorry and how I will never do it again.

And I wonder if the sheriff knew what he was doing when he loaded up the van this morning with orange and angry inmates. I wonder if anyone could see I was hanging by a very thin thread as we all drove down the highway to this shiny new jail in Marshall, Missouri. Because now, alone, as I struggle to get the ink out faster and say all the things I have never said, to make up for time and hurts and mistakes, even I am being caught by surprise. My eyes are blurry and the ink is splotchy, and all I see as I write is Dylan's face—his wide, hopeful, trusting face, looking up at me. My hand hurts and cramps, but that is nothing compared to the jagged edges inside me. I don't care about my hand or my tears or anything except how my little boy is doing. His heart is broken, he doesn't know who to trust and my dumb ass can't remember if she spells her name with one "N" or two.

> ***And I swear to you, no one's disappointment will ever match mine. Those things I could be—a daddy, a husband, someone to change the world—are all lost to the past and buried in here. I'm sorry, Ana. I'm so fucking sorry.***

What have I done?

It wasn't just me that I was ripping apart. It wasn't just me that I killed in those back rooms with needles and powder and lawlessness and spoons.

It wasn't just me that I lost and destroyed in the process. How could my blind spots be so vast, to completely overlook the true casualty of my war with myself. The innocent ones who dared to love me because they thought it was safe.

> ***And I know it's not fair, but I'm asking you to remember me, just not the way I am right now.***

And I wonder if there is a word in any language, maybe Sanskrit or something ancient, that describes a hurt this deep. A hurt that is infused in your blood, in your cells, in your newly-formed DNA as it pushes to the surface.

And the tears help me, kind of. My face is distorted now; I am alone. There is nothing to stop me, so I cry. Like my son who will never know me, I cry. Alone and afraid, knowing no one can hear me, I hold nothing back. Praying for her arms, her voice, her tender kiss. Praying I might hold him. Praying I might die.

> ***Remember me in OUR way. The way you showed me to be. The poet you stayed awake with on candlelit nights. In love. With you.***

And now I wonder, how do I end this letter. Love always and forever? How selfish would that be? What would it even mean from a broken man with an uncertain future who has lost the privilege of ever being trusted again? Because, unfortunately for both of us, that is who loves her. Always and forever.

Dear God, I cry, *I beg you to just let me see her one more time. Let her whisper in my ear as she rubs the back of my neck, lying there in the bed as the morning dawns. Before I become a hardened convict, before it's all too late.*

Tell me that it will all be okay—that my son will be okay, even if that's a lie. Because I need that lie. Because the truth won't set me free. It will only eviscerate me and take away the fragments of my soul that are left. Please, I beg you, just one more chance, one more time.

And so I cry. With my head burrowed deep into my pillow filled with the sounds that come from my mouth, from my throat, from a place inside me I have never felt before…I cry. My eyes ache and my face is wet, but I can't stop crying; because these tears, this grief, has been coming for far too long. So, I press my face harder into the thin prison pillow and let it collect all my tears.

Just like it did for all the men who came before me.

37

She tells me over the phone that his name is Sean Michael and manufactures sadness in her voice and then giggles, then returns to sadness. "He is strong," Nicki tells me.

I sit there on the cold aluminum bench in the common area. I'm numb.

She uses the word 'beautiful', although it seems trite and mechanical, almost like she's reciting the words that real mothers say. Though she swears with conviction the baby is mine, it is almost like a plea, almost like an indictment, almost like an apology because the father of the baby isn't exactly obvious to anyone else.

But even if I believed her, what does it really matter? This child will just be another fragile life for me to break, for me to feel guilty about, for me to regret. Another son to rinse and repeat and destroy like I've done to Dylan.

She giggles again, nervously. See, with Nicki, being faithful doesn't mean you don't have sex with other men.

But who she has slept with or gotten pregnant by is not something I care about, because in ways I can't explain, that would never be considered infidelity in our relationship. The simple fact that she hopes I am the father proves her loyalty. And that's the best I could ever get with a girl like Nicki.

In our world, sex is a tool—a form of currency, if you will. And if life is conceived from the simple act of exchanging money, then who am I to suddenly feel betrayed? Trading sex for drugs is a smart way to survive when the affliction is so heavy on your heart. And it means nothing, little more than the memory of a conversation with a stranger. In this situation, Nicki's only crime is that she's a female—the one with the uterus, the one with the ovaries, the vessel of the meth cook's desire. And, apparently, an inability to remember to take her birth control pills.

She thinks she loves me because she wants the baby to be mine, as if there is a place for her and I in the world—such a distorted, dirty lens she sees this all through. But how smart would I be to believe her? Even with a half dozen of us standing in a lineup, she wouldn't be able to narrow it down to three. And I wish this was a unique situation, but that's just the way it is. The world according to meth. Living in the moment, driven by appetite and impulse in the absence of any good judgment. Nobody said this was an episode of *Little House on the Prairie*.

And let's be clear, Nicki ain't no Laura Ingalls.

38

A MONTH LATER, I'm back. Lafayette County Jail feels like an antique compared to the facility in Marshall. The clang of the heavy steel doors, and the mechanical sound of the locks, and the jingle of the keys, and the echoes in the hallway, are all like cracked, worn scenes from a black-and-white movie. I'm back to being cramped with that shared toilet in the common area. There are new faces and old faces, and I get the impression that not everyone understands that Tuck runs this cellblock.

He's more disrespectful with everyone now, like he has dementia or that evil attitude some men get when drinking whiskey. Only there is no dementia and no whiskey.

And this day starts out like any other day—wake up, turn on the TV, smoke cigarettes, drink coffee. This new guy named Jeremy sits next to me telling me he ran in Northeast, but I don't care. I've never heard of him and I can tell he's a tweaker by the twitching of his jaw, the gleam in his eye when he talks about hitting a pipe, and his common use of the word "pilfer". Plus, his case is breaking and entering, so all roads lead right back to tweaker.

He says he went to Van Horn High School and he's done a five-year bit in Cameron, which explains the demonic clown tattoos all over his arms, and he wants to know if I know some "dude named Mike." I give him a cigarette to calm him down a bit because he swallowed a quarter gram when the cops pulled him over, which may or may not explain why he's so loud, and he replies, "Good looking out," which is how we all say thank you in here. His pupils swallow the blue or green in his eyes; it's hard to tell.

I sit on the tabletop, watch SportsCenter, and tell him to "keep it down, the others are sleeping" and he does this thing where he questions the word "sleep" loud enough for the whole cellblock to hear.

"This is jail, dude," he announces and then dares anyone who is listening to try and shut him up, but I say, "Cool," instead and we both sip coffee and smoke cigarettes, his leg bouncing like the needle in a sewing machine.

But I hear Tuck now, like some kind of radar. His blanket thrown off, the shower shoes put on, the hurried scuffling across the concrete. This ought to be good.

"Who's the badass in here?" Tuck says loudly, threateningly. "Is it you, motherfucker?" He points with his middle finger. A coffee container, full of liquid, lid screwed on tightly, is held with his other fingers.

Jeremy says nothing, just stands there in his wife beater with his arms crossed and biceps flexed.

"You think you're tough, pussy? Well, so do I." Tuck throws the container directly at Jeremy's head, hard. It hits the wall behind him with a low, dull thud. "How badass are you?" he yells and slaps his bare chest with his fists like he's a silverback gorilla.

After being in jail for a few months, almost nothing shocks me. But this does; it really does. Not the fact that Tuck is pissed or that he's standing across the room looking like Tarzan with long flowing hair, pounding his bare chest. Not that I'm watching SportsCenter next to a tweaker who swallowed enough meth to easily have a heart attack. Not even the fact that I have front row seats to a fight that may or may not end up with a dead body. Honestly, by now, that all fits perfectly into this alternate universe.

What surprises me is the fact that Jeremy looks confused, like he doesn't understand why he is being attacked; not only is he backing down, there is this child-like cat and mouse thing going on around the table. Tuck screams "pussy" and "bitch", every word erasing the pride this guy had in being from the hood in Northeast. As they circle the room, Jeremy darts fast to one side, like a boy running away from a parent with a switch. And I smoke my cigarette and watch today's episode of jailhouse reality TV.

Jeremy dashes out into the hallway and into his cell. Tuck walks up and down the hallway, reminding anyone who will listen that this is his cellblock and if anyone "wants a piece of him" he's right here. Truthfully, I feel bad for Tuck. His entire identity is tied up in being the wise one in a bunch of misfits in this small county jailhouse. In his mind, he's scary, he's invincible, he's intimidating, but that's not how it works with me. "Who's next?" he screams from the back of the hall and makes his way towards me. "Who?"

And he reminds me of that dog on the chain, that bloodthirsty shepherd that wanted to rip my face off the night I got arrested.

The more he yells, the more the hair stands up on the back of my neck, the more my blood runs hot in my chest and cold in my veins. I know everything about him but he knows nothing about me. He likes guns, he's willing to kill, and he's mean on the streets. But he's never moved two-hundred-fifty-pound linemen, never bench-pressed three hundred and twenty-five pounds, and never hip-tossed an opponent to the mat. All he knows about me is that I've never killed anyone, I had rich parents, and I dated the cheerleaders. He's one of those people who thinks the guy with the letter jacket has always had it easy, has never built any calluses, and doesn't know how to take a punch. And that is where he's making a big mistake.

"What are you looking at, bitch?" Tuck demands, looking directly at me and that's all I need to hear.

"You, motherfucker," I answer and come around the table instead of backing down, instead of retreating. One of us is going to learn something about respect today.

His eyes widen as he lowers, preparing for the blow. We collide with a low, audible thud. I hear the air leave his body as I wrap my arms around the backs of his legs and lift, then twist and slam him into the table. I grip his hair in my left hand, like a stallion's mane, and punch with my right, which feels normal and good in the moment.

Inmates funnel away, mice scuttling to their respective cells. I hear keys rattling, dropping, and hastily being shoved into locks. Soon the room will be full of mace and overweight, corn-fed cops in brown shirts squeezing their locked arms around the heads and necks of anyone who looks like a threat. But I don't give a shit, and stand over Tuck shouting word by deliberate word, "Don't. You. *Ever*. Fuck. With. Me." I'm committed to this thing as I feel the first couple of streams of pepper spray hit my face.

But he's tough, I'll give him that. He reaches up from the table and sticks his thumb in my face trying to find my eye. I turn my head just as he grabs the side of my face and rakes his fingernails into the soft skin below my eye. I feel no pain—adrenaline is a gift right now—but even I'm aware enough to know this isn't good. My eyes are blurry and stinging, my nose running, but I can feel my hand on his neck. Pushing, squeezing, grunting. I don't see anything but the need to stop him.

The guards yank me from behind, a violent jerk that lets me know who has the authority in this ward, who has the numbers. Three of them shove me into a corner of the common area. I am suspended between them, off my feet, so I can no longer drive with my legs. They do the same with Tuck.

From across the room, we lunge and yell at each other like savage pit bulls tethered to long chains. I still have the taste of blood on my tongue, hate and anger swallows me whole—I'm driven by that primal urge to fight, to win, to dominate.

That's the part of me that Tuck definitely didn't know. Something I hide. Sometimes even from myself.

Both of us scream at the guards to go fuck themselves and say nothing about how this happened. But Tuck knows why the tides shifted. He knows why he lost respect, why the two of us have a problem.

Tell 'em, Tuck. Tell them why your moods are as fickle as the weather. Tell them how we got here, to the point where the cellblock was suddenly too small for both of us and the stories of the girls who "tattooed everything" no longer mattered. Tell them, you psycho bastard. Because for the life of me, I don't know.

I don't know why it happened today or what tipped the scales, but I don't really give a shit. What's important to me is who I am. And what I know is that no matter how much deeper I wind up dropping into this circus, I will never become one of the animals. Because the animals are the ones that belong locked up, that belong in a cage, not sideshow performers like me. I will never be one of them, one of Tuck. I will never be the one you can't trust, the one no one can turn their back on at the end of the day. And I will remain conscious of this, no matter how long I'm incarcerated. I have to; it's all I have left.

In here, in life, we always choose the side that best fits the person we are. And although I have a need to be trusted, a need to be believed in, a need to connect and belong, I won't judge the ones who don't.

They can't help it. They are, after all, the caged lions.

39

I'VE BEEN SEPARATED from Tuck, each of us moved to a place where we can't kill one another, and I desperately hope the judge grants me the change of venue soon.

I hate these new people with their hard looks and preconceived notions about a white boy with scratches down his face being moved from another cellblock. They think I lost a fight and I know what that means, so I anchor in every time I walk through common areas, just in case I have to prove them wrong. They can't help it, though; they are all sheep unable to think for themselves, and this whole fucking cellblock seems shittier somehow as I acclimate to my new surroundings.

And the etiquette is different here, the power structure confusing as the rules present themselves only as people seem to break them. The racial tension is more prominent, the people in charge less clear, and I'm pissed that I'm the one who got moved instead of that long-haired bastard. So much for justice.

Because the unspoken law is that the person who loses is the one who leaves the cellblock and although this isn't the case with me, I know these convicts think it is. I show up on this block after five months in, with three deep scratches down my face and very little desire to talk, so they probably think I'm scared. But I'm not; I'm just growing tired of the stress, tired of the ever-changing rules, tired of my unknown future—and if that's not enough reason to have nothing to say then let's start throwing punches now.

And, as the sand in the hourglass continues to pour, I'm struggling to salvage my identity. Who am I now? The boy I was raised to be trapped inside a cage, or a caged convict trapped inside the boy I was raised to be? Only time will tell.

Lafayette County, where I learn the decorum of the locked away, learn the lies of the guilty soul. Where all my earthly belongings fit in a single pillowcase and home is merely a mattress with imprints of bodies and the weight their conscience carried. I understand them now, I see their perspective, and I wonder—is empathy the seed that harvests a bitter heart? How Machiavellian, how clever, how a man gets duped. Because it's compassion that's the real cardinal sin in here.

That Trojan Horse that allows the convict to imbue your soul?

So I establish my process and work on my poker face, because I have a feeling this is the first of many transfers in this unfolding story.

"Houston," a guard yells my name as the keys twist and clang in the lock, "Get your shit, boy. You're being transferred."

For six months, I spent countless hours regaining the trust of my parents, regaining trust in myself. For six months, I listened to men coming and going, talking about how they got out and got caught and knew it could never happen to me. For six months, I got sober, I gained clarity, and found the inner strength—no, the fortitude—to say no; even if all roads before have led right back to one last burn. For six months, my mom and dad have scraped together the money to get me out, and I am genuinely touched and grateful and emotionally in their debt.

Finally, I get my change of venue—to Johnson County, a place where I can supposedly get a fair trial. And it doesn't take long before I am granted and make bail, thanks to my parents, and am now back on the streets.

For six months, I have role-played in my mind. I contemplate the outcomes, the decisions; and in less than four measly hours of being released, I already have a couple of grams, thousands of dollars, and a fresh U-100 in my arm.

Don't waste your breath, I already know how this ends.

40

It's unbelievable, like a slow-moving dream. Lights flashing, the intimidating sounds of police dispatch, and this cop who is searching my body like he knows—really knows, I'm holding—is behind me looking over my shoulder saying, "that's fucked up," and pointing to the ground.

I don't want to look down because I know. I know what he's pointing at. I know I have the right to remain silent, and I know that it has only been two, maybe three days since my mom and dad posted my bail. Now I'm fucked. Fucked, fucked, *fucked*.

I had convinced myself that if I was lucky enough to make bail, I would be smart, I would be different, I wouldn't become yet another statistic of the revolving door of incarceration. But as I watch the cop bend down in front of me and pick up what I know is a fresh, still wet, sixteenth of pure, white shit, I think to myself what a waste of money, waste of time, waste of emotion I have truly become.

There are no guns pulled, no excitement, just sarcasm and condescending comments. One more for the scoreboard. I wonder if he knows who he has here because this is like any other arrest, and in his eyes, I feel like just another tweaker.

The cop reads me my rights, cuffs my hands behind my back, jams his knee between my legs, presses me up against the car, and searches the rest of my pockets. The cold, damp metal of the car is against my face and I can't overlook how unfixable my life has become. No matter how smart I thought I was, no matter how smart I thought I could be, I am a fucking statistic now.

While I'm in the back of this patrol car, while the cops and the canine units are turning the car upside down, Diego—the six foot one, two-hundred and seventy pound guy who's been driving me around in his new Camaro to make sure I'm safe—is on the phone dialing for dollars. And he's pacing the side of the road, calling anyone who will answer, to collect enough money to post my bail before I'm even booked.

What an unlucky son of a bitch. His seats will be destroyed; all contents of glove box and console and trunk and any other storage space will litter the interior like a gang of Tasmanian devils had a frat party inside. Leftover fast food, registration, loose change, even the smelly thing hanging from the rearview mirror will be crumpled, smashed, spilled, destroyed in their *Law and Order* frenzy to find something to arrest us for.

But they won't find anything, not in his car; Diego is not new to this game. If there were actually anything in there, knowing Diego, he would have shoved it up his ass before anyone could find it. An indignity I haven't had to face in my life, at least not yet. But sitting in the back of this car, contemplating how the rest of this shit materializes—I'm not going to lie—I see it as a viable play in the playbook.

This arrest is different. This arrest is just for possession; less expensive and more manageable in every way for the people in my circle. And besides, everyone in my world already thinks I snitched to get let out of Lafayette County, so from their standpoint, bailing me out is an act of self-preservation, not benevolence. And in an underground world where the consequences are life in prison and you don't have the resources to kill me in jail, the next best option to cover your own ass is to take care of my every need.

Besides, they all know I'll be repaying the favor with a large burn within twenty-four hours of making bail. How in the hell did I ever end up here?

"I have your bail, buddy," Diego yells from the side of the road, the red and blue shadowing his face like a DJ's in a nightclub. "All good." He holds his thumb up and then yells at the cops to be respectful.

The cop who arrested me is walking towards the car, shaking his head. His arms out wide, like John Wayne. He gets in the front seat. "Well, Mr. Houston, sounds like your friends are going to get you out. You'll be tweaking before you know it," then punctuates the sentence with, "probably."

I stare out the window, say nothing, and silently think, *We're all making a mistake. Probably. Later tonight, I will miraculously make bail via friends who wouldn't piss on me if I was on fire. Probably. They will set me up with chemicals and privacy and compliments and strings attached. And I will manufacture meth and it will filter out into the world and you will arrest more people and we will both ruin lives. Probably.*

But what you don't know is I hate my life and kind of wish you would stop me from fucking up again. But then think, yeah, not really. No matter what happens from here on in, I know I'm going to live with this shame, and the thought of my parents and how powerless and broken and utterly gone I am. And this unstable voice, the one at the forefront of my mind that seems to know what it's talking about, suggests only one answer: *Death.*

And it's clear and it's simple, and it's cut and it's dry. An end to my worries.

Probably.

Oh, thank God I'm making bail.

41

And there was that night I almost did it, after being arrested again and after getting out on bail, after it became clear I wasn't walking away. I was so close to ending all my pain, I swear.

And what an iconic scene I chose for my final moments—the basement of Nicki's house in that beat down two-story hovel in Northeast Kansas City. The one where I could back up to the basement door and inconspicuously unload various components of my meth lab for storage. The same house where her kids played war or hide-and-seek, or whatever little boys played when Mommy was busy getting high. The same house where Sean Michael, the newborn infant she swore was mine, was unaware of all of it—at least for now. The same house where Nicki didn't care about the chemicals or the glassware as long as she had dope, good dope, to sell.

I had my mind set, my half-baked plan unfolding as I tried desperately to wrap my head around the fact that I was moments away from not existing. What would it be like? Who would this affect? Where would I go? But it didn't matter; it had to be better than this.

And the basement was cluttered, always cluttered, just like the rest of the house. Rusting tools, old paint cans, and dust collecting on every surface. Everywhere you looked, there were garbage bags piled in corners, empty fast food paper bags scattered and crumpled everywhere, and cobwebs in between the visible floor joists above my head.

I didn't exactly plan it out. I just suddenly felt alone, convinced everything was unfixable in that dark and dank space. In my head, those voices were whispering and rambling—calm, overwhelming, louder than mine—saying *this is the right choice, this is the only way out*.

I searched for a belt, a rope, anything. And, of course, I thought of Mom and how hearing that her son was found hanging from the rafters in a filthy, cluttered basement would crush her. I thought of the boys who played here and would very likely be the first to find me pale and lifeless. What would that kind of shit do to a kid's life?

But as I held the brown electrical extension cord in my hands, the only rope-like thing I could find in that messy-ass basement, I was convinced that I was doing us all a favor.

The voices agreed.

I have to admit now, as I look up between the rafters and wonder how well they will hold my weight, the existential pull of this "step" in the process, is a mind-fuck I can't quite explain. It's kind of like something mechanical inside me—a spring or a belt maybe—just snapped and started smoking. My brokenness that's been held together valiantly has now shattered and, no matter what the outcome of this cord and these rafters, I know I will never be the same.

And I feel it deeply—not wanting to live yet not knowing if I can do something as permanent as kill myself.

I try to imagine the pain, the pinch, the shock of dangling from my neck. All my weight focused on this one thin loop, tightening, constricting air, collapsing in on my Adam's apple as I kick and writhe. A foot, a toe, anything desperately stretched toward the dusty floor. And maybe I brush the surface, just enough to spin my body as I flail and claw at my neck while grasping for the cord that chokes me in a last-ditch attempt to change history. And my eyes bulge, inflated and bloodshot, and my face turns purple as I strangle, as I weep. As I die.

And I wonder, *When I become the yo-yo on a string, will I finally fight for life or will I submit to the moment, to this noble sacrifice, and calmly, quietly slip into the dark?*

But, either way, it is what's best.

I think of my best friend Cooper, of how he must have felt not so long ago, not that far from this shithole basement. When he found the whatever-it-takes to end his own life. When he stood in the doorway of his apartment with a belt around his neck and kicked out the chair beneath him. Did he debate? Did he waiver? Or did he just do it? Is that what unknowingly brought us together? Our yearning for death?

Will anyone spend the weekend locked in their house snorting lines of dope because they don't want to deal with losing me? Like I did for him?

And what will remain after they cut down my body? Will I be a disappointing failure? Will my death be seen as a merciful act? Or will it simply become the thing my family never talks about?

Will I disappear entirely from their minds? Photo albums burned, the place where I used to sit at the table ignored, the team photos of baseball and wrestling and football and swim team and track pried off of walls, because my image is a painful, two-dimensional reminder of the wretched human being who hung himself in the cluttered basement of a two-story rental in Northeast Kansas City.

But it is *what's best.*

How many months, how many years, will my family walk by groups of people as they elbow nudge and fall silent because the whispered conversation is about me—that inconsiderate child who ripped his mother's heart out by committing suicide?

And what about Dad? Will he miss the blonde-haired boy who was so annoying for all those years? Or will this be too shameful to think about? Could he actually erase me? Is that a thing he can do? Shit, now that hurts—the thought of being wiped away, as if I never existed.

The tears are warm and wet as they spill down my face now. I scream. I scream loudly, falling to my knees, my hands in the air. One long, airy sound that transforms from pain to anger to sorrow, all in a single breath. I scream and feel the veins in my neck and the heat in my face and I don't know what to do because it's no longer clear. I have never felt so split down the middle.

It hurts more now as I collapse on the floor, limp and weeping. I am broken. I am weak. I am scared to be alone. This can't be my fate. This can't be my life. This can't be my story.

This can't be my ending.

I jump to my feet and run up the stairs, two at a time, before I change my mind.

Nicki's there on the couch as I turn the corner, surprised to see me with tears and a runny nose that I try to wipe but it all keeps coming. I'm scared, somewhat, as I stand hyperventilating, sobbing like a child, clutching this stupid electrical cord. I need her. Someone to forgive me and make it all go away. I need something to change…this.

"What is it?" she asks, motherly, concerned.

"My father. I fucked up…" I shake my head as if that's not right, and it's not, because I can't say all the words, can't explain all that just happened in that basement. "I can never get it back."

"I don't know what you're—"

"Downstairs," I interrupt. "Killing myself." I pause. "Or…getting ready to kill myself."

Her pale blue eyes are serious but strangely unconcerned. "Stop it," she says. "Come here."

I wonder if this is normal for her. As if numerous meth addicts have stormed up from the basement into her living room after arriving at the frightening realization that suicide is the only solution. She wraps her arms around my shoulders, drawing my face to her chest, and I notice her warm body under her thin, green nightgown and her hands stroking the back of my head.

"Carter came by while you were down there," she tells me.

I close my eyes, not sure if I'm relieved or upset by what I know comes next. "Uh-huh."

"Do you want to get high?" she asks.

I think of minutes ago, downstairs, and how close I really was to doing it. The feelings, the conviction, the knowledge that my life is not worth living. And with my head still against her chest, I realize she's breathing a bit fast and I say the only words that make sense. "Did he leave a pipe? Because I broke all the ones downstairs."

"He left a full one." She grabs a pipe off the table and lights it. The white smoke curls up, like a cobra from a snake charmer's basket.

"Did he know I was here?"

"Yeah. He saw your car." She shrugs. "Are you okay?"

I process the fact that I almost did it, really did it. "No," I say and grab the pipe, take an oversized hit, and release it from my lungs. "But I will be soon."

42

I WANT THE best for this baby, at least something better than this. With a bottle in his mouth all day long, sitting in his car seat in the middle of a room where people smoke cigarettes and smoke meth and have sex with no regard for the curious eyes of newborn life. But I'm not going to invest any emotion into it. Not now. As if I had any emotion to invest. I live in fear, I live in hopelessness, I live my days with insanity shot into my veins fifty cents at a time. I have no soul, so why should I have a heart?

Because everybody knows my days of freedom are numbered and the whole thing is fucking surreal. With needles in the closet and chemicals hidden all over the place, I change little Sean Michael's diapers and try to see myself in his little baby face, and I tell myself I'm doing something good.

Maybe it's because he's only five months old, too early for me to see myself in his features. Yeah, he's pale and has blue eyes like mine. But don't a lot of babies look like that? I see his mother's features but honestly not a single one of mine. And I don't know if that is the absence of innocence embedded in my own self-image that makes it impossible to see a resemblance, or if it's because this child simply isn't mine?

And the only thing that I know I have in common with this tiny baby boy, for sure, is that neither one of us belongs here.

But we don't have a choice, do we little guy?

And if you were my son, I would be so proud because you are a big fella with broad shoulders and strong legs. I can tell you are special, Sean Michael, and I wish you the best. But I'm on my way out, little buddy, while you're coming in, so there's no sense in either one of us getting attached. You're worth more than that, worth more than this situation, and definitely worth more than me, so I hope you find your way out.

Because whether I'm your daddy or you belong to some other meth cook, you come pre-loaded with the sins of your father. A package deal with abandonment and a gaping hole in your heart and maybe even addiction down the road. Only, with me, I faintly remember there were once conscious decisions. But you, well, you didn't choose any of this.

So, I hope you find your daddy and he's brave and strong. I hope he lifts you high above his head and spins you around, laughing and loving, and then you fall into safe, strong arms. Maybe he takes you far away from here, where you might have a chance, and maybe he's a pillar of stability and honor and everything clean. Someone to look up to—a chance, a hope.

And for all those reasons and more, I hope that I'm not your daddy. You deserve better, kid.

43

THE SLOW BUILD of oblivion spreads through my mind, like the expanding dizziness from riding the Tilt-A-Whirl at the county fair, only without the nausea. Lately, I've been mixing the shot thicker, using as little liquid as possible so I can feel the drug inch its way through my veins like a slug on a moonlit slab of concrete. I want to experiment with the rush because my brain starves for more, for different, for better ways to kill the pain. I'm insane, and I know it based on the looks I get from everyone.

Even the dumpster divers from the hood try to avoid long conversations with me, although I'm once again the guy at the top of the food chain. It's probably time I take a long hard look in the mirror. Or better yet, avoid it at all costs.

Sometimes the mix is too thick, like two-part epoxy, and it lags as I try to pull the syrup through the cotton. Even as I struggle with it, I silently rejoice inside my head because I keep hoping that another drop of water can make it feel like the first shot. I still wish for death but don't hold out any hope that the grim reaper is going to visit anytime soon. And I assure myself it's not for lack of trying. I sit on the toilet in a grungy bathroom behind a locked door, head held between shaking hands, staring at my feet while my eyes slowly lose focus and think nobody's life should ever be like this. Now kill me, meth, because what's broken inside me will never mend.

Wait. Did I thump the needle? Did I empty the air, push the bubble? I don't remember, but I'm high. Really fucking high. I retrace, a frantic mouse running through my memory. I didn't, and I don't know why, and I'm not sure what this means, except I know you don't shoot air into your veins.

Will my heart explode? Will I have a heart attack? Do I care? Didn't I pray to die a second ago? Except I always imagined I would die super spun out and fading into the oblivion, not in pain and fear writhing on a dirty tile floor.

Is this how it works? I mean, I feel fine, but I'm really fucking high and I'm scared and freaking out and I'm sure I pushed at least forty ccs of air into my vein. And I'm just so fucking high.

"Nicki," I scream. "Help!"

I stumble, trying to find my footing, but the shot was big, the syrup thick. I manage to flick the lock and lean on the doorknob.

"What's wrong?" she hollers.

"I think I'm in trouble."

She opens the bathroom door, Sean Michael on her hip, takes one look at me and replies, "Fuck yeah, you are."

"Jesus, I'm high." I grip the sink, try to steady myself. "Can you clean that up? I…I just can't. I don't want the kids to find my rig."

"Fuck you," she says. "You do it. It's your habit. Not mine."

"Goddamn it, Nicki! I might be dying!" I try to find her face, but my vision is wiggling like dice being shaken in a back-alley craps game.

"You are so high, dude." She laughs, and I'm pissed and scared and wish she'd take this seriously. "I told you to take it easy."

"Nicki, stop. Please. I shot air into my veins."

"Is this because I didn't really give a shit the other night?"

"You're a fucking idiot!" I scream. Twice now she hasn't given a fuck that I almost died. I hear the baby start to cry, but to me it's just white noise. "Nicki, I can't get into this right now. Don't we need to call an ambulance?"

She shrugs, adjusts the baby, and doesn't even look at me. "Maybe you're fine."

"Maybe I'm not."

"What's it feel like?"

"Fuck you, Nicki." I stumble out of the bathroom, brushing past her and the crying baby. "This isn't… I'm too high to think."

"When has that ever stopped you?"

"Get your kids in the car," I demand, tripping over the car seat. I can't walk, I can't think; and now, I swear to God I'm feeling that bubble of air inching toward my heart. "Where's my shirt?"

"In your hand, you dumb shit." She grabs her keys and straps the baby into the seat. "You better be fucking dying." She hollers for the other children.

We're inside the car now and the kids are driving me crazy as the windows struggle to defrost in this fucking Missouri winter. Sean Michael is crying, another kid is hungry, everyone except me is complaining about the freezing temperature, and I'm praying my heart doesn't explode. My head is spinning out of control.

Nicki, wearing three-day-old lingerie and a tweed trench coat, stops the car in a side alley, gets out and calls 9-1-1 from a payphone on the corner.

"They'll be here soon," she tells me as she gets back in and slams the door.

The small of my back is aching, partly from stress, partly from the shot. And in between the loud kids and the fear of what my heart might do any minute now, I'm not sure if I want to sit in the warmth of the running car or fling open the door and sprint home. I elect to stay.

"I thought you were just going to ask the 9-1-1 operator if I was going to be okay with what I shot into my veins, Nicki."

"Yeah, well, if you don't like it, go do it yourself," she tells me as I hear the sirens in the distance. The lights flicker in the mirrors. And they're not just red and white. There are also blue lights.

"Holy shit, Nicki, that's not just an ambulance."

She doesn't look at me. "Stop screaming. Your son just stopped crying."

"Holy shit, why are the cops—"

"I didn't get a chance to tell you," she says.

"Holy shit." What the fuck has she done?

The swirling lights ricochet off the walls of this otherwise dark alley. I slink down in the seat, and then a paramedic raps on the window.

"Mr. Houston?" he asks. I open the door and say yes. Nicki is staring at her fingernails. "Come with me," he says. "Let's get your vital signs."

I follow behind him, wary, slow. "Why are the police here?"

"Standard procedure," he says but nothing inside me believes it. The cops are getting out of their cars and ambling over to me.

I sit on the ambulance's bumper while the EMTs check my vitals and explain that I'm fine and that I would have to "shoot a lot more air than that to cause problems."

I say, "Oh," and then ask why they couldn't have said all that to Nicki when she called. Because then I wouldn't be sitting here with the cops breathing down my neck.

"Because this lady here said you were a threat to yourself, Mr. Houston," the paramedic says. "And we take that very seriously."

"She what?" I look over to the car. Nicki looks back and mouths, *I love you.*

One of the cops moves into my line of vision. "Mr. Houston, did you know you had a bench warrant out of Johnson County?"

"That's not possible," I say. Across the way, another cop walks over to Nicki and she straightens the tweed coat and sits up taller.

The cop with me gestures for me to stand, then he pulls my arms and cuffs them behind my back. "You have the right to remain silent. Anything you say can and will be held against you…"

Nicki is over there, with her messy hair and lingerie and four kids with two different daddies and she's shamelessly flirting with the cops. She doesn't give a shit about whether I'm going to die or get arrested.

The relief that my heart won't explode is eclipsed by the fact that I'm going to jail. Out of the frying pan and into the fire.

It's only been a couple of months, and in that short space of time I've already caught another felony, almost committed suicide in a dingy basement, and managed to lose the respect of every person I know. In two years, I've gone from a young, up-and-coming entrepreneur to a wanted criminal with track marks running up his arms. And I honestly don't know what's worse—the fact that Nicki probably called the cops herself, in spite of her claims that I'm the daddy of her fourth son, and her claims to love me; or the fact that none of this should surprise me at all. That bitch.

And as I look at her telling some story, laughing on cue with the cops who stand around her, I wonder if this is symbolic of the last shred of dignity slipping from my loosely held grip or the undeniable proof that, for me, dignity vacated my life a long time ago. I'm shoved into the backseat of yet another lonely cop car, and I wonder if this will finally be as low as I go?

Please life, please God, let this be it.

Let this finally be rock bottom.

44

WELL, SHIT THE bed. Here I am again. In jail. All so familiar and so —I don't know—not surprising, I guess. I'm pissed and I'm sad; and, if I'm being honest, I'm scared to death. I'm twenty-eight years old, I've burned every bridge I've ever built in my entire life, and I'm facing thirty years in prison. I'm alone, really alone, and there is no one to ride this out with, not even my own mother. Because how am I ever going to face her again?

I don't want anyone else to say "At least you're still alive" because they don't have a clue what they're talking about. God didn't do me any favors by sparing my life. This cell, and the clang of the lock keeping me in it, is too real, too permanent, too painful of a cross to bear, because nobody is handing out do-overs in the courtroom across the street.

I am so fucked.

And I literally want to hit everyone in the mouth. Anyone who says something cross or vaguely pissy to me or thinks they want to make their time more enjoyable by messing around with the quiet guy in the corner, quickly regrets it before they get the last word out of their mouth. Right now, in here, I'm not in the mood to talk about anything or in the mood to listen to banter. I will punch, swing, and kick until I'm worn out before I waste any energy trying to discern what their words really mean.

I get one hour to shower and enjoy what they call 'recreation', which rarely means seeing sunshine. My bed is a steel slab with a two-inch mattress that does very little to separate my body's contact points from the metal. Bruised hip muscles, a bad back, and chronic neck and shoulder pain take the place of a good night's sleep. And the freezing, uncomfortable seat of the toilet bowl forever just a foot or two from where I eat. Loud conversations about the inflated success of criminal activity being exchanged between convicts is the lullaby of every night. I can't see the guys in the cells next to me but I can talk to them and hear their yammering. But if I want to put my earphones on and drown them out, I can. And I do. Often.

And I try unsuccessfully to stop thinking about that night down in Nicki's basement. I try not to focus on how much easier it would have been for everyone if I could have just wrapped that goddamn extension cord around my neck and stepped into the abyss. The darkness that I didn't just stare into but lived with, now only seems to be deeper and more unforgiving.

I try not to go there, but I can't get it off my mind. I can't let it become just a passing thought. Because the tragedy of that suicide seems so much more appealing than the shame of whatever this is going to be.

God, you really didn't do anyone any favors sparing this life. I'm hurting, dying on the inside.

I miss you.

45

THE INMATES TELL me a guy named Tuck hung himself in his cell, not just his cell—this cell, the same one I'm in right now. They don't know that I knew him and they don't understand why I cut them off when they explain to me how he did it—on his knees with a towel tied to the bars. I just say, "Yeah, I know the drill."

He had gotten his change of venue to Johnson County, just like he had coached me to do, and then he ended his life, silently, drawing little attention—and I bet that just bugs the shit out of Tuck.

And I wonder what straw broke that camel's back. Did his parents finally make it clear he was unforgivable or did the girl who "tattooed everything" tell him that he wasn't worth being remembered. Or did he finally realize that he's fucked and he's doing his time and he wasn't as tough as he wanted everyone to believe he was? Who knows? All I know is I understand it more than I want to admit while sitting in this jail cell, only a couple of feet from where they found his body.

His jail cell; I'm sure he'd want me to know that.

And although our last encounter was him trying to shove his thumbs into my eyes, I forgive him. I won't forget him and I hope it all works out for him on the other side.

So long, brother. I guess another one bites the dust.

The real coincidence is how close I was to heading down that identical path. Weird. Creepy. Cosmic. Except my Ground Zero was a dingy, damp basement and an electrical cord. And the irony or coincidence or whatever you want to call it, is that I didn't do it. I didn't kill myself, as close as I was in that moment, but wound up here instead, in the same cell where he was successful at the thing I couldn't do.

Aw shit, Tuck. I'm sorry. It must've been lonely, must've been heartbreaking to stand on that proverbial ledge all by yourself, making the most permanent decision anyone could ever make. Were we standing close to the same ledge at the same moment in time?

No judging. I hope you know that. I know if you were here, you'd hook me up with coffee, hell, probably even cigarettes, although these heartless bastards won't let us smoke. You'd tell me to be careful of the people who give you things and call karma a real motherfucker, and this time, I'd laugh right alongside you.

And hopefully they let you smoke wherever you are and listen to music in the dark. It just isn't going to be with me, brother. Not now. Not yet.

Because, although I'm frightened and lonely, I didn't really know it until right now—I'm going to face this thing, this life. I'm going to square off, grit my teeth and fight. Something I know you would approve of.

Until we meet again, rest well, my friend.

46

THEY MOVE THIS behemoth of a man into the cell next to mine. He's got to be three hundred pounds, with huge hands like stumps at the end of hairy arms. Because of his case, they had to isolate him on my cellblock. He articulates his words with a voice that sounds like a radio announcer. And it's pretentious and contrived, and it feels like he's always lulling someone into letting their guard down. I don't like him. What can I say?

Further down the row, there's another big fella who loves referring to himself as a "convict". Now I've got both these big bastards, like two peas in a cozy little pod, bullying the little guys, talking about the good old days when prisons were like a biker rally. Without the women, of course. And they hype up their street cred and think they are at the top of the food chain by impressing or frightening or whatever effect they're going for. And I listen, but I'm not buying into their shit.

Big guys rarely see an attack coming and most of them haven't been in a lot of fights because they're so big and, well, intimidating. So, when a real fight happens, they're complacent and ill-prepared.

I don't have that size advantage. All the respect I've ever gotten I've had to earn, especially in here. But it's no different than it was on football fields or wrestling mats or bar rooms—I have the same singular approach to handling aggressive situations. And it has come with scars, and it has come with pain and a lifetime of recurring anger, and hate, and triggers. They have become these overpowering natural instincts I will one day be forced to deny, forced to channel in a different manner.

But not here. Not in jail.

Still, the new guy is a bona fide killer. Unlike the inmates who just talk about killing, this fella is a sick sadistic psychopath. I know this because a friend of mine, a trustee, saw his paperwork. And, although this isn't my first rodeo with a murderer, this twisted son of bitch has gone to depths I can't comprehend. He's different, with real blood on his hands, and that is a huge consideration in how I handle him.

The story I was told begins like a lot of stories I know: two guys were hired to rob a drug dealer, hired to send a message. Real biker shit. But somewhere along the way, things got out of hand.

Hey, it's the drug game, after all.

And although I have no idea what component of your brain you have to switch off in order to dismember a body with a circular saw, I cling tightly to the Judeo-Christian philosophy I was raised with: thou shall not do shit like that.

For me, the saddest part of the story is how the task force that kicked in the door found the seven-year-old son of the murdered guy hiding under a pool table with a pellet gun, trying to protect his dad's body. That's enough to make me squirm because it's too close to home, too close to my son's age. And while I'm not exactly Sigmund Freud, in my clinical opinion, if this asshole felt remorse for what he's done he'd stay nice and quiet, disconnected, like a good little murderer.

Now, because I'm me and have found myself entangled by the sticky web of incarceration, I want so desperately to formulate this universal and well-thought-out postulate that states that, sometimes, good people go to prison. But the more I dwell with the criminals of the world, learn what amuses them, and climb inside their heads, the more I realize I have to be careful bandying around my formulated principles. Some people just might always be like oil and water when it comes to civilization. And one thing's for sure when it comes to this guy, the courts got it right.

And I grow tired of all these predators—real ones, professional ones, violent ones. So, I find myself formulating an opposing but equally true postulate: some people do belong in prison.

And here's me, smack dab in the middle of all of them.

It's hard to explain what it's like being this close to him—listening to him, getting to know him, and understanding his personality. It's unsettling. Especially since he seems like a regular dude, albeit a schoolyard bully.

But I was once a regular dude, too, and meth has this way of making us different people. Maybe not that different, but it definitely dampens your spirit, your morals, your sanity. As much as I'd love to believe I could never go that far, is it so unreasonable to at least imagine this person was once like me?

I mean, two years ago I would've sworn I could never become an addict, never use a needle, and there's zero fucking chance that Kyle Houston could wind up in a prison cell, facing thirty years.

Yet here I am listening to a murderer brag and use big words with this 'I'm in control of my emotions', mind trick thing, like some kind of hillbilly Hannibal Lecter.

Don't come into my world, with your loud mouth and your new death row status symbol, and try to disrupt what little peace I've salvaged. Don't act arrogant because you read a few Louis L'Amour westerns. Nobody gives a shit. And most of all, don't plop your fat ass in the cell next to mine and have me questioning how close I came to being you.

I don't want to see parallels between us. I want to believe that your parents tied you to a tree in the backyard for weeks and fed you scraps like an animal. Because all roads don't lead to murder, dude.

Do they?

And I have to wonder if this is the only difference between this cold-hearted killer and everyone else in the world, simply just a few experiences along the way. Are the only real things that separate any of us in this world the fear, the hate, and the interpretations we pick up on our winding paths?

Who knows?

All I know is this guy's entire act is pathetic and causing me to grind my teeth, so I interrupt one of his sentences and eloquently suggest he "shut his fat ass up." Not my proudest moment but it did the trick.

So now, we all sit in silence, the ball in his court, and we wait until morning when the guards take us to the shower. And, if I'm being honest, I'm nervous as hell.

But one thing is for sure—tomorrow I'm going to swing like it's personal. And I'm doing it for the seven-year-old boy with the pellet gun. I'm doing it for the seven-year-old boy who's waiting for me to get out. And, most of all, I'm doing it for the seven-year-old boy deep inside me.

The one buried under all my fear, my hate, and my interpretations.

He thinks I don't know what's coming. They both do. I let them think I don't see their sideways glances because I'm pleasant, just like every other dumb shit who doesn't see it coming. I carry my soap and my towel and my toothbrush and a thick hardback dictionary that nobody seems to notice. It's not much, but it's all I have.

In another world, this would be abnormal. But not mine, not anymore. The idea of protecting vulnerable body parts from two men who may or may not have a knife is like some natural yet subconscious next step in the unfolding drama that is my life. As if months of solitary confinement contemplating thirty years of incarceration have somehow made this seem normal. And feeling that pain, realizing that incredible amount of loss—really living it out inside your head—makes this scenario, relatively speaking, just another day in the life of Kyle Houston.

And the one thing I have going for me on this fine morning is I just don't give a fuck.

The door closes and I hear the key turn loudly in the metal door. The guard is gone and I no longer smile. The men say a few words and Tiny, the taller of the two men, walks to the shower and turns it on.

The silence between us is awkward, unsettling.

I put my towel and toiletries down on the table but hang on to the book.

"We need to talk," the three-hundred-pound killer tells me and it echoes throughout the room, the steam of the shower starting to drift our way.

"About what?" I glance over to the shower. Tiny has his shirt off. I can see his tattoos, sleeved and detailed. I wonder how many years of prison it took to get that far.

"The words you chose last night."

I look at his hands, his waistline, and his towel for a weapon. It appears to be safe. He's making a mistake.

"What words?" I ask.

"You know what you said, Houston."

I put the book on the table but keep my eye on his hands; the same hands that held a man down, duct taped him, and sawed the limbs off his flailing body. The same hands that could squeeze the life from me. And, for a split second, I see the psychopath that he suppresses most of the time standing in front of me, ready. Like a tiger just before it pounces on its prey, desperately trying to contain its excitement, suppressing its breathing, but its body is too attuned to the kill.

That little boy must've seen the same thing when his daddy screamed for mercy. And if I'm being honest, as I stare down a man who I'm certain wants to kill me, I'll bet I have the exact same things behind my eyes.

One of us has got to go.

My calculation is that I have maybe twenty seconds before his partner jumps on me and then it's two on one. My goal is to be efficient, effective, and cause as much damage as I can in ten seconds. We are going to be loud, so guards will be here soon and I want to be done before that happens.

"Yeah, I do know what I said. So do you." I look him in the eyes and then ask, "So what the fuck are we talking about?"

He turns towards the table, adjusting his stance, telegraphing his next move. And I feel the blood in my body rush to some invisible center, like lightning to a lightning rod. I hate this man and I don't even know him. I hate him because it helps, somehow. I hate him for what he is. I hate him for who I might've been. In this moment, I hate him more than I hate myself.

He swings, but it's slow. I drive back and then I punch him hard in the face while he is still off-balance. He falls and then struggles to get back on his feet, so I rush him, pushing him into the corner. We collide with a small bench riveted to the concrete.

"I'm going to kill you, motherfucker!" His huge angry hands are faster than I anticipated. He grabs my face, my eyes, my skin. He tries to turn, but the bench blocks him and we end up in a weird violent wrestling match.

I grip his hair with my left hand, so tight I can pull it out. I am brutal in these moments; I always have been. And his soft chubby face is vulnerable and open and teed up, for the power from every hay bale, every weight, every push-up I've ever done. He is in danger, not me, as long as it's just the two of us.

I strike as hard as I can—one, two, three times; fear and anger and adrenaline smacking against his oversized head. One of the blows lands awkwardly and strains the ligaments in my thumb. His body goes limp but only for a second. He's definitely scrappier than I thought.

Then my twenty seconds are up. From behind, his partner grabs my shirt with one hand and lands hard blows to the side and back of my head with the other. He pulls the non-elastic collar, choking me, but I keep swinging. "Get off him, motherfucker, or I'll kill you," he demands. Then I finally hear the guards frantically fumbling with their keys outside the door.

"Fuck you." My words have a raspy spitting sound.

I hear a key slip into the lock. I mule kick the guy behind me but he has my collar with both hands now and my movements just serve to pull it tighter. The killer's now scratching at my face, trying to tear into the soft flesh of my eyes. I can't breathe. I'm losing consciousness. And I hear him say, "You're dead."

A door flies open and guards flood the room. "Separate! Now!"

Orange streams fill the air, splatter our clothes, our bodies, and the floor. A searing stinging assaults my eyes, my nose, and I'm coughing now, but neither one of us stop fighting.

His hand, his oversized fist, is still seeking, grabbing, pulling. He wedges a finger between my teeth and my cheek. I try to bite, try to pull away while still protecting my eyes but his thumb is under my jaw, my shirt is choking me, and the mace is making it hard to see. He buries his fingers deeper inside my mouth, then yanks his hand away, and as he does, I feel the flesh tear away from my jaw.

A second later, the guards are on us and my feet are off the ground; suddenly I am easy to carry.

Three guards lift, push, and drag me into a cell and all the time I am still trying to get to that son of a bitch. I am maced, I am beaten, and I am tossed in the cell and left to cool down. The inside of my cheek is ripped to shreds, the flesh clinging loosely to my gums. I need painkillers. I need stitches. I need my own pound of flesh for what has been done.

But instead, I get salt, I get water, and I get time. That thing that heals all wounds.

47

There is a haunting difference between being alone and being lonely.

If left alone for prolonged periods of time, the mind will awaken. Not so much the intellectual mind, but the feeling and emotional center of your mind that you can normally ignore when it gets too intense. Hit the local pub, watch a new release, give a friend a call, and the mind will scatter all those thoughts to the wind.

Not in jail, though. Not in a single cell where you are alone for twenty-three hours every day. Not lying on your metal slab, wading through your memories, being pummeled by the bad ones and watching even the good ones splinter off into regret. Not left alone, truly left alone, with nothing to comfort you except the images of moments you will never live again missing, yearning, aching in a cold, callous six by eight concrete cell—an environment that never relents.

Time is no longer linear in jail. The past is like an incoming tide that keeps battering you with waves, but with no timeline. One second I'm reliving the Christmas when I was seven and the next moment I'm sixteen and my grandmother is crying because I've disrespected my mother. The internal life is vivid, rich, and cruel.

The irony of the whole thing is that I have finally arrived at a place where I can truly understand the capacity of my wrongdoings, and want so badly to say *I'm sorry*, but I can't reach any of the people I hurt in order to make amends. And chances are, even if I was standing right in front of them, hat in hand, there's a fat chance they'd ever believe a word I said. At that very moment, when karma is shaking a judgmental finger in my face as if to say, "I told you I don't play nice," I realize my only choice is to sit there and take it. Shut up and do my time.

Phrases like "Time heals all wounds" or "This too shall pass" become the ancient wisdom I hold on to in the dark and quiet, because I'm hoping to God they are true. Knowing that both hope and God are as unfamiliar as sunlight to my eyes in this concrete box, but no matter how thin a thread I hang onto, hope and God are all I have left.

But something about "This too shall pass" feels profoundly different; like somebody, somewhere, at some time, understood all this. I believe these words—not because I decided to, it's more like they reminded me of something I already knew. A reminder of something always true. The instant the words entered my head, I felt something familiar but I'm not sure what. As if the first person to say these words sent them out into the universe thousands of years ago to find me now, in my darkest hour.

But I wasn't strong enough in those days of silence and solitude to imagine anything good. Because I was getting clean and I was gaining clarity and what I saw was that I was all alone— forgotten, desperate, and homesick, with the realization that everyone in this world loved somebody…yet, possibly, nobody loved me.

And that was the exact moment when I understood the haunting difference between being alone and being truly and utterly lonely. So, I'd say it often and I'd say it out loud among the concrete and the steel and the despair: *This too shall pass.*

Because in that cell, even death would have been less lethal than getting clean.

48

THE CLOSEST I have ever felt to my mother was when she was the only person on the planet who would come to visit me. As difficult as it must have been, she found a way to push it all down and be there for her child. Again.

In those moments, when I sit across from her, aching to re-engage, I'm not empty, I'm full. But when you're locked up and have no outlet for overflowing love, being full is like a can of Coca-Cola that has been wildly shaken…with no one to pop the top.

I'm not sure what getting sober is like for other people, but for me it seems to be a lot of crying. I've been sober now for three months, with the backdrop of life in prison looming over me. And I doubt I'm ever going to become sorrier than I am right now.

And she doesn't quite understand. I see it in her face as she watches me cry. She constructs her sentences with "it's okay, sweetie," or "I know you're sorry", but she has no clue that this is a part of my healing process. Some of my words enter her like the sharp blades of a utility knife, but other words bounce off the glass between us. It's not her fault; she's as new to this part of the game as I am. And she listens to my apologies—detailed, verbose apologies about things I did when I was sixteen, nineteen, twenty-two. And she listens to the poetry I have written—none of it is any good—but the message is clear: *I'm sorry*. And she watches me break down like a man sentenced to death, who's headed to the gallows, reluctantly being put to rest.

"It's okay, sweetie, I believe the drugs blurred your vision," she says as we sit in a soundproof room where we can, and do, talk openly.

"It's no excuse. I can't believe what I did." I'm sobbing again, apologetic, wanting to talk.

"It's okay," she repeats and glances at her watch. She doesn't think I notice.

I laugh a little, as I wipe my nose with the palm of my hand. "I know it's all crazy. Mom." I pause, searching for the right words. "It is drug abuse,

I guess." It's the best excuse I have for her. For me. Even though I know she wants to hear something that makes sense, I don't have anything better. Why did I go so far off the rails? Why did I throw away a perfectly good life? Why did any of this have to happen? Maybe the answers will come when I'm done with all these fucking tears.

And like everybody else, I'll probably eventually blame others for everything. Like so many men in prison, I'll find some way to be pissed or ashamed or destructive toward these feelings that seem to be the deepest, most enriched emotions I have ever experienced. And I want to do us both a favor and ride this one out. Because if I'm just going to ignore it all later—the embarrassment of red distorted looks and snot barreling from my nose—then why not make the memory a doozy so there's no way I can deny it later.

Even to myself.

"Your dad says hello," she says, changing the subject. "Says he's sorry he couldn't make it." Her gaze drops to the floor. I can tell she made that up.

"How's Keenan?" I ask. "Has he asked about me?"

The subject of my brother hangs in the air between us for a second. Then my mother straightens but avoids direct eye contact. "Of course, he has."

"Not even Keenan?" Something's not right. There are too many memories, too much history, too much love between Keenan and I for him to count me out.

"You have to understand…" Her words trail off. "Damn it, Kyle, don't back me into a corner."

"How's he doing?" I ask.

She says nothing.

"I love you, Mom. Your heart is good." There are so many things I want to say, but nothing I can say is going to help her.

She scoffs. "I'm glad someone thinks so."

"Then you should be happy to know the son on his way to prison thinks you have a good heart." I try to make it sound like a joke, but the words fall flat. My mother shakes her head and buries her face in her hands. She's crying now and I feel helpless, I feel responsible, I feel guilty. "I'm sorry, Mom."

"They just don't understand. None of them." She reaches into her purse for a tissue and then adds, "And I don't know what to tell them."

"Tell them I'm sorry." *Like I do all day*, I think to myself. To the walls, to the silence, to God, in hopes that it will make me feel differently.

"Everybody knows that, honey." She blows her nose, takes a breath, and stops crying. "Kelly says—"

"Kelly says what?" The mention of my sister makes me cringe. We haven't had a civil word in years. "This should be good."

My mother shakes her head again. Add Kelly to the list of taboo topics. "Something's wrong with your brother."

"It's okay that he isn't asking about me, Mom. It doesn't mean there's something wrong with him." But the words feel fake, they lack conviction. Because I think I would be asking about him if the roles were reversed. I'd be sitting here with him. Well, if I wasn't on meth.

"It's not that," she says. "He sees things."

I look at her for a moment, trying to read her body language for answers. "What are you..."

"Sees things, thinks things, does things," she interrupts. "The other day I came home and he had barricaded the front door. Said people were after him."

I see myself in that place, wired and frantic, convinced there was a conspiracy of people in that kitchen, in the warehouse, in the trailer park. "Mom. Sounds like he's on meth." And my heart breaks because I don't want to think that. I don't want to imagine my little brother stumbling down the same path I've taken. I don't want to have to accept that I can't do my job as a big brother.

"No. I don't know. Maybe..." She thinks for a moment and then says, "I don't think so."

"And what's Kelly say?" The two of them had their own relationship, separate from me. Although Kelly doesn't understand the first things about drugs, she knows her baby brother. I'm curious what she sees.

My mother wipes her face and says, "Honey, I don't have much time today. I'm sorry." She dabs at the corners of her eyes, careful not to smear her makeup. "Is the food getting better?"

She's changing the subject. I'm sure to protect my feelings. "No."

"Your face is filling out. You look like my Kyle again."

Her Kyle. I don't know if I've been that for a long time.

Her eyes are red-rimmed, bringing out the deepest blues in them. And I remember this drawing I did when I was in high school of her senior picture. I was fifteen, maybe sixteen. I remember how unavoidably mesmerized I was with my mother's beauty. She was so small and pristine, at a time before life started kicking her ass. Back when she was just a pretty girl from a small town in need of someone to shelter her from a world that didn't give a shit how tiny or pretty she was.

And as I look at her now, I can still see the girl in her face behind her crystal blue eyes, and I wish I could be those arms to protect her. I wish I could be the man who cleans up the mess and casts the net that ropes it all back in.

But I can't. Hell, I can barely pull the rope to keep myself on solid land.

My mother is a tough woman. She's been through a lot. But I think I broke her this time. I think, just maybe, this episode with the drugs and the arrest and being in prison is the one that might be the final nail in the coffin. And if it isn't, it sounds like my brother might pick up the slack.

She reaches for her purse, about to leave. I clear my throat loudly. "Mom…" My voice is dry, cracked, the tears welling up for the thousandth time today.

"It's okay, sweetie," she tells me, but she looks away as she says the words. "I know you're sorry."

49

I'm ten, and my three-year-old brother Keenan thinks I'm a superhero. His Titan, a God; there is nothing his big brother can't do. Grandma Mimi tells me story after story of how Keenan brags about my abilities. If she points out a water tower, Keenan tells her, "Kyle can climb that." If she points out a baseball field, he'll swear, "Kyle can hit a homerun over that fence." It doesn't matter what the task, not only can I do the impossible, I can do it better than anyone on the planet. That's my job. I'm a big brother.

Keenan is Tom's son, so he's technically my half-brother, but we are the only family we know. And I love this kid with all my heart. And all I want to do is protect him and teach him to be a boy and how to be cool, and tough, and athletic.

That's my job. I'm a big brother.

Tom left about thirty minutes ago to grab something from work. He and Mom have been fighting more often, longer and louder. I hear it through the vents, through the floorboards at all hours of the night, and it makes me nervous because I'm afraid they might split up; and it makes me nervous because I'm afraid of his temper if mom isn't around. And I am always so tense and anxious, like something big is going to change, like I'm about to lose something important but I don't know what.

The new cardinal rule is to never piss him off, at least not when Mom isn't home.

And right now, I'm in charge of Keenan while Tom's out. My best friend, Brent Pearson, teases him and lets Keenan chase him up and down the stairs in mock fear of being captured.

"Hippity-hop," Keenan tells him. "I'm the Easter Bunny. And I'm going to get you." His bright yellow onesie is baggy and loose on his tiny body as his footies hop in unison.

Brent finds it hysterical that the most frightening thing my baby brother can come up with is the Easter Bunny. I agree. And we laugh and we patronize as we run up, back down, and up the steps again.

"Oh no, not the Easter Bunny!" We laugh, and Keenan growls and giggles a little as he stays in character, hopping up and down the stairs.

"I'll put a stop to this. I am Kyle, the bunny slayer." And I stand one foot on the floor, one foot on the second step, whirling a dish towel like a lasso above my head.

Everybody's having fun as I whirl the towel faster, off the steps now, pacing the floor of the entryway. Without thinking, I walk underneath our chandelier and swing the towel into the dangling diamond–shaped fixture and knock one of the small pieces into the air, high above our heads and then watch it plummet to the floor.

I freeze for a second, hold my breath and pray the whole thing doesn't follow, crashing down on my head. The room is silent. Nothing falls. Just the single crystal glittering at my feet, still whole and undamaged, and Dad can probably reattach it with some minor modifications.

"Oh shit!" Brent says.

"Shit," Keenan repeats.

Brent glances at the chandelier, then back at the piece on the floor. "Maybe no one will notice. It's not that big."

"I can't just lie about it. What if I get caught?" I say.

"Shit," Keenan says again, but quieter and it seems more out of interest for the word than being worried about the chandelier. He then hops down the steps.

"We're done messing around," I tell him and Brent. "That's for sure."

"What are you going to do?" Brent asks.

"Tell my Dad. I have to."

"Am I going to get the blame?" Brent asks.

"No man, I'll make sure he knows it was me," I say. "Besides, it was an accident."

Outside we hear the crunch of tires on the gravel. He's here, pulling into the driveway. I'm so glad Brent is with me to buffer his temper, to keep his anger in check.

"Shit," Keenan whispers again.

"Keenan, look at me," I hold my brother's face between my hands and look him in the eye. "Don't say that word. It's bad. Brent shouldn't have said it."

Keenan nods. I can hear the thunder of Tom's boots on the front steps.

"Kyle!" He's calling me now.

Butterflies fill my stomach as I yell, "Coming." I then turn to Keenan to make sure he understands. "Don't say that word, Bubs. I'll be the one who gets in trouble."

When I walk into the kitchen, I can tell Tom is already angry. As always, the emotion is palpable; it fills the room, fills my body like a flammable gas as I try to tread lightly. Brent stands beside me, silent and still.

"You boys need to eat," he says, his face stern and his temples pulsing. Whatever happened when he was out didn't improve his mood at all. "Is Brent eating with us?"

"Dad," I say.

"What?"

I shoot a quick glance in Brent's direction. "Well, um..."

"What? What now?" Tom sighs and he seems to get bigger somehow.

"Well, we were playing with Keenan, and he was chasing us, and..." I hesitate.

Dad stands in front of me now, staring down, casting a large shadow over my body. "What is it?"

Now I know most kids my age would pick their words, soften the impact, maybe even lie, but not me. There has always been something about him that forces me to want the truth to come out. To get it out in the open where no one can say I'm lying. I want to feed it to him bluntly, maybe to proveto him and to myself—that I'm not scared; maybe to remove some of his power and intimidation; maybe to piss him off worse, I don't know. But now, as I face my dragon with fire in his eyes and anger in his belly, the only thing that I can say is the truth, unpolished, with no punches pulled.

"The chandelier, I broke it," I say quickly. And in an instant, everything goes black. Just like when the baseball hit me in the mouth as a rookie in Little League, only this time it's Tom's fist to the side of my head.

As I'm regaining consciousness, I hear whimpering and realize it's me. "Goddamn it, boy!" Tom is screaming at me. "I was gone thirty minutes."

Keenan hides in the corner, crying. Brent runs out the back door and I am on the dining room floor, crying, and confused, and ashamed. And heartbroken.

The anger, the intolerance, the short fuse, all of it feels like my fault, like I'm unacceptable. I know this isn't normal because he doesn't do it to Kelly or Keenan. He's picking me up now, looking closer at my face, as I repeat, "I'm sorry, Dad."

He says nothing and I feel worse. I'm sorry I broke the chandelier but also know it's fixable. Just like the bruise on my face, it will heal. What's not fixable is the way I feel, the feeling that is with me all the time now, because I have figured out that I am cursed to push people away, cursed to not be loved, to not be wanted.

Cursed to always be the kid who screws up and lets people down.

And I don't know what it is about me that is not worth understanding, that is not worth listening to, especially when I always make sure to tell the truth. And I would trade all the friendships in the world just to know that I was worth the love of one of my two fathers. And although I want to run out the door and chase Brent down, it's not because I'm afraid to lose his friendship—that's never going to happen—it's because I don't want him to tell anyone or to think I am lesser, now. I can't bear the thought of someone knowing. I'm scared that if anyone hears the story, they won't understand that I am not something to be pitied or rejected. That although some little boys get punched in the face, they are still good, they are honest, they are worth loving.

I cry harder because I'm bad, because I can't be trusted, because I can't be loved. He can hit me all he wants; I can take it, but what I don't want is to lose another Daddy. I'll heal. Nobody has to know because nobody really knows about any of this. Let them all believe he loves me. Maybe if I'm quiet and good and stop messing up, eventually he will. In spite of broken chandeliers. In spite of how I look like Jerry Sam. In spite of what I'm worth. He will love me if I'm loyal enough, he will love me if I hate what I've done, he will love me if I'm sorry enough, if it bothers me deeply, if I realize it's all my fault that he hits me.

"All you had to do was take care of your little brother," he says and turns toward the kitchen.

Please don't leave, Tom. Someone needs to show me I'm enough.

50

I PUT MYSELF here. It's a fact that I suffer through, with unrelenting clarity, alone for twenty-three hours a day, every day. Where the cold, hard concrete that boxes me in from the world is also the brick and mortar that boxes me in with my thoughts on replay. And in an entire world bent on keeping society safe from worthless criminals like me, there is nothing left to protect me from myself.

In silence, I replay that bizarre conversation with the U.S. Marshals. The one, less than a year ago, during those first forty-eight hours, that now seems like a lifetime ago. The moment they asked me to rat out the people I got my chemicals from. And now I wonder—not that I would change my answer—but what if? What if I had handed over names? What if I had cooperated?

What would've changed had I been nicer, more compliant? What would have changed if my body wasn't screaming for sleep, or my ear wasn't oozing unexplained and alarming amounts of pus, what then?

And keeping my mouth shut wasn't necessarily misplaced loyalty—although, where are any of those people now? I would chalk it up to integrity, or pride, or maybe it was a fuck-you to the feds. I don't know. I just felt like I got myself into this mess, and, well, you know the saying.

Those thoughts are punctuated by the life-crushing idea that my entire existence could possibly become a cautionary tale or, worse, an after school special about the loser who serves thirty years for being an idiot. What. The. Fuck?

Dear God, don't let that be my life.

I think of my family and all the people who used to say I would be somebody someday. I am somebody now—just not somebody they would recognize.

But with fresh new perspectives and fresh new scars, I'm not so sure what is right or what is wrong.

Only that I am all alone.

PART THREE

SUFFER

51

AND NOW I am thirsty. After I exhausted every angle about whether I was here for good, after I threw in the towel on the idea that a judge would ever post bail and let me run the streets again, after I had agonized over the sea of "what ifs" and came to the impotent reality that none of it mattered, I turned within.

This didn't happen after a couple of hours lying on a rack and miraculously coming to life-changing conclusions. This was weeks of punching walls and screaming at people in the cells next to me. Wondering what the Universe wanted from me as I sat alone at night with the misery of my life pouring over my tortured soul.

I could hear a whisper inside my head, but didn't know what it was saying; maybe I feared the answer because I was unaware of the question. Because I had been there before. And I'll be goddamned if I wasn't there again.

Then I wondered (at least I think it was me), who's really steering the ship here, who's asking the questions, which eventually morphed into something existential or spiritual or something -itual. Is there really a God? Is there purpose to any of this? Is there a soul, life after death? I then did something radical, at least for me, and released the rules and labels and religion from this pursuit. I made a profound and life changing decision in that jail cell:

I was going to figure "Truth" the fuck out.

God hadn't done me any favors by sparing my life and now He needed to make it up to me. I wanted to see how far this knocking at my heart really went and God, with a southern accent and six guns a-blazin', said, "Strap on your chinstrap, son. We're just getting warmed up."

So, I went full-frontal and put a shit-ton of faith into that guy. And I did what any smart seeker would do—I covered my bases and prayed that if there really was a Hell, I was going to need a free pass. Because I wasn't going to just fall in line with the Bible thumpers' view of the world. Shit was about to get real.

And so here I am, pacing and pacing around this godforsaken cell, asking questions and breaking down my spiritual philosophy to include only what I believe wholeheartedly. Not what I am *supposed* to believe, not what I was bullied into believing or too scared not to believe. Only what I actually, truly believe. Not the fluff or the confusing stories that are so easy to poke holes in like the Virgin Birth or people rising from the dead. Having grown up a Christian in the Bible Belt, it's no small act of courage to take this sort of inventory in one's heart. When you are raised with the mindset that Hell is your destiny if you think any differently than what your preacher tells you, playing around with the rules is far more terrorizing than death.

And I am not wasting my energy petitioning God for mercy. I am not going to waste my time groveling for scraps from the table or some miracle to set me free. And I am not going to waste a perfect opportunity to find Truth by diving into the existential vacuum with preconceived notions or the distraction of scripture. Yeah, I said it.

This is me and you, God. Mano y mano.

And just to be clear, I'm not seeking Truth because I'm scared. I'm not searching the universe for some unseen force that can save my ass and put me on a beach in Hawaii. I am simply in a place in my head and my heart and my life where figuring out some of the most perplexing aspects of the human condition seems, I don't know…possible.

But my question isn't so much, *How did I get here?* It is more like, *Why didn't I die?*

Why, with all the perfectly good reasons to let me go, why am I still here?

What do you want for me, God? No, really, what? If You're truly up there, I'm asking because I've got time on my hands. And I want some truth. My hunger is insatiable, my thirst not yet quenched. And don't knock at my door and whisper in my ear if You're not going to go all the way and tell me what I need to know. I want to know Truth and I want to know what's real.

It's not just about me and my life; I'm confused by war, I'm confused by pain, and I'm confused by all the messengers You've sent to change the world. I'm not sure what I believe but it seems to start here—with this conversation, with this cry for answers, with You. I guess. Otherwise, who else am I talking to?

So how about it, God? What else is there to do for twenty-three empty hours a day? Because, although I can't guarantee any of the shit people say about messengers and prophets, I do believe in You. I believe You are there and You hear me, but the verdict's still out on whether You love me; Truth that I'm sure You'll feed me like a swift kick in the pants.

So I bare my chest and open myself up to You without a single distraction to get in the way. This is the first time, in I don't know how long, that I want something more than I want death. I want Truth more than I want oxygen, and I don't want to fight or argue or wrestle.

Bring me Truth, God.

I am open. I am listening.

And like the flutter before the cough when the methamphetamine enters my vein, I can feel it. It's coming. It's coming. But will I be able to survive it? Will this be too much for me to handle?

And do I really give a shit if it is?

The liberation, the euphoria, the deliverance, is like taking ecstasy around people you don't particularly care for; suddenly you love them all. And if this is what giving your life up to a Higher Power is all about, I'm in. Not only that, but I could kick myself in the ass for not doing it sooner.

I feel an awakening, but I am not sure what that really means. And I'm changing, seemingly overnight, although I realize that's never the way it happens. But what do you call it when so many of your strong convictions instantly, and without warning, change into something opposite and all-consuming and, for lack of better words, usable? Or when the stranglehold of your childhood religion—where you memorized the stories, recited the verses and leaned heavily into the God-fearing part—abruptly means something different? In a matter of what feels like seconds, but really is a lifetime of thinking, I'm going from the paralyzing idea of eternal damnation to realizing maybe…just maybe, that's not exactly how it works.

And now I have this overwhelming feeling that giving up my life to something divine is not the death of my personality but the realization that I might be pretty freaking amazing to the universe exactly as I am. That just being myself could be all He wants and that the motivation of God is simply to offer joy and fulfillment and abundance.

What's the word for transforming, for unfolding, for seeing clearly? It is either an awakening or pure insanity, and I'll be damned if I'm going to rule either one of them out just yet. I'm still sitting in the same gray concrete box, but it seems lighter somehow, brighter, like someone whitewashed the whole cell. Whatever this is, I'll have some more, please.

Now that I've been asking for this serious one-on-one time with God, I feel like this has been an ask of mine that has been waiting here forever, patiently hanging around in the crowd but so damn subtle. Until now.

A week ago, I prayed. With pureness of heart and the sincerity of a child's love, I prayed that God, the universe, the infinite spirit, would reveal the Truth.

And it all started with identifying what I fundamentally believe to be true. Such an interesting exercise, breaking down the core of what I was really seeking. And it wasn't religion or life after death or any of the crap that wages wars and creates friction at holiday parties. I mean, don't get me wrong, all that is certainly pretty cool stuff to scare the children with, but I needed to narrow what I believe down to something more universal, to what I truly believe if this moment in time is going to be meaningful. So, here's where I landed. Ground Zero, where my spiritual mushroom cloud balloons out across the sandy desert of disenchantment:

One: that there is an all-knowing intelligence in this universe. Forget conditions, forget whose image is whose, forget the names or rules or whatever other bullshit hinders our beliefs in God. Forget it all and just start with the idea that something created the universe and knows a hell of a lot more than we do. At least it knows the Truth, which is a hell of lot more than we know.

Two: if I ask this all-knowing being to reveal the Truth, I can, at the very least, count on the idea that it won't maliciously send Satan to my door with a pack of smokes and a bottle of tequila to say, "Trust me."

Three: I have to believe that if I mean it and I release my desires and expectations then I will get the uncut, unfiltered pure powder directly from the Source. My job is to listen. Nothing else.

If any one of these beliefs are false, I decided, we are all pretty much fucked anyway, so what's it really matter? And voilà, I had my religious foundation. I prepared to unfold.

And as you would expect, all the heavens opened up, a light shone brightly from above, and this man who strangely looked like Obi-Wan Kenobi entered my cell.

Yeah right, if you believe that shit then there is probably some Kool-Aid with your name on it down in Jonestown. But still, I feel the presence of a teacher in this six-by-nine cell and I don't care how crazy that sounds. The presence is subtle, always subtle, but this feeling and these incredible thoughts I've been having are radical for me. Yet they seem to somehow make sense of so many unanswered questions.

Even though He wasn't exactly invited, I have this crazy feeling Haysoos is also here, just not the one in Scripture, not the one that's so…Jesus-y. This Jesus seems to hang out here in the trenches. Calm and loving, like that friend who always has your best interest in mind, who you know is the one you should be hanging out with most but tend to ignore on Friday and

Saturday nights. This guy doesn't seem to judge, doesn't make me feel guilty and just wants to observe as I unfold. This Jesus seems to be buddies with Buddha and Mohammed and Hare Krishna, and it all makes so much sense as long as I exclude everything else I've been told my entire life.

I sit cross-legged against the wall in my cell and forget whether it's day or night, while this

Jesus tells me that the message of Truth isn't that difficult, that it is about Love and Oneness and the process seems to have a lot to do with just being ourselves and learning through the hardships along the way. This guy lifts the weight of getting it wrong off my shoulders and lets me know that His message is for everyone, that there is no such thing as "God's chosen people". And He doesn't care if you've ever read the Gospel or even know His name; the message has been the message long before human beings decided everything needed a label. It's the good news and it's Love, that four-letter word that gets mistaken for all sorts of crazy shit, available to all, even a lonely bastard like me. And, in the old days, I'd be burned at the stake and on my way to hell for even thinking all these thoughts, but this is what I'm getting, so take it up with God.

I have wasted so much valuable time, so much precious energy in my life worrying about the divisions in religion. And as a result, I realize I have clearly lost sight of God. But He is here, lying with me, His arm over my shoulder as if I'm four years old and watching TV with my dad. It feels like warmth and acceptance. Like home.

I see clearly, somehow, how the mind of God works…kind of. How sin and iniquity are only about us. How hate and intolerance are what we need to unlearn, which is why the world is such a mess, because we humans are so stubborn that only pain and grief will ever teach us these valuable lessons. And, even though I am not qualified to have these thoughts, I can't shake the realization that if the only path to salvation truly is through pain and grief, then the most benevolent thing God could ever give us is that eight hundred-pound gorilla in the corner of the cage waiting to tear us limb by human limb.

Maybe it's the tough love of the universe that we find out, in the end, was the kindest thing of all. Medicine that is much easier to swallow after the ass kicking is over. But I'm not there just yet.

What this is has no label, which is kind of the point, I think. There is no straight path, no two people arrive at this in the same way. And I honestly feel so much less encumbered by what I should be and more grateful for what I am. Not the drug addict on his way to prison; that's not what I am.

As ridiculously silly as it is coming from me, I'm grateful to be an Eternal Being without beginning or end. But who talks that way? Still, it certainly takes a lot of the pressure off my shoulders, that's for sure.

Now here I am, alone, with deep intense thoughts and no brake pedal. I don't dare call them revelations because they're so new, seemingly so far removed from my firm philosophies as a child or a young man or whatever part of my life I straddle now as an inmate in this lonely county jail. My heart wants to burst like fireworks over the castle at Disneyland, and there is this still quiet voice that assures me it's all real. Still, I'm scared. Love and Oneness galvanize me, illuminate a better path to define the world, appear to be some truer guideposts to navigate the storm but also a radical concept compared to the jealous tyrant I'm familiar with from the Old Testament. This new God seems too soft, too passive compared to who I've been praying to for almost three decades. Regardless, He fills me with hope and understanding and faith like never before.

That's right, faith.

Unconditional Love may be impossible for my three-dimensional mind to grasp, and I have no idea where to begin trying to define Oneness, but somehow believing that these two concepts can move me toward my Higher Self gives me solace in the gray and cold and solitude. I feel safe, I feel protected, I feel the empathy of a saint when I try to imagine that it is simply Love and Oneness that is all that matters. And maybe, in this moment, I'd put flowers in my hair and strum an acoustic guitar encircled by people with flowing white gowns if I could get my hands on any of that. But I still can't shake the feeling that this is Truth. Why should I? This ride is exponentially better than the one I've been on.

Somehow, two books have arrived in my cell for me. Not, like, fell from the sky, but I honestly can't remember how I got them. And I read them word by word, precept upon precept, and feel something push me toward something else, but I'm not sure what quite yet. One is a story about an amazing man's journey to understanding purpose and his struggle to stay true to the Gospel. I feel your pain, homie.

The other is about these twelve steps that never quite pertained to me as a drug addict but are super relevant now that I'm a seeker on the path to righteousness. Who knew? And the more I read, the more I see what an amazing set of guidelines these steps are for anyone who just wants to be a good human.

Unlike when I was sitting in the circle in that rehab with Cam and Sandy, these steps are more like feelings in my wake and not guidelines or rules I have to follow. These twelve things that I follow are now twelve things that also follow me as they pass in and out of me like a guiding light. It's all just a history lesson of everything I have done—accepted, admitted, repented, forgave, faced fear, and loved. These steps are like the strings that suspend my life as I move on my own but connect to something unseen, available to all, guiding me to something new.

These two books, coupled with my life's situation, are slowly becoming my chiselled commandments, my burning bush. Although I'm no Moses on the mountaintop. I'm just a dude in prison coming to deeper realizations and hoping it's not too late.

Truth, damn it. Give me more Truth. I lie in this rack and count the tiles on the ceiling and never once do I ask for a miracle or a wish or a leprechaun or anything of the sort. I only want Truth as I lie awake in an environment that holds little more than me and time, and a really good opportunity to listen.

Be still and *really* listen.

Or I guess I could go back to driving myself crazy with guilt and regret. No, I think I'll take Truth, especially since there doesn't seem to be a lot of that going around these days.

And this word "humility" seems to be all I see, maybe not every word but every other word, in bold and raised like braille, reaching all the way to my heart. I have been contemplating God and how He could love me and this word keeps ringing a bell in my chest.

Humility. Humility. Humility.

This seems so familiar, like I've been curious and thought of this before. And I remember back to a moment, years ago, when I was standing on my back porch, smoking a Marlboro and sipping a cup of Joe while whispering a prayer into the wind. A prayer I thought no one heard. A prayer I released, like tossing a pebble into a pond as I watched the ripples build, and then instantly wanted to rescind. This moment, I realize was the first ring of that bell in my mind.

I see a vision of me, not too long ago, a pompous young man flying high with judgement then crashing and burning in a warm, steamy heap of humility. Who stood up, spitting mad that I ended up that way, completely forgetting that I had prayed for God to somehow, some way, some time, help me understand the struggle of others. In one sense, I feel super connected to something vital, visceral, safe. In another sense, it's like, what the hell? This is what I get when I simply want to understand why some have it easier than others? This is the path I unwittingly chose the day I decided it wasn't fair that things come easy to me? That, just because I was once good at high school football or tested well in algebra or owned my own business, I could still find myself in a heap of shit over a rogue meth binge.

I didn't know any of this was coming in that moment back on the porch, but it is clear to me now—blaring and shouting and in my face all day long as I find myself unfolding with these twelve steps. The word leaps out at me, anchors into my heart, more than all the other words. *Humility*. Why? It's not the first time I've read it or seen it or known about it.

I'm not sure I'm buying that all of this—the addiction, the prison, the tragic turn of events—was some lesson in humility because of that prayer.

Is the secret to fulfillment and the meaning of life only discovered when you understand not only what a hopeless wretch you are, but that everybody else is going through their own shit, as well?

I can formulate hours of words and amazing pontifications about what all this means, this business of Love and Oneness, but who's to say I got any of it right? Who's to say I'm not just stumbling around with my own fucked-up version of the Truth? I mean, there's been a lot of wars waged, a lot of humans tortured and oppressed all over these abstract concepts that torment our minds during this long, drawn-out human experiment.

I come back to the one thing I do know—how I feel. Like I'm connected to a source that is in me or through me. One that drives a new type of thoughts. Not tumultuous ones of fear or anger or confusion, but thoughts that seem to know something, to have some sort of authority. Some type of experience that I lack.

Which brings up another point, God. I absolutely refuse to use religious jargon when I talk. Please don't let me cheapen what's been given to me with all those trite, unoriginal terms I hear from churchgoers. Because You and I both know that's not what this is, right? Please don't let other people's definitions of Heaven and Hell get in the way of what we are doing here. As far as I'm concerned, Hell is here, God, in this cell, imagining the rest of my life forgotten and worthless.

Don't let my fear of fire and brimstone or the chasms between dogmas get in the way of understanding Love and Oneness. Don't let scripture stand in the way of a worthwhile revelation. I'm not going to be able to be a beacon of light if I have to say words like "have a blessed day" or "scripture is my rock" because these will never sound genuine pouring from my lips.

And I realize You have the power to change me. Hell, You already have. I know You probably have the power to transport me right out of this cell, to change the evidence into wine, to change the hearts of the prosecutors, to change the very laws that bind me to this dreary, dark cell; but You're not doing any of that, so let's not start throwing powers around to change my vocabulary.

I'm not perfect. I know that. I like football because people get hurt, I like shit that blows up, and I really like boobs. I like cigarettes and black coffee, Lord. And even though I wish it wasn't true, I like three-day cocaine benders with lots of whiskey and the occasional lap dance. That's who I am, part of the man I'm going to curb and change. But I'm not one of those "bloom where you are planted" kind of people. I hope You're okay with that.

I'll fall in line with what You've told me. I'll open up, dear God, and listen to this feeling, to You, to this Truth that I hope isn't as fake as the one I've been fed for the last twenty-eight years. How could I not?

Because I finally believe that humility just might be the key to true happiness and that the meaning of life can be found within Love and Oneness. And I also really like the word fuck.

So where do we go from here?

52

THE TERM "JAILHOUSE religion" seems to be reserved mostly for the suckers who come into prison afraid and convinced they can be on the Almighty's friends and family list as long as they recite scripture and change their ways. I've seen it hundreds of times and I have never witnessed— they love that word—it to be permanent. These selfish bastards are so used to running a game on the people around them that they even become delusional about fooling God. But just as soon as they get sentenced, just as soon as they find out that their prayers weren't quite as good as the pious prosecutor petitioning the same source, just as soon as it hits 'em between the eyes that God didn't intervene and they are doing the time they had coming after all, they go right back to beating people up for their commissary. Onward, Christian soldiers.

But I'm not a sucker. Am I?

I'm certainly not going around promising that I'm going to be perfect from here on out. Staying clean is a slippery business. I didn't exactly do a bang-up job the last time I was out, so how arrogant would I be to stand around and proclaim that I'm forever clean, that I have some exclusive lifetime membership to clarity just because I got to peek behind the curtain a little? That just sounds like horseshit, even to me, whose cup runneth over. But I know one thing that is never going to subside, and that is my hunger to understand Self. Who'd a thunk it?

So, now I'm sitting here in this cell with that and a shit ton of the usual suspects—worry, regret, fear—but the difference is now I'm committed to finding out how far this ride will take me. I am strong. I am fierce. I am ready to set the world on fire.

But I am also here, in a concrete box, separated from the world for who knows how long.

Feels like the lost lyrics to an Alanis Morissette song. Isn't it ironic?

Maybe I'm the last to get the memo. Maybe everybody else knows this. Maybe they don't. But here it is, better late than never. Except here I am exposed—together, yet alone. Stuck on a shelf.

Just plain fucking stuck.

Everybody in my life seems to be addicted to something, attached to a thing that clamors at their life: drinking, anger, power, fighting, smoking, eating, sex, lying…you name it. Hell, even religion. And how is anyone else ever going to find You, God, when all we worship is our damn religion, and not actually *You*?

I understand weakness, I understand people who need help. I understand I'm one of them. But it's not clear to me how this place is going to help anyone. And, because we're cool, you'll tell me…we're going to get out of here, right? Right? Take Your time answering that one; I'm not going anywhere.

And this is what I want Tom to see; this is what I want my family to know about me, to tell the people who ask how I'm doing—that I have an amazing spirit after all. I want my family to hold their heads high and tell the world that Kyle Houston has all his shit in one bag now. Dare they say, *he's doing amazing or wonderful or at least not as bad as they thought*. I'll take that.

And now that it's here, now that I am in touch with my higher self, I don't want this to be *just a bunch of fancy new words. Let's make this important. Let's do some epic shit, God. What do You say?*

It's like that age-old question—if a tree falls in the woods and nobody is there to hear it, does it make a sound?

Does it make a sound? I don't know. But my bet is that this tree wants—no needs—to make an impact.

And I am no different than the tree as I sit here, living and changing, growing with conviction and the disturbing realization that I am sentenced to fall.

And now, after all this, the only thing I want in this world is to make my sound. To have that chance. *Put me in, Coach, I say to God, and let me make some noise.*

What scares the shit out of me with all these newfound wakeup calls, is that I realize meth ain't the problem. But man, how easy would my life be if it was? Like, oh, you mean that powder I put up my nose or in a pipe or in my veins is the problem? Cool, I quit. Now I'm complete.

Substances are merely the distraction from that vortex in the center of your chest. And maybe that yawning emptiness is God shaped or love shaped or purpose shaped. All I know is that it sure as hell isn't meth shaped.

And if I keep going through life blaming my issues on an illegal, albeit beautiful, crystalline flake that I tend to like—and clearly, I tend to like it a lot—then all this pain and tragedy and loss will have been nothing short of some cosmic circle jerk.

Put that in your pipe and smoke it.

But what am I going to do with all this insight if I am sentenced to deal with convicts for the rest of my life? Should I help them heal and find God? These angry, hateful, shitty human beings…for the rest of my life? Is that really what I signed up for?

Can't I just hide inside books and cells, surrounded by cinder blocks and shiny silver toilet seats? Am I a coward if I hide my brand-new light under a bushel—*oh no, I'm going to let it shine*—to stay safe, stay quiet, keep to myself and spend the rest of my days as an introverted recluse? The next Andy Dufresne in *Shawshank Redemption 2*?

All these questions crush my spirit but, honestly, the answers hurt worse. Every one I arrive at seems to make me lonelier, more scared, more saddened about my future as I prepare myself to never again stare into a girl's eyes, never fall in love with someone who is in love with me, and never know what it's like to feel the warm embrace of people who think highly of me.

Sobriety is like giving your heart to a wandering lover—you spend your nights sleeplessly trying to find out where she is and knowing that, once you do, she's only going to break your heart again. And, yet, a part of me craves her respite because it would take my mind off all these *nevers* I don't want to think about.

So, somebody please tell me which step this is? Is this the one that no one really talks about, the one with both good news and some bad news? The step that says, "Hey, the good news is that if you open up to your higher power you will find out all your sins are forgiven. The bad news is, nobody gives two shits."

If I get out, I want to show everyone that I am different, I am new. And it's not jailhouse religion, please don't let it be jailhouse religion. I am committed, I am atoned, I am fulfilled, and I swear it's all real. Someone please, see me, believe me, have faith in me. But don't take too long.

Come get it while it's hot.

53

My lawyer is young, green when it comes to law, but likes me a great deal. Ashley is sweet and compassionate. And she's almost hyper-interested in my life, way more than the facts of the case. *How does someone like you end up in a situation like this?* she asks, not so much with words, but with everything between the lines and with her body language. If we have an hour together, alone in a private room where it's against the law for anyone to listen, maybe ten minutes is spent discussing my case. And I try my best to satisfy her curiosity, at least by communicating between the lines, but the truth is I'm still trying to figure it out myself.

And she told me the news about a month ago, about the possibility of my rights being violated. "Fruit of the poisonous tree," she said. "You could beat this."

And I sit in silence as she smiles primly, curiously, because watching me wrestle with this decision was another side of life she wants to experience. And I don't give her the answer that she wants. I don't jump for joy and declare that we ride into battle on white charging stallions and "beat this fucking case." Instead, I just sit there and relish the fact that God just threw me a bone.

My choices are clear—I can either go to a jury trial and prove that the officer had no reason to pull the car over that night in the trailer park, therefore all evidence uncovered after the traffic stop is inadmissible; or take the new offer from a disappointed and frustrated prosecuting attorney. Nine years and a class B felony—a reluctant offer from a man who truly seems to have taken this case on as a personal vendetta. In my mind, from my point of view, here is how the cards spread out before me—I can take the nine years in the state of Missouri and do a third of that because it's my first time down. Since I've spent eighteen months getting sentenced, and it all adds up, I'm looking at doing another eighteen months and walking out with six years on parole. On the other hand, I can go to trial in front of a jury of my peers—kind of a misnomer since my peers would never be chosen to sit on a jury for anything.

If we prove I was pulled over without just cause, which should be a cut and dried argument, I walk free. If I lose, I get thirty years in one of the hardest, most violent prisons in the state. Highly unlikely at this point, but the possibility has my attention.

"What would you do?" I ask her.

"Kyle, I like you," she says. "I'm confident we have precedent on this one." She pats my hands.

I stare at her for a moment. "That's your answer?"

She smiles, her teeth so straight, so white; her perfume faint but intoxicating. "I'll do whatever you think is best." She nods. "But we have precedent."

Precedent. Do I dare trust in that?

For a month, I've wrestled with this. Quite possibly the most important decision of my entire life, but not for the reasons Ashley is thinking. The true consequences of the decision I'm about to make are hidden from the naked eye. Because I am awakened, well aware of what happens to the soul that doesn't face the music, even more aware of what happens when an addict is released into the wild with unchecked desire. Suddenly uncaged like a bull pinned too long behind the gate, there is no telling what mistakes I might make, whose heart I'll break, or what transgressions I might commit against my soul if I get an easy pass on a sin I've a hundred percent committed.

I have grappled with choosing prison or freedom; and the unfathomable fact that it is essentially my choice—not Ashley's, not my mom's—*mine*. And I have prayed, and I have meditated, and I have communed with the thing that is taking place inside my heart. And the two answers I have come up with, the only two that are clear and unequivocal are: One, I am guilty of the charges that are brought before me. If I'm going to honor the awakening in my heart, if I'm going to have the best chance of returning as the son, the father, and the human being I was raised to be, it only feels right to accept responsibility. And two, I am far more concerned with what I might do if I get out too soon, before my head is screwed on straight, than what might happen to me behind bars.

"Kyle, where's your head at?" Ashley asks. "Today's the first day of the rest of your life."

"You've got that right," I tell her.

"So glad to see your smile is back."

"Me too." I take a deep breath and place my hands flat on the solid, sturdy table. "I want to take the plea."

Her smile drops a bit, but she recovers. "Ohhh-kay. Let's do this." She pauses. "You're sure?"

"I have to."

Silence for a moment, then, "You are a special person, Kyle Houston."

"I want to be," I tell her. "Maybe someday."

Outside, my mother, my father, my grandmother, and my aunt all sit ringside waiting impatiently, nervously, for me to come out of the private office where I'm meeting with Ashley. Earlier, I explained my options to them with a low, whispering voice, like in the pews of church just before service. As always, Dad listened…

And then he surprised me.

Throughout my life, Tom has been a wide range of voices. He's been a bully, a stick, an unfair tyrant, a guardian, and a teacher. At times, he has stolen my joy; at others he has used a gentle, understanding hand to guide me to be more. But most of all, he has been the voice of righteousness and integrity that echoes in my mind when he is nowhere to be found.

And today, less than twenty minutes ago, he looked me in the eyes, with his thoughtful, blue piercing stare and said, "This is your decision, Kyle. And your mother and I will support whatever you decide. The choice is yours."

No dictating my decision, no lectures, no advice. And no strings attached. I know him. It was a real moment.

Just like now.

Because this case is no longer the State versus Kyle Houston, this is now the case of Kyle versus Kyle. And I have such a clear understanding of my opponent, a broader picture of his strengths and weaknesses. My eyes are now open to the fucked-up decisions this son of a bitch can make, given certain situations. I know what he does, what his habits are, how he acts, how he reacts, how he feels, how he hurts, how he bleeds, and how he takes his poison.

What I don't know is how he succeeds, how we beat this curse. But time will reveal that. Because, although I can't see it and I can't imagine it, I know that life is beautiful, life is free, life is out there waiting for me to grab it by the balls and live, really fucking live this time, with love in my heart and the past in my rear view mirror. The only thing I need now is forgiveness—to give and to receive—that elusive siren's song I have never quite embraced. And I think I'm close, but what do I know? I'm an addict who plays tricks with his own mind.

Guilty, Your Honor. It is all mine—the iodine, the phosphorus, the glassware, the needles, the heartache, the despair, the sins, the consequence; all mine. I take it on. I accept it. I am ready.

I've learned my lessons—keep my head down, stay under the radar, get in and get out and never fucking come back to this place. Besides, I'm a brand-new man.

Peace, love and understanding…that's my world now. Now, please, get out of my way. I have work to do.

54

Boys will be boys. What a cute way to sum up the prison experience. Because I'm here now, in the Department of Corrections, and I'm starting to discover what that statement really means. I have discovered that prison is a think tank for criminal enterprise. I have discovered what loveless boys who have been neglected their whole lives grow up to be. And I have discovered that, even if you mind your own business, somebody is going to fuck with you just because they can.

Two weeks into my prison sentence, and another inmate shoves a long piece of metal into my hands, whispering, "Keep it hidden."

He's told me that "they" might be coming for me. So I'm lying awake on the top rack and holding this unsolicited piece of metal, wondering what I will do when they show up with their weapons and bad intentions.

On the streets, this would be attempted murder or assault with a deadly weapon, but in here it's a really good idea. But still, as I lie awake, I can't help feeling I am definitely in way over my head. Fighting doesn't bother me at all. I've already been in at least fifteen—no shit. But in no small way should a guy like me be given what feels like cast iron and told, "Use this if they come."

And how the hell do you know how hard is too hard to hit another man in the head, across the face, or in the chest with a twelve-inch piece of a sink stolen out of a janitorial closet?

Holy shit, how did I get in this position?

Well, I have always been lucky when it comes to networking and good at meeting the "right" people. Like at my carpet store, like in the industry of my father's business, like the meth cooks and the bikers who mattered; and I guess, now, like the convicts who supply murder weapons while you're still in the honeymoon stage of incarceration.

And what if the guards catch me with this thing? Do I claim I just found it under my pillow, while I'm clutching it like the "oh shit" bar above the door of a Jeep Wrangler?

God, I hope, for everyone's sake, these convicts don't show up because I know me. If they do, it's going to happen. Although I've never done it, I will yield this bitch like a pony Excalibur, screaming, "Fuck you" and "I'll beat your ass" while I hit everything within a three to four feet arc. I'll want to see sparks off the wall. I'll want to hear the thud and see the blood because I know that Kyle. He shouldn't be given a club. I know the Kyle who was a crouching gladiator, who loved to hit in football, who ran the ball like he was playing defense, taking hits and running through the other boys like they were the goal line.

It's in my blood, you motherfuckers, so please don't make this happen. Because you have no idea what I'm capable of, and what scares me the most is neither do I.

Boys will be boys? Tell that to the white guys who get tattoos in back rooms and control the traffic of meth and weed and hooch on this compound. Who decided I was a problem they needed to take care of, out of entertainment or irritation or just plain boredom. Who knows? But I got lucky when they came for me, because when one of them went to hit me in the head with his lock in a sock, the weapon ricocheted off the wall first, deflecting the blow. So I turned and dropped his partner with a haymaker.

After that, I walked up and down the hallway pounding my chest, filled with adrenaline, the taste of battle on my tongue, screaming to anyone who would listen to have my back, to come with me so I could go after the two and finish this bullshit off. Nobody, not a single person, wanted to get involved. And just when I was prepared to kamikaze into the room and take my chances, I heard the voice of an old friend who grew up in the next town over from Higginsville. Lawrence Baker—a black man, in for child support or a DWI, I'm not sure—who was as unassuming in a fight as he was mean.

"I gotchu, Houston," he yelled and put all the prison rules aside, put the fact that I was white on a shelf, and did what literally no one in prison ever does. He stepped up, out of love and reverence for the person I was a long time ago. I can't explain to you the strength it took for him to do that or the credibility he jeopardized by aligning with me—a newbie, a white boy, a friend. Just like I can't explain the loyalty I have for him. But we went in like warriors and took care of the two who had tried to jump me, and planted a flag in front of a few others.

And if I could share this story with Mom, if I thought she wouldn't worry herself sick, I'd tell her what Lawrence did for me. Putting himself out there as a black man protecting a friend who happened to be white. In a past life, he worked for her and I'm sure she remembers him as a challenge. And maybe he wasn't the model employee—he was always late, smoked weed on the job and fell asleep. But when her son needed someone to stand back-to-back with in a room full of thugs, Lawrence was there to make sure I wasn't alone. Lawrence and I, ebony and ivory, surprising the shit out of everyone. And I love that dude from Mayview, Missouri. It's a small-town thing.

But I'm unsure what the repercussions are to any of this. I am new; I am green. Will I be jumped tonight in my sleep by a band of midnight assassins? Or will the black dudes see me as a sitting duck? Or will it all be good in the morning and I'll wake up and have the respect of them all? Unanswered question number seven hundred and fifty-two, asked while I lie awake in bed during my first two weeks in prison, gripping the weapon under my pillow tightly.

55

Now that I'm actually in a prison with room to move, a job, a library, workout equipment and a means to remove myself from most of the bullshit, I am able to really start my personal journey. So, I have. It's like county jail was the incubator for spirituality and prison is how I will get ready for the outside world.

So, I play games with my mind. Although alcohol is readily available, and the people I hang out with drink, I don't. I have even quit smoking. I figure, if I can't quit while locked up in prison, how can I ever imagine quitting my vices when they're all staring me in the face? I associate my ability to curb my appetite for cigarettes to my ability to stay away from meth. I am building calluses, I am listening to my mind, I am training the machine to become what I have defined as meth-free.

Oh, and I have rediscovered the power of that old proverb: *If a job is worth doing, it is worth doing well.*

I don't know what kind of employment convicts find when they get out, but I'm willing to bet it's not the pick of the lot. Something tells me if I want to climb up out of this shit pile, it needs to start now. Something tells me that if I'm ever going to be great, I need to harness greatness in here. And I have committed to doing an exceptional job at whatever it is I'm asked to do.

So, I wipe tables like my life depends on it. Because maybe it does.

And I take pride in what I'm doing. I feel peaceful, and enlightened, and ready to take on the world, or at least be a productive member of anything I can get my hands on. I get the cracks and crevasses, and even underneath the table where no one can see, and my heart is in this work. Hell, I even swap out the dirty rags with clean ones, which nobody ever does. And in it, I see programing. And in it, I see conditioning. It's about the calisthenics of success and inner peace all rolled into one.

But I tell these convicts my OCD cleaning is part of the residual effects of meth use, not because I care what anyone thinks but more so I don't have to listen to any shit over actually doing a good job. I mean, how foolish would I feel getting in a fight and going to the hole because I was trying to Tony Robbins the tabletops in a prison chow hall? Trust me, it's easier this way.

My light is bright behind these bars, even as I wipe tables and mop floors. With joy and peace, I am renewed. With joy and peace, I lower my head and barrel into the darkness and illuminate the possibility. Where there is concrete, I see the cracks that burst forth with life, beautiful green and yellow life. Where there are criminals who talk tirelessly about the next crime, the next burn, the next infraction on society, I see a dude who needs direction.

My shell is hardened through thousands of push-ups, through dozens of fights; because, after all, it is still prison. But I hold no hate; I hold no animosity. I only hold the realization that their lives have been different than mine. Up to this point.

I have never been so full, so happy, so excited to get to live. I have never felt as free as I do behind bars. I am alive so much more than ever before and I'm going to ride this wave like the offspring of Poseidon to the shores of the place that has been waiting for me my whole life.

And no, I am not high.

But I'm sure the judge probably thinks I am. The letter I wrote to him last week was clumsy, awkward, superfluous in its seven pages. Distilled down, it was a simple plea from a convict to a judge who passed down the sentence and has inevitably heard it all before. But he hasn't heard this—a convict asking for drug treatment in a way that will prolong his time. And if I was him, I would believe there was a catch because who in their right mind does something like this?

And maybe I'm naïve to think that state-run treatment will do me any good. But I do. I remember I tried this once and got kicked out when the stakes were much lower. But this fucking drug is so clever and unfair, fooling us all into believing we are safe, that we are cured. Complacency is an arrow in its quiver; confidence, its kiss of death. And my biggest fear is still becoming a statistic, a cautionary tale, and dragging my son down with me.

I am a father but unsure of what kind. I swear that I love Dylan. Out of all the items on my laundry list of fears, disappointing that boy, even one more time, is the thing I can't bear.

My freedom is useless if I can't unite all that has been divided. My freedom is useless if Dylan sees anything other than strength and stability from the stranger who has promised to teach him the man things of life.

Because, up to this point, his life has been hijacked, like a terrorist, like a thief, like a junkie pretending to be a father, pretending to care.

The daydreams I have while I'm wiping those tables have me raising children, kissing babies, mowing the lawn on Sunday morning just before the game. Not drinking instant coffee, wading through a world of instant karma, and wondering where my son is at in this very instant. I miss my child like he misses me, like my mother misses me.

Like the drug misses me.

I don't know a single person who has quit this drug and taken back their life, but I believe I can be the first. So, I beg the judge to help a wretch who deserves nothing except possibly a chance to find the answer to the two questions that haunt my every moment—is there life out there or is sobriety nothing but a lost hope?

So help me, judge, so help me God. I humbly threw my pride on the mercy of the court because I'd rather push my release date back another year than be sentenced to life with my conscience if I ever come back. To this.

And I keep my head down and keep working my job. I am of service, and people trust me, and inside all of that is the meaning of life. Show me a single person who knows that outside these walls and I'll kiss my own ass.

And here I am happy, fulfilled, and free of the distractions and pain and sorrow. And I will be ready, if I stay the course, when I get out.

In less than a year.

At least that's what I tell myself.

56

DYLAN SEEMS SO happy during our visit. In this room with guards and cameras and vending machines where men in gray clothing and slicked-back hair and muscular arms all sit at tables with family members and try not to say "fuck" every other word. Where convicts smile, trying to be different than they are on the yard, and pretty women, who are giving up their best years, hold infants on their hips and do what they've been told. And the smeared syrupy candy wrappers that lie crumpled on the table, discarded and used, are biodegradable metaphors of the lives wasted inside these visiting rooms, and all I can think about is how Dylan just seems so happy.

In prison visits, we get to sit face-to-face, without the glass, where I can reach out and ruffle his hair or he can lean his weight on me with his tiny pointy chin on my arm and hug me to his heart's delight. In prison, we can whisper to one another so closely that I smell my son and memorize how soft his skin is, how blonde his hair is, how perfect he is. His hair is combed, his shirt tucked in, and he looks so…I don't know, *proud* to stand next to me.

For hours, we've been cracking jokes as I learn so much about his mind through his humor. He's witty and smart but clearly broken, because the shadows of sadness behind his eyes never leave. I wish I could erase his insecurity, but I don't know how, so we mask each other's pain with jokes and laughter. And I pretend that's all good enough because, honestly, it's pretty damn funny and it's all I have.

But I see his disappointment, now that it's time to leave. His smile is different; there's something like fear in his expression. So, I kiss him on the side of his head and secretly hate myself because this is happening and it's my fault, and it's one more hurt in a lifetime of hurt for this kid and I hug him, and whisper that I love him, and stand and look down. There's something he wants to say before I go back to the concrete and the chuck holes and heavy, locked doors.

“Dad,” he says in a dry, strained voice.

“What’s that, buddy?” I ask with the huge smile that has become my poker face in these moments.

“Get in here,” he points under his shirt. “I’ll sneak you out.” His words are shaky, his eyes glassy, his voice high with hope that this silly joke could become a reality.

I put his face between the palms of my hands. “Not this time, buddy. Give it a couple more months.” I hug him tightly and inhale the faint scent of shampoo in his hair. “I love you, Dylan. I will be out soon. You have my word.”

And I stand and I turn and I leave the room knowing I’ve done the best I can as a daddy in this situation. I assured him he is loved, I assured him he is not alone, and I assured him that I will be out soon. Gave my word.

The one thing they will never be able to take away from me.

57

If you want to know the value of compassion, sit down with a fractured soul that is battling depression. If you want to know the value of hope, ask a patient with a terminal illness. And if you want to know the value of a moment, sit down with me and I'll try to explain.

The only thing that keeps me from falling further down the rabbit hole is the memory of the two of us, Ana and I; the images of moments when I was still ignorant of my dark side. The part that could fade into my new surroundings, in the wrong ways, to do my time protecting myself in the ways that men protect themselves from the pain of knowing that life is passing them by. Prison is a locked gate that houses boys who cling to their sad stories, as if inside them redemption was somewhere to be found. So, I live in those moments when Ana and I drove through construction barriers, down the freshly paved street close to where the two of us lived, singing at the top of our lungs, celebrating the moment, celebrating the future, celebrating life. Together.

She was kind, smart and comfortable with the intangibles of life, the unexplainable essence of that thing living behind the veil. With her, I existed differently. And we shared time that was electric, emotional, and a reprieve from all my insecurity. In her presence, I felt whole and renewed because her vision of me was strong enough that I could see it too. And she gave me someone to love, and she allowed me to cherish every drop of life we were able to share, and in return I broke her heart in ways I could never imagine.

She took me in like a stray dog because she saw something that I had been hiding. That intrinsic luster held close to my vest. And we wrote the rules for the very first time on how to be in love when you really don't fit. So many late nights, listening to music, touching her soft, beautiful skin, memorizing the curves of her silhouette as we smoked cigarettes and spoke like the world was our canvas, and love and youth were the colors of our pallet.

Time always stood still in her bedroom. In my mind, it still does.

But we talked, recently, over the phone, after multiple letters and multiple years of separation—finally, we talked. After enough water had run under the bridge for her. I was so nervous, so afraid that I wasn't still the stray dog worth taking in anymore. She hadn't changed. She was still beautiful, and smart; and I think I embarrassed myself trying to impress her, using new words that I've been reading in books and putting on airs of being in control, when all I really wanted to do was cry and beg for forgiveness.

I did try. I tried to explain how the hamster wheel ran in my head, how the interior life worked for a junkie, but didn't use that word. To me, it all seems so logical, but when I put all of that into words, spoken to someone sane, someone who hadn't been where I was, I realized nobody will ever fully understand. The philosophical angle on intent, the deep voids of reality, all sounded like bullshit excuses to a person who had to own her pain. The pain inflicted simply because she believed in me.

And I listened to her stories of how it had been for her when I went missing. How she would stop at traffic lights in downtown Chicago and start weeping uncontrollably, broken and unsure how to move on because I had never said goodbye. Was I dead? Was I hiding? Had she done something wrong? All she really knew was that I was absent. Absent, when only weeks before we talked every day.

And I was amazed at how she could tell me this without being mad. How together and strong she was while she shared her perspective with me. And I have no words to explain how self-absorbed the junkie really is, living moment to moment in a survival mode that makes us overlook what's going on in the sane world.

She told me of a boy that she really liked and I wrestled with the thought of what a compromise he must be. I wanted to be big and congratulate her, but inside my head I was screaming and telling her she was making a mistake.

This guy will never love you the way I can. He's never going to see how cute you are when you're mad because you've had enough, or how you fight to be in the front row at every concert even though you're only a hundred and ten pounds, or how excited you get when you think about a road trip. He is not going to stay up late at night making love because you can't help it.

And he's not going to ever have to listen to the story of you crying at a stoplight because you're confused and tortured and wondering if he's dead. He'll never have to hear those words over the phone in the Department of Corrections, biting his tongue because all his explanations only make sense to himself.

Instead, I told her that I will always love her and that I will leave her alone and that I never wanted to hurt her. She wished me luck and it sounded like closure. For her.

Words still come, but I write them down on the back of envelopes or pages of a library book or notebook paper folded up and saved under a mattress, knowing she'll never see them now.

She found closure but I will never let go. Because I need those moments or I will lose myself completely. And when I need her most, I will run off to quiet places and I will find her in a moment, and I will remember who I was, who I can be again, if I just stay strong.

So, if you want to know the value of a moment, ask me. The heartless convict who held tightly to the scattered remains of his story before he hurt the people who mattered the most.

Before I broke her heart in ways I could never imagine.

58

Not this God, not now, is all I can think as I stare down at the document, so official, so black-and-white. The emblem, the district, the federal government.

The word: *Indictment.*

The same crimes, same evidence, same sins I'm doing time for right now. And it's got to be a mistake, but I'm buckled at the knees, weakened from the blows that seem to come from everywhere at once.

This is the reward of goodness in my heart? This, the result of trust?

Finally, God, the simple things all make sense now, like the smell of a baby, like the warmth of my son, like hugs and smiles, and love and understanding. You've given me a glimpse of happiness and how to live—then You yank it away.

I know You don't owe me Lord, but don't throw it all away, don't throw me away. I can see my value; I think I might bring joy into this world, like a bee that pollinates the flower. I am good, now. I am open. Please, not this, not now.

By far the worst lie I ever sold anyone was the one I believed was truth. Now those words are just another empty promise that will haunt Dylan and me for the rest of our lives.

And I can't believe I sold Your lie to Dylan. With conviction and belief, I sold it hard. Why shouldn't I have? But You knew, didn't You? The whole time it was a lie and You knew. So, You tell him, God. See how easy it is to watch his trusting blue eyes well up with tears and confusion.

He is innocent; he didn't do shit to anyone. I am the one who made the choices, who made his own bed. I am the one who held my middle finger up at life and said, "Take me, kill me, remove me from this pathetic existence," but not this.

Because he'll never understand that I didn't commit another crime, that I didn't do another thing wrong. My only sin was having faith; my only crime here was owning my mistakes.

By admitting everything, I thought I was correcting the problem; instead, that testimony is being used as the stake in my grave.

How should I define hope, now? As the consequence of that gullible, naïve, small-town boy who once believed in Santa Claus the same way I believe in You and Your benevolence? The same way I believed in justice. Until now.

The guards are here to get my things, to put cuffs on me and to eventually parade me across the yard while curious convicts stop and stare and whisper a million different reasons why I'm being taken away. They'll make up stories about how I slept with a female guard, or got into a fight, or got caught with weed. They'll tell them so many times that it soon becomes fact, but none of them will imagine the truth.

That I'm being thrown in the hole because I'm getting transferred to a higher security prison until the U.S. Marshals pick me up.

And as I sit here watching the guards shove all my belongings into trash bags, they sigh and shake their heads and I tell myself it's because they know I'm one of the good guys. And I'm thankful we're not talking so I don't have to lie and act tough and say things like "I'm cool" or "Do your thing," when all I can think about is how badly I want to go home.

Fuck you, Lady Justice; fuck you, federal prosecutors; fuck you, Kyle Houston, for all the stupid shit you did to wind up here. The deceit, the lies, the disregard—take your pick, you reap what you sow, dude. And here I am, trying to regain my balance from this ambush, wondering how the Feds can cherry pick a fella already doing his time and shove him deeper down the rabbit hole.

I'm not going to lie, God, I'm fucking angry. I feel cheated. I feel abused. I feel like You're trying to pick a fight, and that hurts. If it's a test, You can keep it. If it's to teach me a lesson, why couldn't we talk it out? If it's because You really are the jealous tyrant of the Old Testament, then stick all of this up Your arrogant, unfair ass, dear God, because this isn't right. I am not Job. I don't have patience. I don't have grace. I don't have the heart to go through this again. Not me. Not now. All that I have is love and the trust of a little boy, and now You're seeing to it that even if I ever make it out, I won't make it out with any of that.

I have now discovered that my most redeeming quality in this moment is hate. I hate the food, I hate the music, I hate the ugly words that echo through the yard. I hate prison, I hate convicts, I hate a world where everything is betrayal, where everyone is a predator with ulterior motives. *No different than You, it seems, dear Lord.*

And most of all, I hate all these prosecuting attorneys with their judgment and their unfair rules and their fake conviction that their motive is simply to make the world a better place. To protect the world from people like me. But the truth is I could've made a difference, in a way they never will. In a way I never will now.

The United States of America versus Kyle Dean Houston.

Not this, not now.

The hole turns out to be quiet—more comfortable and more familiar than I care to admit. No longer new to isolation, no longer new to breaking rules, to unanticipated consequences, to paying a debt to a collection agency I will never meet.

But I am new to this…new fears, new heartaches, new pieces of me, broken and scattered on the floor with nothing to sweep them up with, to collect them in, to catalog for another day.

I sit there in the silence, on another shitty bed in another shitty prison cell, and wonder why I ever trusted God. I mean, look what He did to His only begotten Son. I think I understand how Jesus must've felt when He saw clearly what the future held for Him. And I get that a path was created, that if you believe, His death opens the door to salvation. And I can see where people think the crucifixion was worth it to everyone. But the truth is, it was worth it to everyone except Jesus.

So, don't tell me to have faith. I don't want to hear that bullshit. Because I didn't know I had to have faith. I didn't know this was a part of the game. Where, in the middle of serving a nine-year sentence, I should pray that no one arbitrarily decides that justice would be better served by stomping out my life like a hot boxed Marlboro on a busy city sidewalk.

This Too Shall Pass? I don't wanna fucking hear it.

There must be something about this that I don't understand—a loophole, an angle, a way to beat these heartless people in their ornate marble tower in downtown Kansas City. Because I could've taken the easy way out, been let go scot-free, with my mom, with my son, with my faith.

But now, not only is that gone, but You will also use that defining moment as the evidence of my guilt and ensure that the last hope, the last bit of light, is extinguished.

And the truth is, God, I am growing pretty ambivalent about our partnership. I'm simply just trying to work off this debt to society and hopefully enjoy some borrowed time in the process. I'm not sure what Your plans were, but I think it's best we loosen the reins.

I probably gave you the wrong impression, so my bad.

Let's just start fresh. From here on.

And now that I'm not seeing so much red, I know it's not Your style to get hung up on the dumb shit we do. Somehow, through all of this, I think You love me in a way I don't understand, in a way I haven't necessarily earned, in a way that overlooks my raw unchecked emotions.

You know I hate clichés but You have a plan, right? *And it's not to just consistently have me surrender, because I'd rather go back to meth than continue to feel lonely. I think You and I can both agree that would be a bad idea.*

But this indictment was a sucker punch and my jaw still hurts; but I'll heal. I want to know my higher self; I want to figure out love. I guess I want more wisdom, but I'm not sure I have deep enough pockets to pay the fiddler all on my own. I need You to help, God. I need You to meet me in the middle. Because, honestly? Between You and me, You're all I've got.

And I keep circling back to the same question over and over again: *What about my son*?

What does this do to a nine-year-old boy who is trying to figure out the world? Whose early worldview is that shit for him isn't going to be the same as it is for all the other kids? He got the ultimate booby prize; and I can see it all now, the hurt in him that will eventually make him want to cause hurt in me. He'll want to see me grovel and beg for forgiveness just so he can look me in the eyes and tell me, "No."

Because nobody gives a shit that I've been telling him "I will be out soon" and that he should ask his grandmother to buy him a football so we can play catch like other dads and sons, the way he has always imagined. And that this orange jumpsuit, which are the only clothes he can remember ever seeing me wear, would soon be a thing of the past. And I told him to open up, to trust, to have faith that something good was about to happen.

Now I have to tell him about the indictment. The extra time. The broken promise. Me, the piece of shit father. Now I have to drag him, kicking and screaming through the mud, because I am no good. This is Karma, baby, with a smidge of What the Fuck?

I think of Dylan's face when I break this to him, and I can't breathe. *God, I don't want to cause him any more pain. Not one more ounce, not one more word. So, You tell him because I can't. Not this.*

And let's just forget about how angry I was earlier, because if You're wondering, I forgive You for clearly taking it too far. Although I'm hurt and confused, I still have a semblance of faith—faith that You and I will work through this. I'm hoping You're not insulted by some fit of anger, some loose moment of humanness, because we're better than that. Right?

So, let's move forward from here. I mean, what choice do I really have?

But let's not kid ourselves, I've got one in the bank.

Because I'm cool; but You owe me one, God.

59

I STARE INTO his eyes through thick, smudged glass again and, almost in a whisper, I say the words, each one hitting like nails in a coffin, and swear I can see the trust leave his body. His eyes start to water, confused, as my knees grow weak and my energy evaporates. But I give him nothing—no hope, no despair, no bullshit that might come back around because he deserves better, much better than this, as I utter the words, "I'm not coming home."

In my head, I am screaming, I am cursing that this isn't fucking fair, and I think he sees it because he studies my face. A signal, a joke, a chink in my armor, anything to make this news go away. And I'm crushed under the weight, like a steamroller in reverse, slowly coming back to flatten my life.

"How much longer?" he asks, and I shake my head. His little chest pumps faster.

"I don't know."

He thinks for a moment then repeats, "How much longer?" This time a little louder. His eyes well up, he refuses to blink.

I say nothing. Afraid to give him hope. Afraid to take any away. I feel like a total piece of shit.

"But I believed you!" He buries his head in his arms. I grip the phone tightly, pressed hard to my head, and hold in all the pain. The smell of coconut lotion and stale remnants of other men's conversations waft up from the phone. My mother looks at me nervously and tries to comfort him, but he shrugs her off. And I watch, and I pray, and I shout in my head, and I hate everyone in the world.

Especially myself.

He picks his head up, his face red, pain stricken, and grabs the phone. "Why?" he asks, his eyes begging, pleading. "Why?"

"Dylan," I say. I press a hand to that glass and wish he could feel how much I love him. "I need you to listen."

He just stares at me, holding in his tears, my brave, angry, wounded boy.

"This isn't my fault," I tell him. "I promise. I don't know what's going on."

Mom wraps her arm around him and squeezes. He sits there, a stone.

"I would never break my word. Never betray your trust."

He quickly swipes his forearm across his face. I look at Mom; she nods her head.

"You mean everything to me. You're my son. I…I swear, I didn't know this was going to happen, Dylan." Now, I'm the one trying not to cry.

He looks down for a moment. I study his face. Something I'm seeing for the very first time ignites inside those pale blue eyes I love so much. It's anger and it's familiar. And it's all my fault.

"I'm sorry," I say softly.

He blinks and a tear escapes down his cheek. He swipes at it immediately. "I know," he says, his voice unsteady. He stares through the glass, holds my gaze with his own, so tough, so strong for such a little boy. "I trust you."

And the word 'trust' is like a bullet. And the word 'trust' is the death of the man I'm supposed to be. And the word 'trust' becomes a five-letter thing that has finally destroyed what remains of my son's childhood.

Wiped away, like the tears he refuses to shed.

60

I'm fifteen now. I'm a sophomore and starter on the varsity football team. I'm small, I guess, but somebody forgot to tell me. At five foot eight and a hundred and fifty-two pounds. I can bench press two seventy-five, hit like a Mack truck, and practice like I have something to prove. Whatever I lack in size or possibly talent, I make up for with hunger and determination.

My sister is in her senior year. She's popular and pretty; and, because I'm Kelly Houston's brother, I'm accepted by the upperclassmen. Kelly is modest, and holds her virtue high, and is a straight-A student. I am none of that.

Some of the seniors don't like the fact that I got a spot on varsity; especially since, only a year earlier, I was the water boy for the senior squad. Because I was a freshman and wanted to be a part of the team so badly, I would have done anything to open the door. I took stats, ran water bottles, fetched tape, and felt so lucky and important to get to do it. To me, riding the bus and walking the sidelines with an entire hometown cheering us on, was a rite of passage. And for an underclassman who coach was already talking about, I believed that I was somehow more important because I was on the field, front and center.

And now that I'm on the team, I'm even more obsessed.

Attention is like oxygen to me, although I'm not sure why. I thrive on it. I listen to the broadcasts of our game on the Lexington radio station, which I always record. I listen just to hear what is said about me or my friends. And I try to imagine what it's like listening in on a Friday night, and whether or not I'm possibly almost famous.

But the thing I enjoy most is watching the films. Some from school and some from this huge, clunky camcorder that Tom purchased from God knows where.

And this week was homecoming; it felt so good to be me. The whole week, our focus was narrow with singularity of mind as we showed our spirit with tissue-stuffed floats exploding with blue and gold, driving down Main Street, and young girls in short miniskirts kicking and clapping and screaming in cadence with the rest of us in tow. And, as always, the entire town took off work to watch the parade and remember what it was like when they were in our shoes. Words like "fight" and "kill" and "beat" rolled off the tongues of God-fearing Christians. We threw candy to children who will someday do the same, and people cheered like we were soldiers serving something greater than ourselves because homecoming is a timeless tradition to our town. Where the consensus is that this might be as good as it will ever get, quite possibly the only experience in life that will live up to its hype. And we rinse and repeat every year, forever.

The game was great. The dance was great. I didn't want either to end. Tom's video is priceless, with images of the after-party with adults, and neighbors so intoxicated, so happy, so alive. And Tom is, too. He is un-serious, un-stern, and un-judgmental as he chuckles about silly things, like everyone in the room. There are moments of proud smiling fathers in sports jackets whose daughters rode in the back of nice, shiny convertibles during the parade—the queen candidates; my sister was one of them.

And I watch the recording of the game because I want to see myself running the plays, but the video of the game is disjointed. One second, there are boys getting up from a pile, the next someone kicks the ball into the lights and I can't find it until someone gets tackled. The announcer calls out my name and number as I am wedged beneath the pile; I am always the first to the ball.

But now I can't make out what's going on but hear steps and see the camcorder is heavy. Tom must think the camera is off as he videos the turf for a good couple minutes.

"How's it going?" I hear Tom say to someone.

"Great, and you?" replies an unfamiliar voice.

"You're doing a great job, Ref," Tom says as a man's shoe appears on the screen.

"Filming for the team?" the man asks. "Looks heavy."

"No, I've got kids out there."

"Mmmm," he grunts.

"My daughter is a queen candidate and my son, number three, is in the game."

"Oh, that's your boy? He's talented."

"We're proud of him," I hear Tom say.

"Good luck, game is starting back up."

And it ends and I sit here, alone, tempted to rewind a hundred times. Am I the boy he sees from the other side of this camera? Is he the father who pack-mules a cumbersome camcorder in hopes of capturing me doing things that make him proud? How different would life be if we took all those feelings we express indirectly, through other people, through casual conversations, and actually say them to the people we love? Where I talk about how smart my dad is, and how hard he works, and how people respect his last name. The things

I never think of when he's around. What could we share, if we weren't scared and full of triggers and history and preconceived ideas of what the other is thinking? Would we lift one another up and never sigh again?

And I wonder to myself, how many times this happens, but goes unnoticed? And why can't we live our lives in unexpected moments with good feelings and acceptance and no eggshells to walk upon?

But no matter how I heard it, I still heard it.

He called me his son. He said he was proud of me.

I just wish he would say it to my face.

61

HER UNFAMILIAR HANDWRITING reminds me that we haven't had a meaningful interaction for over a decade. Maybe longer, since we ended a conversation with an "I love you" or "see you later". Still, my sister picked up a pen and scattered her feelings all over a stack of papers, then stuffed them in an envelope and sent them out into the world.

How old was I when it started—maybe fifteen, maybe sixteen? I can't really remember. I only know she used to always piss me off and now, for some reason, she doesn't.

I feel something stir, something absent that I was unaware was missing. Something subtle and fragile that awakens now, like a sleeping giant, and it makes me feel more complete somehow. Quiet, like the tap of a pebble against the glass of a bedroom window, but permanent like a ton of bricks; I am reminded, after all these years, what it really means to have a sister. And I love her. And I miss her. And I will never let her go again. No matter what. No matter how things look. No matter how mad I get.

And as I sit here reading Kelly's words, feeling the sadness in her message, I can't remember when, why, or how our differences began. Only that she has known me since the day I was born. She cheered when I did great things; she has suffered her own unique consequences of Jerry Sam and the mother we share. Kelly is the only other person on the planet who derives her talent, her heart, and her insecurities from the same chromosomes. In many ways, whether we like it or not, it has secretly been her and I against the world.

Although she didn't live through the same childhood as I did, it's not her fault. I was a boy, a reminder of Jerry Sam. It's not her fault she didn't get hit and she didn't get called a liar. It's not her fault she was never taught that little boys are to be dominated, are to be put in their place, are to be crushed under the weight of mistakes they never made. But she does know what it's like to be forgotten, to be looked through, to be second best to a pot of coffee in some truck stop just off the highway. She knows that Jerry Sam wasted precious moments and precious time, doing absolutely nothing but breaking our hearts.

And she is telling me that nothing matters except that she loves me, and she is asking for forgiveness so that we can forget and move forward with love and understanding. I agree and craft my reply, then fold up the letter and place it on top of my chest, and lie there, alone in the cell.

Instantly, I miss her. I realize I have missed her for years and years and years. And I know, even though I can't tell her to her face, that she somehow knows that whatever "it" was is now over. Because we will fill empty places between us that only we can fill, possibly places that only we created for one another. And Kelly will shelter me like the big sister she is. And I will be better for her because I am her baby brother again. And we will never talk about all the time we lost together, never lament over how it could've been different; only set our eyes straight ahead, into a future that has a place for both of us. Together.

And that is that.

62

By now, I have been to a lot of, what are affectionately nicknamed, Gladiator Schools, since I was one of only three white men in a cell block in the Jackson County Jail and have also had to prove myself in two state prisons. But the CCA federal holding facility outside of Leavenworth, KS is by far the most violent place I have ever been. Not "everybody-gets-raped-in-the-showers" violent, more like "twenty-five percent of the population gets beat down in their sleep with locks in a sock" violent.

Every week, it seems, I hear about a new, creative, and unique story of the way a man can get his ass whooped. Here is where I have learned that a mop handle split in half becomes two weapons: one end to be used as your everyday, garden variety dagger, and the other end—the side where the mop head goes, with metal and heft—can be a very effective club. And the fights are eye-opening. Men who know they're outnumbered stand on an island of dry concrete and pour water concentrically all around them so that the men who are coming for them slide around as they swing whatever weapon they have. Because we wear these thinly-soled shower shoes, liquid on the ground is very difficult to overcome. I learned that the hard way.

I have also learned terms like "Buck 50," which is slang for the hundred and fifty stitches you receive when a tuna fish can lid is slashed across your face. And let's not forget the insane, but widely-held, belief that if you boiled baby oil in a microwave it will melt the skin off a person's face.

Every type of criminal imaginable—murderers, domestic terrorists, professional athletes who smuggled cocaine, and the man who was spreading the gospel of LSD across the planet—is all housed in the same facility. You never know who might cut your throat or attack, or even how they will do it or who might take advantage of someone's stupidity, but you always know that someone amongst you will do something at some point. It is only a matter of time if you aren't careful.

Turns out this was my time.

There's this kid named Ian from Independence, who is a real piece of work—young, weak, and known as a cook. He has enough street cred and enough money to shoehorn his way in with some real convicts. His insecurity is obvious to everyone but himself, so he polishes his act a little more every day with his speech or the way he holds himself. It is annoying. But for the people in the pod, he's the benchmark for a sucker and has lots to offer, so they put up with his false bravado and…well, the rest is pretty obvious.

Now Butch is a bona fide son of a bitch. He's an Aryan brother wannabe who doesn't really like me much—and trust me, the feeling is mutual—but he tolerates me because I am funny and the others decided I was "okay". He is a malcontent, stocky asshole of a dude with tattoos and a long red goatee, who always sharpens the ends of spoons and makes weapons for when the Black vs. White Armageddon goes down.

Nico is different. He is for real. Easy to respect, very quiet, calculated—and, by the way, another killer. Rumor has it he has beaten at least two cases for murder. In one of them, he apparently followed a sixty-five-year-old man back from the riverboat casinos and gut shot him in his own garage for a couple thousand dollars. The surveillance footage from the casino showed him following the unsuspecting man all night. But nothing after that except a corpse in the man's garage in Northeast, so they couldn't connect him to the death. Nico is an Italian from Queens and, although not a "made" man, is definitely connected in many ways that are above my pay grade. A man of very few words, which makes him seem more mysterious and intelligent. He is athletic and never too emotional. Clearly the leader.

Prison is a microcosm of the real world. Oh sure, violence, harsh language, and unstable emotions are certainly more concentrated, but it's also a mirror image of the heart of man. Really. Because, once you get past the unchecked impulses and decay within the collective moral compass, you see that life in prison, no different than society, is an ongoing series of power struggles and wars over geography. Only, instead of fighting over traditional things like oil or rules of government, the fights are over a sixty-nine cent Ramen noodle soup.

And conflicts are handled slightly differently. Instead of sending tens of thousands of troops to foreign lands to implement some hidden agenda, these guys ambush a poor unsuspecting bastard in his sleep and stab him in the neck with a pencil.

Same thing.

The environment of our pod has a lot to do with how those three catch me off guard. In our district, we have an unusual split of Hispanics versus Black. About 40% Black, 40% Hispanic, and 20% white. This is a completely different dynamic from state prison, which quite honestly had very few Hispanics. At least non-English speaking Hispanics.

Nico is always secretly teaching the group how to act out in the pod—show unity, use force, show no signs of weakness, yada, yada, yada. The type of conversation that's a wet dream for Butch. Nonetheless, one day Ian got mad at Butch, probably because Butch took some of his commissary, and they started yelling where everyone could hear. The whole pod waited for something to kick off but their interest died when it quickly became clear Butch and Ian were both full of shit.

"Hey," Nico yells as he puts an arm across Butch's chest. "I need you both to settle down." Punctuating his sentence with the word, "NOW."

Butch exhales and his chest deflates.

"Don't get in my shit without my permission," Ian whines.

Nico looks pissed but says nothing. He stands at the top of the steps with Butch, Ian on the bottom step and looks out over the room. "Go into my cell," he tells Butch and shoots Ian a glare. Butch and Nico go into the cell and everyone goes back to what they were doing.

Mario, a stout but athletic Italian, and I go back to doing our push-ups. I thought nothing of it, for the most part. Just that Ian was clearly out of his league.

Later on, as the five of us are finishing up evening chow, Nico has us all meet in Butch's cell. Nico gives a serious speech about how we can't have the other races see us divided. That it's a show of weakness and to make sure any disagreements are handled in the privacy of one of our cells.

"I don't care if you want to rip each other's throats out," he says. "Don't do it in front of the other kind." Nods all around. It all makes sense.

It's amazing how quickly your choices shift, how visceral and primal your life becomes—the further you get away from civilized life, the further you're trapped in survival mode.

A couple of days later, Ian and I have an issue. Ian goes and gets the fellas and I'm invited to step into a cell to "sort out our differences". In my mind, we are going into this cell to talk about the argument, which of course sounds like the oldest trick in the book; but, in light of Nico's speech, it seemed like the right move.

As I step inside, Ian hits me in the back of the head. I'm caught off guard but unconcerned. And when I turn around to knock the shit out of him, things start getting a little fuzzy. Someone drops coffee in the middle of the floor and someone else hits me from the side, and I'm wearing shower shoes and the floor is slippery, and the next thing I know I'm hearing my mom's voice, so soft, so soothing, as she nudges me to wake up.

"Come on sweetie. Time to wake up," she whispers. "It's time for school."

I want to answer but sleeping feels so good. The bed, my childhood bed, too warm for me to want to wake up just yet. Mentally, I ask for a few more minutes because if I make a sound it will be hard to go back to sleep. And I'm comfortable and cozy and why the hell would anyone want to get up from this?

"Come on baby boy, not now," she says. "I need you to be strong."

"Just a few more minutes," I beg. "I'm having a dream."

It's the wee hours of the morning and I'm young and the sun is coming through the window, the one that overlooks the large cornfield in my backyard. There's a squirrel outside, chewing on a walnut and the breeze moves the curtain like crashing waves during high tide. I am content, I am free, I am home. Soon I will walk downstairs and smell the faded scent of fried bacon and hot coffee and everyone will be at work and—

I hear angry men's voices, saying things I can't make out. They're cursing, almost in rhythm with the pounding that seems to be closer now. Mom's voice is nowhere and my room, the breeze, the warm cozy sheets, are all gone, too.

I feel my body jerking, air leaving my body, a strong, violent something that I can't stop. And as I am ripped away from that beautiful world, into this vicious, cruel, violent environment, I am like a child coming into the world for the very first time after leaving my mother's womb—I am confused, I am disoriented and all I want is to go back in.

Wait. I had an issue with an inmate…I'm an inmate…in Leavenworth, Kansas.

I'm in a cell. I'm on the floor. I'm a convict in a trap. No, just in a trap. Being beaten by men. That's it; I'm being beaten by men.

Shit, I'M BEING BEATEN BY MEN IN PRISON!

The whole thing is surreal. I never saw it coming. And I've been knocked unconscious, and the men are on top of me, stomping my head, my neck, my fingers. I'm frantically trying to figure out what is going on, running through a triage of very limited options with very limited time.

It's clear to me that I've taken on damage. I can't see, I'm fading in and out of consciousness. I catch a glimpse of light—the doorway—and I barrel my body in that direction, head down, legs pumping like a fullback once again dragging defenders across the goal line.

Once outside the cell, I put some space between me and these bastards. And take a second to start piecing together what happened. My head feels numb and fat, like your cheek when you leave the dentist after a filling. Only this is my entire head. I'm full of rage and adrenaline as I spit blood and scream "motherfuckers" more times than I can count. And I don't run, I don't hide, I surprise them all by widening my stance, balling my hands into tight, angry fists, putting them close to my face and preparing to finish what's been started.

I can taste the copper of fresh blood. We are on the second story balcony and the entire pod is watching, settling in for a show. The men back up as I continue to advance and all I can think about is throwing one of them, all of them, any of them, over the balcony and onto the concrete floor. There is no doubt in my mind they will do the same thing to me if they get the chance. But the difference between them and me is I no longer give a fuck. Oddly, I feel more like me than I have in a very long time. There isn't enough mace in the state of Kansas to keep me away from these pieces of shit. They have no idea what they've gotten into.

Besides, at this point, what do I have to lose?

63

THE CAMERA IS aimed directly at my bed but far enough away so it captures the whole room. I've never seen what the camera sees, or even who is on the other side staring at the screen. All I know is I am being monitored for "serious issues" and anytime I speak a request into the camera—water or salve for the stitches on my face—I get it within fifteen to twenty minutes. My face is tender now that the adrenaline has subsided and I vaguely remember they took me to the hospital, a hospital that I think had normal people, not convicts. But it all seems like a dream because I've got this severe concussion.

And it disturbs me that they watch me for "serious issues". As if holes in my lip from where my teeth punctured through isn't serious, or the swelling in my brain or the debilitating sensation of vertigo anytime I sit up or lay down in bed, which oddly feels like the drunkest I've ever been just before I puke. It concerns me, just a little, that I can't recognize the face staring back when I look at my reflection in the mirror, and how my first reaction was pity, then sadness, then concern that the scars would be yet one more permanent stain from prison.

It's not like this is the first time I've been sewed up or had vertigo or spent a night or two in some hospital being monitored. I was a curious and accident-prone little boy, after all. It's just the first time I've been alone as I recover, with no one to hug, no one to talk to, and no one to care. Only me, inside my head, listening to the electronic hum of the prison door locks, fading in and out of consciousness.

In a way, I'm lucky because I have a room with multiple beds all to myself. It is quiet and dark, lit only by the soft red glow of exit signs and the blue/white glow of secondary lighting that illuminate the hallway outside this medical ward. In another way, it's like the carrot held in front of the horse that it never gets to nibble because I can't get comfortable in this condition with the excruciating pain, the lack of equilibrium, and the utter fact that I don't know what the repercussions of this fight are going to be.

I agonize over the what ifs, and the constant tight worry in the pit of my stomach that feels equivalent to being cheated on by a lover. And I'm also pissed off. Not so much at the men who tricked me, who trapped me, who stomped my head like a campfire spreading too quickly, but more because it all makes me feel so naïve.

I sit here praying for God to make the outcome better, to remove the fear of retaliation from my overactive mind. And for this reason alone, I am grateful that I have a concussion and that it weaves me in and out of consciousness. But I can't deny it forever. This won't go away on its own.

I replay the incident over and over. How they enclosed on me, how easy it was to keep me down, like a clubbed marlin tossed up on the concrete, surrounded in blood and violence and indignity. If I turn the other cheek, I will need to prepare to fight every day until people see I'm not a guy they want to mess with. But the truth is, I don't really care. I don't care how bad they beat me because, somehow, they have it justified. I don't feel the cold auto-drip of revenge creeping through my veins. I don't have a need for a rematch because they caught me slipping and they caught me good. And I know that weasel prick told them I was a bully, that I was taking advantage of the weak, and lied to get us all to this point. And if there's any consolation in all of this, it's that they respected me enough to send three in after me once I had slipped and couldn't get up.

But the truth is, Nico's a killer. The kind of convict you want on your side and not against you—one with no remorse, no respect, and a component to his thinking that I don't possess. At least, not yet. And it's no small consideration that, for him, this will never stop; I'll come for him, he'll come for me, and it won't be to settle things like men. That's not the way it works with guys like Nico.

And I have to decide how much of my soul I'm willing to sell in this part of the game. I see it all now, how men go down this path, the one they never come back from. It's not because they're sociopaths, it's not because they are killers—at least not in the beginning; it is simply because they are frightened little boys who are backed into a corner with seemingly no other choice.

But that's not the way it is for guys like me. I'm not giving in to any of that. I'm Kyle Houston, one of the cool kids, and I'm not giving in to peer pressure. It's never been my thing. I'm not swinging a knife; I'm not stabbing a human being; I'm not sacrificing that final remnant of my virtue hanging from a thread that thins more every day I'm in this place. But I will hold my head high and brace myself to fight anyone and everyone who thinks I'm weak, who thinks I'm vulnerable or that I can't handle my business. Because this is about so much more than the salty sting of pride; this is about saving my soul. Here, right here, in this fucking holding facility in Leavenworth, KS where I'm not so much being baptized as I am giving in to something higher—my dad's son.

And I'll pray to God that I make it home soon and return as the same man I was raised to be. The real battle of a fallen warrior. The temptation of the warrior soul.

The fight comes back to me slowly and in chunks of time, like black and white clips of a movie, only some of the images are of the fight and some are the hypothetical scenarios of how well life is going for old friends. I recall now that I slipped, my shower shoes were unstable, standing in the middle of a puddle of coffee. It was probably planned that way. And then I think of old girlfriends and where they are in life, who they've married and how many children they have.

I recall the faces of the men in the cell block looking up at me on the second-row balcony, like viewers of a drive-in movie too close to the screen. Then I think of my closest childhood friends and where life has taken them. Do they live in large houses? Did they marry women who love them? Because one thing is for sure, they aren't holed up in some prison medical ward worried about how permanent the damage really is. They have careers, they have dental bills, they have 401(k)s. They live a good life, the way it was supposed to go for me—eating Sunday dinner, barbecue grills, October hayrides. Not licking your wounds in some lonely moment with the sterile stench of institution filling your senses. And I want to be happy for all of them, carrying on with their lives, becoming the good people of the world, but it hurts and makes me feel left behind. And the thought makes me miss childhood, makes me yearn for the savory smell of corned beef wafting through the house and the piles of dirty shoes from all the neighborhood boys collecting on the back porch as we all play video games in my mom's den, staring at the TV screen like moths captivated by a flame.

I sit here replaying the moments when we were all innocent, when our biggest concern was a bad grade in English or how fast the grass grew before I was forced to mow it again, before life in prison was ever a thing. I remember them all—my friends, my girlfriends, my memories that have kept me warm in the past; but tonight, they all seem to make me feel lost somehow, forgotten, swept under the rug. Because those people are adults now, vicariously living out memories of their youth through new faces, through new versions of themselves, and I'm in here getting old, finding new wrinkles, new gray hairs, all alone.

I feel so sorry for myself. I feel so angry but I'm not sure toward whom. Maybe them, maybe life, maybe me. Tonight, I have no distractions, no ear to bend, no TV, no music, no book; only the symphony of my loneliness inside my mind and the images of lost memories that never got to happen unfolding in my thoughts.

This pain is unstoppable, unrelenting, but I will lean in and make it hurt more. Because, tonight, it is all that I have to hold onto, all that I have of myself. And I have never needed pain more than I do right now.

64

For reasons I don't quite understand, I am moved from the medical ward. In the middle of the night, a female guard, who sounds soft and compassionate, comes in, asks me to gather my things and follow her.

"Where are we going?" I ask.

"To the hole," she tells me.

"The hole?" I stop what I am doing and stare at her. "It is clear that I got my ass kicked, right?"

"Oh, I can see that, sweetie," she says with a little laugh. "Come on. You'll be all right. Captain wants to talk to you."

The captain's office is nothing special—walls, gray; door, gray; desk, gray, and all of it anchored by stacks of papers neatly sitting in each corner. An American flag juts out of the corner of the room and reminds me of reciting the Pledge of Allegiance when I was in grade school. To the captain's left is a monitor with a keyboard just below it and a single manila folder with my last name first, first name last, sitting in front of him, closed and ominous.

"How do you feel?" he asks.

"Worse than I look."

He laughs uncomfortably. I sit there straight-faced, no smile, afraid my stitches might open.

He asks me what 'this' was all about, telling me he read my file and that none of this seemed like anything from the streets. I say nothing. He tells me "that kid" was in the hole but that he suspects Ian wasn't the one who did this. At least not alone. *Hint-hint, this fucker wants information.*

Again, I say nothing. Then he leans forward and his tone drops into grave territory, and he tells me I'm going to be transferred to the hole… unless I can tell him who else was involved. If I do, I can go back to the same cellblock, an option he makes sound like a great deal.

"Skip the hole," he says in his I'm-the-best-friend-you've-got tone. He thinks I'm stupid.

"Yeah, right."

"Look, I know y'all have your code, but—"

"But you're not the one who has to go back in there, after skipping the hole," I say, pointing over my shoulder back to the cellblocks. Nothing screams *snitch* like a visit to the captain and no punishment.

The captain nods. I tell him I'm glad he understands and then I get to my feet, struggling to maintain my equilibrium, and turn to leave.

"I heard you held your own, Houston," he says to my back. I can hear him shuffling papers. "For what it's worth."

"That's not the way it feels to me." And I walk out.

It never ceases to amaze me how these guards have cameras, numbers, jail house snitches and, in my case, practically a trail of blood leading them right to the gutless fuckers who did this, and they still can't figure it out. Go find the bastards with my blood on their boots. Go find the sole that matches the imprint still criss-crossed across my face. Go find the son of a bitch with bruised and bloody knuckles, the one who punched my teeth through my lips; the one who was inevitably sitting in his cell still gasping for air when you found me, because kicking my ass was a workout.

You don't need me, Captain, just do your job—the one where you get fat and out of shape sitting in your dull boring office trying to imagine if you could do time like us; and I'll do my job—the one where I drag every possession I own down an empty hallway with shiny wax floors and into a cell full of nothing but concrete and me. Where I get to deal with all the fucking idiots who go to the hole. The jail inside the jail.

The hole here is different than what I'm used to. The cells are laid out in a horseshoe, curved around a common area that has a desk and a guard sitting in the middle. Inside the cell, it is all concrete with a drain in the middle so they can simply hose down the degenerates when they are done doing whatever it is they do—spitting, pissing, or shitting, as an act of defiance. And the cells all have bars, like in the prison movies where inmates clang tin cups off the bars and scream at the guards.

But in here, it is silent, with the exception of a faceless asshole a few cells down who won't shut up about some miserable bastard, someone either he beat down or his friends beat down. I don't know. I don't care. I've been trying to sleep.

Then the one-man conversation turns. "Hey you! White boy who got his ass kicked."

I say nothing as I slowly sit up. *Not now, motherfucker. I'm not in the mood. Let me get the stitches out before I have to argue with an idiot who thinks he's got an easy target.*

Officer Williams looks up from his desk. He's tall, athletically built, and Black. Not that it matters to me, but it makes a difference with Black inmates. These convicts will tell you that all guards are the enemy, wish they'd all go to hell, and "If you think one gives a shit, you're a sucker, you're a bootlicker, you're a jail house snitch". In prison there is a language, a code, and a set of rules that generates from a source I will never see, and the convicts never stray too far from.

"Look man, give it a rest," Williams says. "You don't know."

"You ain't my daddy. I know enough."

"Okay, if you say so." Williams pauses, as if he's contemplating something.

I can't see the inmate. For all I know, he is big and powerful and affiliated. For all I know, he can fight and is a worthy opponent. For all I know, I should be aware that going toe-to-toe with him won't be easy and will come with spilled blood and fresh scars, that he won't go down easily and I should brace myself because it's not going to be a cakewalk. But something I know that he doesn't is I'm not putting up with his shit. Because of that, I might be forced to listen to his mouth, might be forced to call him out, might be forced to have a new debt to pay before I even get out of the hole. Because he has no idea who I am or what I'm capable of, and I'm pretty fucking sure this fight is already going to perpetuate another fight. I'm lying here in solitary confinement, in pain, in agony, while another asshole is calling me out before the boot mark is even off my face. The experience has no parallel in the real world. Just imagine every bad emotion you've ever had, swirling wildly inside your conscience as you waste energy on the types of things that shouldn't matter. Except in here.

"You know what? I usually don't get into this kind of thing, but I'm going to do you a huge favor," Williams says.

"Oh, you gonna do me a favor?" The faceless guy snorts.

"Yeah. Just in case you think this guy's a lame."

"Fuck him. He ain't said shit all morning. And I've been calling him out."

"I don't know anything about that." A half smile is on Williams' face, maybe because he has information the other asshole doesn't. "I just know that he got jumped by three guys but he had one on the ground and was beating the shit out of him by the time we showed up."

The inmate says nothing.

"That's right, he was screaming gangster shit like, 'You think this is over because the guards are here?' And you know what… most of you convicts make all that noise so we come in and break it up, but not the guy you're trying to fuck with right now. It took four of us to pull this guy off. Four." Then Williams adds, "And if you think I'm some weak-ass bitch, you're wrong."

"You's a bitch," the inmate says and laughs.

"I've been doing this long enough to know y'all are sneaky motherfuckers. People get jumped all the time." Williams shakes his head and then laughs a little to himself. "The difference is how you show up when it happens."

"What the fuck do you know, Williams?" The other inmate wants to challenge Williams now.

"Not much. Just that I'm out here and you're locked up, playa." Williams pauses to let that sink in and then adds, "Oh, and that this motherfucker over here ain't no punk."

There's a moment of quiet. My head aches, my stitches are bruised and I'm tired of being stressed all the time. Williams goes back to his work and I go back to lying on my bunk and minding my own business.

"Took four of you, huh?" The other inmate calls out. "Good for him. Don't take shit, white boy!" He yells the last bit and then, just like that, it's silent again.

And for the time being, I'm back to dealing with the simple things about prison life.

The simple things like a looming life sentence.

65

I'M SEVENTEEN NOW and Mom's in my face. She's always in my face. Pulling me in, deepening the pattern that has etched a groove between us. She is bent on control, not love, not nurture. It's a ritual she learned somewhere before I ever came along. And I hate her, I'm sure I do because she's obstinate and intolerant, incapable of changing.

And I'll be damned, wouldn't you know it, I am too.

This is my life's work these days: daring anyone to hurt me again. I won't have it. They can't do it because I am strong now and have to be heard. I have to stand proud, stand brave, and believe I know everything with conviction and vigor, especially when it pisses her off. She has passed it along so perfectly to her best student, her worst opponent…moi.

We are always at an impasse, even before we speak, so we skip the meaningless small talk and head right to where harsh language overpowers understanding. Confrontation is our connection; anger proves our love. It's where we are comfortable, at our very best. That place where the gloves always come off.

And we have all these buttons that we push and observe and deflect and deny, but never admit, because that might render the advantage. Instead, we just get mad, dig in deep, and see who can hurt the other the most. In my heart, I will fight to the death and, honestly, I don't even know why. But I have decided she will no longer chew me up, no longer spit me out, for we have arrived at that point where the student has become the master.

"Why? Why can't I go see her?" It's more of a challenge than a request. And it could be anyone—a friend, my girlfriend, a lap through town—because all I want to do is get out of the damn house.

"Because I'm the mother," she reminds me. "Period." Her arms are crossed, her face contorted, her stance dares me to continue down this path.

It's the end of summer. I will begin my senior year soon and I have just been diagnosed with mono. The doctor says I can't play football because "it could be life-threatening", but for me, life without football is as good as death. I've spent three years of my life waiting for my senior year, the year when all the practices, all the talent, all the emotion in my heart is sure to pay off. And now the universe wants to take away the one thing that brings me love. I am devastated, pissed off at the world, and unwilling to be under anyone's control.

"What's the harm?" I ask.

"The doctor wants you to—"

"I've done what the doctor wants. I've been here all day." I pause, then, "Mom."

"Sleeping and watching TV," she clarifies as if that means something. Her face is tight and cold, the way it always is just before the fight.

"Yeah, no kidding," I tell her. "It's what the doctor said to do."

"You're not going. That's final."

Tom enters the room now, his brow furrowed and his arms folded. His presence makes me angrier. Typical—now it's two against one.

"I'm going," I announce.

She shakes her head. "In what car?"

"I'll walk." Then I don't need anybody to do anything.

"Watch your tone, kiddo," Tom tells me. That vein in his temple is pulsing and his face is already red. When I was young, that would have scared me, but now, I tell myself that he doesn't.

"This is so unfair. I'm a senior." I pace the living room, ten steps one way, ten the other.

"Yeah. Under my roof..." Mom puts one hand on her hip and stabs at the air with a finger. "...my rules, you little shit. What makes you think you can talk to me the way you do?"

"Why do you have to call me names?" My voice is loud, probably too loud. I don't care.

Tom unfolds his arms and leans into my space. "Lower your voice, young man."

"Because I'm the mother." She throws her hands up and shakes her head. "Do you think other kids talk to their mothers—"

"Do you think other kids have a mom like you?" I interrupt, biting my lip now, trying not to say the word, the one that brings pandemonium.

"What do you mean 'like me'?" Her arms are crossed again. "You're not leaving this house. You're not getting in your car. And you need to realize who is the boss here." She hesitates, and I can see the words forming in her mind, before she delivers the last blow, "Little Jerry Sam."

"Fuck you! I know what that means." I hesitate. "Bitch!" The word explodes out of me, and it feels good.

Without warning, Tom charges the room and grabs my chin, so hard and fast, it makes us stumble into the couch. My head hits the windowsill and everything goes dark for a moment. When I come to, my head is pressed into the wooden frame and he towers over me, shaking and red—the way he is, the way he's always been since I was a boy.

"Get off," I mutter softly, but I'm not all here yet.

Whatever reply he has is inaudible but has violent undertones. His weight is so heavy on me now and he's squeezing my jaw hard.

"Get off me, Dad!"

Then he's telling me to apologize, to show some respect, because "this is your mother". And I'm reminded of the bruises around Mom's neck a few years back and this elaborate story they spun about a dream that he had. That when he came out of the dream, "somehow" he was choking her. Somehow? Whatever. But I don't care about the story because, in my mind, the fact that nobody has killed anyone yet is the silver lining here.

I feel the rage consume me. I feel the emotion of hundreds of moments just like this—him standing over me, him shaking my face, him feeling bigger than me. The anger fuels me, and I jump up and toss all two hundred and thirty pounds of him off and to the side of me. I push him across the end table, through a lamp, and then I strike twice with a closed fist, as hard as I can. Two crushing blows—almost exactly the same— and straight into the orbital bone of his left eye.

Now this dominating presence, this powerful man, is wounded and in need, helpless. His eye is out of the socket, his face is full of fear, and I know this image will haunt me forever because of the way it haunts me now.

"Dad!" I scream and throw my arms around him, tight as I can. "I'm sorry, Dad. I'm sorry, I'm so sorry," I repeat endlessly as the tears stream down my face. My chest hurts, it's hard to breathe, and I squeeze like I'm never going to see him again.

"What…what happened?" he asks, confused, frightened.

"I'm sorry. I'm so sorry." I repeat.

"What do we do, Tom?" I hear my mom ask. "Let go of him, Kyle."

I release my grip slowly, reluctantly, because I don't want to see. I don't want this to be true, to be permanent. I'm crying uncontrollably and I won't let him get too far away. I feel like a child. In this moment, I am a child—a boy wanting approval, feeling so guilty, unworthy, ashamed. Again.

And I would give anything to change the last five minutes, to go back and let him do what he does, what he's always done. Because, at the very least, I know he cares when he's mad. But if he is afraid of me, what do I have? Does he ignore me now? Shift all that attention to something else, to someone else? I want it to go back, I don't want to conquer anything. I want to be tiny and fragile and weak. Because every smack, every harsh word, every painful moment is a reminder that he loves me. Please, let me be nervous again, erase my self-esteem because it's better than this—the sorrow and shame, the passing of something sacred. And that tone in his voice is a sound I can't take, a sound that won't leave.

A sound I never want to hear again.

66

It's a Saturday visit that brought my internal world crashing down. Because it's sad, like real *Cat's in the Cradle* kind of sad, and I realize that my vivid hopes of getting back to where I started, circa 1995, is never going to happen. All the memories that I have been so desperately clinging to, hanging my hopes on, and using as a target for where I wanted to go, are going to be just that—memories.

Dad sits across from me, sixty pounds shaved off his frame. He is so gaunt, so confused, and keeps trying to scoot himself—no, drag himself—in front of that fucking glass that separates us. I don't know what this means but I know I don't want it. I imagine he doesn't want it, either. But the world has a very specific job to do and that is to spin, to move, to pull time through all our lives, not to give two shits what the two of us want.

His eyes are dim, as if something is missing inside him. And that rubbery, saggy skin with the cheekbones and the sadness and the strength that no longer exists, is a genuine gut punch from life itself that reminds me, *Hey Kyle, the world ain't slowing down.*

Whether I am locked up or not.

This man who entered my life at a very young age to raise me, teach me, love me—in his way—sits two feet away from me, wordless and stoic, and I can't reach through that thick glass to wrap my arms around him or help him stand. I struggle to accept that making amends isn't going to be in the cards for us.

The more I look at him, with his tired, bloodshot eyes, exhaustion pressing him into the hard, plastic seat, it's eerily clear that *This Too Shall Pass* sometimes means even the ones we love.

"Doctor says we have nothing to worry about," Mom says in the background, trying to aim her words at the phone pressed to Dad's face. Her smile is fake, almost too big. "He's pulled through as planned."

Dad's face is flat, devoid of reaction.

"How do you feel?" I ask him.

He shrugs his shoulders. "You," he grunts. It's supposed to be a question, but the word seems to be so much for him to get out.

I lie and tell him I'm doing fine.

Mom grabs the phone out of his hand and starts telling me how they took a cantaloupe-sized tumor out of his body. She puts her hands against the glass and makes a circle with her fingers to show me the size. There are some other words, something about it being attached to the kidney, but I'm not listening. His clothes hang off him, big and floppy and I think to myself, *Why can't she buy him something new?* The man's in pain, probably dying, and he has to walk around looking like this?

It's been months, maybe even a year, since I've seen him. And his skin reminds me of one of those rubber Halloween masks of past presidents, like Richard Nixon or Bill Clinton, that make your face sweat and never fit right, and it wobbles so much on your face that your eyes never line up with the holes.

They're his eyes, but that's not my Dad.

My God, this all makes sense now. I stand up, put my hand on the window and shout into the greasy glass, "I love you, Dad."

He nods and closes his eyes for a long time. I hear the faint sound of my mother's voice saying, "Honey, just sit down please. Your father just wants to have a normal conversation with you."

And I watch him, and I pray that the cancer doesn't hurt but everything tells me that it does.

But he still came to visit me, to sit in that hard chair and trade small talk.

And in this moment, I try to imagine how he sees me, his son, behind the frame of the glass, and in my orange jumpsuit. Does he know that I love him? Does he know that I am sorry? Does he know what he means to me because we haven't had a chance to talk or share our feelings, that's for damned sure. There are the things I remember, and the things I forget, and most of all, there is how much I want to thank him for all he's done. I always thought I'd have time later, but now everything feels so urgent. So where to begin?

How about *I'm sorry that I lost your kite.*

I want to be that five-year-old again, standing in the field across from the house, but this time I'll hang on when the wind gusts hit. This time, I won't let go because I promised that I wouldn't. If I could go back, I would, because that mistake is where I think somehow our problems all started.

But, in this moment, that just feels like a silly memory of a boy and I can't bring myself to say it or take the last two decades and condense them into a few sentences.

So I hope there are kites in heaven, Dad, and little boys who tell you they're sorry and you get to hug them and teach them and tell them all the things you won't get to tell me. You deserve that. Because I'm afraid you're leaving this world and you won't get the chance. And your heart won't get to heal. And neither will mine.

I sit down and put the phone back to my ear. Dad opens his eyes and sighs. "Is he all right, Mom?"

"He will be, sweetie." Her promise seems to be missing something. She doesn't turn around to check on him, or offer a smile, or anything to put the stamp of honesty on the sentence.

"How are *you* doing?" I ask her.

She tells me she's fine, but it takes too long for her to get the words out and I get the sense that none of us are being honest. And I want to unload, to beg her to tell Dad that he has to hang on. If for no other reason, for me. I need him to be there when I get out because we have too much to do, too much to repair, too many wounds to heal. But I don't. Instead, I think for a second and search for a lie. Because if anyone needs one, it's her.

"Don't worry about me, I'm doing just fine." The lie is chased by a truth that makes a smile wobble on her face. "I love you, Mom."

And she promises that everything will be all right as she struggles to help Dad stand. He's like an old and withered prize fighter who feels the repercussions of a lifetime of punches. His legs are weak, his movements precarious and fragile, and something has clearly been beaten out of him. And he half-smiles as he looks at me as if to say, *I'm sorry, son*. Then he pivots and shuffles toward the door while the scent of bleach and desperation hang in the air.

The door shuts behind them. A hard, solid thunk.

A noise that sounds far too final.

67

THE PHONE RINGS on the other end as I stand here looking out into the pod at the faces of men who were once little boys. Scared, abandoned little boys. Before life did its thing, before the world lied over and over, before they were taught to strike first or they will be hurt. Before the humanity inside them sharpened and hardened until it was unrecognizable. *Please, God, help me get Sean Michael safe so he will never end up like them.*

Somewhere in the state of Texas is a child who is confused and lonely and crying. And he is my child, my son, my sister's nephew.

I can't leave him where he is. I can't personally go get him and I can't bear the thought of how he must feel. I don't have the words to explain how I feel about this four-year-old son, a boy I haven't seen since he was a baby, who has been a thought in the back of my mind for years. But now that I know he might be lost and vulnerable and afraid, the papa bear inside me rears up with an overwhelming need to protect him. I'm now desperately scrambling to make sure my cub is safe, sheltered, and somewhere I can see him. Because, although I can't put my finger on the psychological phenomenon that is taking place inside me, or the case study that explains how I feel, the truth is, I love him.

More than I expected to.

And how does a person like me find the chutzpah to ask his sister to fly to Texas and pull a child out of foster care?

Like *Hey Kel, I realize we haven't exactly been connected at the hip for the past fifteen years, but there's this thing I need you to do. Um…would it be too much to ask for you to take on my illegitimate child, your nephew?*

Where do I get the audacity to ask a favor like this? From my heart, from that thing that is thicker than water, from the simple fact that I have no other choice.

But what is she going to think? Will she think I'm one of these manipulative convicts who plays games and lies just to connive their way back into other people's lives? With selfish fucked up ways of seeing people as a mark, a pawn, a means to achieve some ulterior motive. Or will she believe the truth—that all I want, all I need in this moment, is for her to rescue a child who is my son, her nephew, from a life of abandonment and institutions and a loveless childhood?

That if I can somehow save my boy, then maybe I can save a bit of myself and the soul I lost along the way?

God—yeah, it's me again—please protect Sean Michael. Don't let anyone touch him or change him or do permanent damage. Show him love. Help him trust the world, even though it has been nothing but confusion and broken promises. Put someone brave and strong and genuine and honest in his life. Let it be a woman, let her be maternal, let her be soft in all the places a little boy needs and firm for the exact same reasons. Let her be nurturing, let her be righteous, let her be the source of everything he hasn't had up to this point.

Let her be Kelly.

"Hello?" I hear her voice as the automated system announces that her brother is calling her from prison. There's a pause when my heart stops and I wait for her to accept the call.

"Hey," I say. "How's it going?"

"I'm tired," Kelly says. "I just got back from the kids' soccer practice. How are you?"

"Good." How the hell do I bring this up? What if she says no?

"Did you get the money we sent?"

"Yeah. Sorry. Thank you." Damn it. I should have mentioned that right off.

"Good. It breaks my heart thinking you can't just go get a snack from the fridge whenever you want." She pauses, and then, "Mom is not doing well."

"Kelly," I begin because if I don't say it soon, I feel I might explode. "I need to ask you something."

"Of course, Kyle. Ask me anything."

When people say *anything*, they don't really know what they are saying. It's an automatic response and in the outside world it can be about picking up a quart of milk or doing carpool the next morning. But when your brother is in prison because he's a needle-using meth junkie who cooked enough meth to supply a small country, *anything* can open you to a world of trouble.

"I need you to listen," I tell her. "I need you to understand."

Silence. The pause lasts long enough that I ask if she's still there and she confirms she is, that she's going into the bedroom, that this sounds serious.

"Know that I love you," I tell her. "Know that I will not judge you for any type of reaction you have. And most of all, know that I hate that my life is this perpetual nightmare of baggage."

"Okay. I know those three things now," she says with a half laugh, half sigh. "So, tell me what you really need to say."

I start by telling her about the court-ordered paternity test that happened a month ago. The paperwork, the legal jargon, and the cotton swab inside my mouth.

"Why didn't you say something?"

"I don't know," I answer, but the truth is I didn't find it necessary. Not until I found out what was happening in my son's life.

How do I tell my sister, with her well-defined ideas of relationships and one-night stands and mistakes, that there is no way to sum up this kind of situation? That the mother is a meth whore. That even though I have no desire to ever speak to this lost and cruel and fucked-up woman again, at one time Nicki meant a lot to me…and I maybe even loved her. How do you manage the flow of information inside that ball of yarn?

And I apologize to Kelly for the hundredth time, telling her it's not fair but that I have no one else. I am the black sheep of the family who deserves nothing from her and it's wrong to ask such a huge favor.

"So, what do you think?" I ask her.

In a calm, low voice she asks, "What's his name?"

"Sean Michael," I tell her.

"Sean Michael," she repeats.

I close my eyes and press my head against the hard metal phone bank. How I wish I was anywhere but in prison, that I could stand up and be the dad my son deserves. "I am so sorry to ask this of you."

Kelly pauses again. In the background, I can hear her kids laughing and running down the hall. They're happy and loved, and oh, how I wish that for little Sean.

"I know you're sorry, Kyle." I brace myself for her to tell me it's too much, because it is a lot. Instead she says, "But now we have a little boy to save. My brother's son. My nephew."

And for the first time in maybe forever, I feel like I am not alone. Like maybe there is hope.

68

I'm twenty-one now and somehow, in fits and starts, we have become father and son. It's how we introduce each other on business trips and over the phone and within the company. And, although I can't quite pinpoint that single, lightbulb moment, when everything suddenly changed, I do know that we have gradually begun to read each other better or try a little more or whatever mystical thing happens when two men bury the hatchet. I do remember one specific moment when I told my mother I'd never felt accepted, never felt wanted by him. Like I was too flawed to be his kid.

Tom overheard us talking. When he came in the room, I steadied myself for some bullshit argument. But instead of blame, or denial, or excuses, he said he was sorry. He said he never meant to make me feel that way; he just didn't know how to be a father. Then he held his arms out, we embraced, and he squeezed me tighter than I remember ever being hugged before. The embrace was clumsy, not something either of us were any good at, and then he started to cry, something I'd never seen before. Something I'll never forget because it might have been the most honest exchange the two of us ever had. And he was sorry, and nobody yelled, and I had been heard for what felt like the very first time in my life.

He didn't know how to be my father any more than I knew how to be his kid.

But now, I'm so proud to be this thing, so honored when he says, "my son"; and I learn from him, of all people, the strength in being kind and caring. He's no longer the man who insisted I was lying or physically took everything out on me. I'm not sure where that man went, just that he ebbed into the shadows a little more each day.

My role has more depth now, more meaning. No longer am I the stepchild or the package deal. I am his son. And I have his attention and his respect, and I would take a bullet for him although he would never ask. Saying "Dad" in his presence brings together the loose ends of our relationship. Hearing him call me "Son" quickens something in my heart, each word forming new skin over old scars. My urge to be destructive is replaced with a yearning to be better. The emptiness to have a father is filled with my passion to be his child. I forgive him and my sincerest hope is that he forgives me as well.

When I needed a job, he brought me into the family business. I worked so hard, worked my way up from the very bottom for something far greater than earning money. I worked to earn his approval. At work, I am his right-hand man. Someone he needs. Someone he lets tag along. I am in awe, witnessing his empathy and compassion for every single person who works for and with him. At tradeshows, business owners pull me aside at cocktail parties to share elaborate stories of how Tom Runge helped them when they needed it. In the beginning. Before they mattered to anyone else. They tell me as if to thank him through me. They buy me drinks and make it clear that they wouldn't be where they are if not for "your father".

But gratitude isn't what drives Tom Runge, it's not what he feels he deserves. He's modest, humble, something I lack the capacity to understand; but I can tell letting go of that hunger for praise takes strength. The kind of strength I don't have at twenty-one. The kind of strength I will pursue for the rest of my life.

I see what it means to be a good man. I watch him as a new ice cream parlor comes to town and he quietly supports them by buying things he doesn't need. I hear him encourage the owner because he genuinely wants him to succeed. Because he knows what it's like to put yourself out there, and he admires people's courage and wants to help in any way he can. Even if it's just to buy an ice cream cone and say good luck.

And I see him struggle to always do the right thing for his employees. And I see people follow him and I'm happy that, for a brief moment in time, I am led by someone as positive and upright as my father—a man who is now gentle and understanding, and wants nothing but good things for me, too. The rest has all just become water under the bridge.

He teaches me that the world is not so cruel, that there is a place for gentlemen who are honorable and live by their word in business. And when you are a business owner, every employee becomes your responsibility, even if you have to take their salary out of your own paycheck. Even if none of them ever know it. It may seem naïve, but that's how he lives his life; and through his code of ethics, I catch a glimpse of how I want to live mine.

Now that I can see there is a me and there is a him and there is simply an us with a past and a present—and even though I believe we could have done better—all of it plays a part in what we are now: Father and Son. And the bond is strong, and it isn't misplaced, and it has become unbreakable. Because "I love you" took the place of "I'm sorry". And heartfelt pride between us took the place of "I forgive you".

We have never spoken about the way I was handled as a child. Suddenly, I can see how much better he wished he could've been for me. For him. Because, although he fucked up in a lot of ways, I know he would take it all back if he could.

Suddenly, the loyalty of a five-year-old boy is something to be treasured and kept. Because, in so many ways, I am still that little boy, still wrapping my arms around the man and squeezing with my eyes closed tightly, praying for love, his love.

And finally, it's mine.

Better late than never—I am a son. And he is my Dad.

69

THIS DUDE NAMED Dante is laughing about the terror on another man's face as he tells me about how he stabbed this guy with a switchblade knife outside a bar in Kansas City.

"They always be surprised when the knife go in," he says, then claps his hands and chuckles, like he just delivered the punch line of a joke. "Stupid motherfuckers."

I raise my eyebrows and nod my head and try not to look so caught off guard. But, inside, I'm thinking, *Are you shitting me?* How does someone casually mention a possible murder attempt? More importantly, how do I casually take it all in? His choice of words, like "they" and "always", make it clear this ain't his first rodeo.

"What about you?" I ask. "You ever been stabbed?"

"Look," he explains, slowly dropping his smile. "The big dudes know they got it comin'." And he turns toward the TV and pats the cornrows in his hair with the palm of his hand as the bouncers on *The Jerry Springer Show* flood the stage.

And none of this is exactly new to me. I mean, this is prison, not daycare. I think I know my way around alarming conversations with men who have a propensity for stabbing "big dudes" with switchblades. Honestly, I've heard much worse, but normally this kind of stuff is none of my business. Not something mentioned out of the blue, not between a thug and, well, a fella with three years of piano lessons under his belt. I'm a little fuzzy about how exactly we're bonding here.

Dante is a Black man from Kansas City. He has a medium build but is very strong and clearly has no hesitation to "equalize" his opponents. With his silent, calculating presence and his lazy, tiger-like movements, it's clear he doesn't have the patience to argue. In his world, he's a man who keeps things close to the vest, which makes him dangerous and unpredictable, and those are the guys you have to look out for. And, typically, his facial expressions remain hardened and mean because he's a master at that inner-city emotional stoicism thing. It's unusual to see him smile; but this time he does, because, apparently, a guy shitting his pants with a switchblade in his kidney is funny.

Although I don't care for him, I decide it is good that Dante is opening up to me. After four weeks in the same pod, it means he is done sizing me up. The fact that he opens up like this, at the very least, means he doesn't find me weak, which is good, I guess. Because in the land of never-ending transgressions, it is weakness that is the only unforgiveable sin.

God, I miss normal people.

The lock clangs and tumbles as the guard's key turns. The pod is quiet now, except for Jerry Springer on the TV, as callous, angry men sit in baggy orange suits on the tabletops and turn in unison toward the noisy door.

"Houston," the guard barks. "Here." He hands me a small Post It from a pad that probably sits next to a phone on a shared desk where there are donuts and coffee and contempt for people like me. There is something different about this exchange, something about the quick, unsure glance he gives me that seems out of place.

Three words that make my stomach sink and my breath race. *Call Family–Dad.*

Shit. Not now. The one postulate that is universally true is that Death has its own calendar, its own seasons. It doesn't give a shit if I'm in prison and want, no need, my father to be there when I get out. Death does what it fucking wants.

It's hard to recall how many months it's been since the surprise visit with my mother and Tom. The one where "everything was all right". Kelly has done her job keeping me abreast so I knew that, not too long after that visit, Dad was handed an expiration date. Well, more of a range—six months to two years, but who's counting at this point?

I dial the phone, equally afraid to be in a hurry and afraid I will take too long. When the line rings on the other side, I hold my breath. I'm not ready for this.

"Hey, how are you?" Kelly asks when she answers. Her voice is soft, calm, but nasally, I can tell.

"How's he doing?"

"What? I can barely hear you."

"How is he?" I ask louder. The goddamn phone has been acting up all week.

"The doctor says he doesn't have long." I hear her struggle to keep it together, then lose the battle and begin to cry. "You should talk to him."

She covers the phone, muffling her voice. I hear her talking compassionately, deliberately. Then there's a rustling and I hear, "Kyle?" Dad's voice, weak and breathy.

"Dad," I say. "Dad, it's me. I'm here. I'm so sorry I can't be with you."

Nothing from the other end.

"Dad? Are you there?" I pause. I cup my hand around the mouthpiece and lower my voice so no one in this shitty prison can overhear. "I need you to know I wasn't a waste of time. Shit, I'm not even sure what that means." I feel tears welling up. I turn around and face the wall.

And this is such a fitting scene for how my life goes. Kyle Houston on an intermittent phone connection, in one of the most vulnerable moments of my life, in a prison of all places, futilely trying to find the perfect balance between gaining closure and not getting jumped for showing weakness. It's like, Good news—your dad is still alive and you get to say goodbye. Bad news—you have to yell it loudly in front of an audience of hardened criminals who never had a daddy.

With the way the phone has shit the bed and Dad's inability to talk, I have no idea if I'm making an impact or if I'm making a fool of myself, or if he can even hear me. I might as well be saying goodbye to Helen Keller.

Suddenly, I fear that maybe he has already passed or worse, he is in so much pain and struggling because I asked to talk to him. How fitting of me to send him off writhing in agony. Please don't let that be true. Please don't let me be the source of more pain for him.

"Okay, if you're blaming yourself, don't. That sounded better in my head. I'm sorry. Maybe it's all been said." Silence again, and I try to make light of the situation. My armor, my default, my position of defense—make someone laugh. "You're not exactly helping here, Dad."

"Can't talk. Just listen." The words sound like one long whisper. This is worse than I thought.

A prayer runs through my head, an undercurrent for this conversation, the words I can't say, the hugs I can't give. *Please God, bring closure or grace or some synonym for relief to me, to him. If You want my faith, here it is. If he is hearing my words, then help me say something that makes sense, let me offer something real.*

I mean, soon enough people will be spewing out sound bites to the family like "you're in my prayers" or "he's in a better place" and I really just want to call out how much this sucks. I know my mother isn't going to be able to handle losing Tom. She's a hot mess. I think whatever thin thread she's been hanging from is going to die with him.

And I realize it's not his fault, but I think his timing stinks. For real. We all need him, his quiet wisdom, his strength, his innate ability to see through life and guide us. And if I'm being honest, there's a huge part of me that resents that he drank so much. Because maybe he wouldn't be dying right now, when I need him so much. Maybe he wouldn't be dying if he'd put down the bottle a little more often. Thinks the meth junkie sitting in prison—but dammit, what if? What if he took better care of himself? What if I would have stayed in rehab? What if I was there right now, where I could give all my energy, my love, my positive vibes?

What if I could've been his real son?

"I love you, Dad," I say and wait and hope and pray. "Not sure we have time for anything more complicated. Although, who are we kidding, that's not exactly an easy thing to unpack. I just want you to know I love you."

I hear the hum of static, then a click and a faint, "Love. You." But I can't be sure.

"I'm sorry, Dad, I'll do better," I say, and I hear the words of a child, words that might make him sigh and shake his head if he could, yet they're all that I have. "Shocker, right Dad? Seems I'm always sorry for something, but—" I catch the emotion in my voice and stop, look over my shoulder. "I get it. This time I really do. I wish I could be there to show you but, well…"

And here I am caught somewhere between what I think I'm supposed to say and what I want to say. Because what I think I'm supposed to say is what a great dad he was and how the memories will never fade. That he provided well for us, gave us a better life, and that he's leaving a legacy behind that will be admired for generations to come.

But what I want to say is, "Don't you dare fucking leave me now. Not now that I have all this shit figured out, and maybe we can finally fix all of it, and be a family again." What I want to do is fall to my knees and scream, "Please, please, please, don't leave me, Dad. I need you. Nobody else can take your place. I can beat this fucking drug. Watch me. I will be good, just don't leave me. I'm not a liar. I can watch my mouth. Even though I thought it a hundred times, I never wanted any dad but you. You. Are. My. Dad. Don't you dare fucking bail on me."

But I don't say any of that.

I am composed. I am conflicted. I am confused. And I sit there and try to figure out what I can say that is honest and peace-giving and heals every scar between us. I remind myself that this is it, kiddo. These are the words you leave him with for eternity. So, I clear my throat, close my eyes, and think.

We are silent, the men behind me the same, and I'm scared shitless as I clamor for the appropriate words to send my father off into the abyss.

Then I hear myself say, "I will be amazing someday," as loud as I dare into the broken phone, "because of you, Dad." But the last words are caught on a sob and stuck in my throat somewhere.

And I listen for the final words uttered from my father's lips, hoping selfishly they will be about me. Kyle Houston. His son. I clutch the phone so tightly it leaves an imprint on my hand, and I lean toward the wall as if I can get even closer to him. I listen attentively for these words, hoping they will validate something I just told him. I listen. Like a child on his father's lap, I listen.

But nothing ever comes.

It's late now. The door to the cell just closed and I am alone with only one other convict. I crawl into bed and bury my head under my pillow and cry uncontrollably; and I know, beyond a shadow of doubt, he has passed. I don't know how I know, just that my heart hurts like I've lost something I can never replace.

The father I hoped for all my life. The father I had for too little time. The father who gave so much to the man I'm going to be.

And he is gone.

70

"HOUSTON!" I HEAR the guard shout as the keys clang against the heavy metal door.

"Me? What now?"

The guard says, "Transfer," then tells me to hurry up and pack my shit. It's standard protocol, not telling anyone about a transfer until it's time to leave. It's their safety measures to prevent planned escapes—shut the phones off, keep the destination a secret, first thing in the morning, etc., etc. It is a federal holding facility, after all. And unlike me, many of these offenders definitely have the connections and the resources to pull off a Hollywood-esque escape. And a lot of them will, if given a chance. What do they have to lose?

My hopes are up, but it feels irresponsible—naïve—to hope for something good. But I can't stop thinking that maybe this isn't exactly a transfer. It just seems too coincidental. Kelly planted the seed weeks ago, when Dad's last days were quickly diminishing to hours and she told me about a connection through Dad's network. Somebody who knows somebody who knows somebody who could pull some strings.

And the fact that today is my father's funeral and, out of nowhere, I am being transferred and told to gather my things all seems to connect the dots, and it feels safe to do something as foolish as hope. Intellectually, I know that it's crazy, but I choose to believe I am headed out of this place to bury the man whose absence I will never replace.

The two and a half-hour ride from that backwoods town to the federal courthouse in Kansas City takes a lifetime. All the "what if?" scenarios play in my mind. Holding in, bursting at the seams, nervous, excited, cautious—I question whether I deserve this, but then decide it doesn't matter. I worry how my presence will be received, how everyone will look at me with my hands cuffed together at my beltline.

I imagine a quiet funeral home with me being escorted up to pay my last respects and how the shackles around my ankles will rattle with each step, like an animal on a chain unable to roam freely. And how the orange of my jumpsuit will be impossible to ignore, or how the guards on both sides of me, who may or may not have shotguns, will frighten people and they will lean over to whisper and pass judgment. Forced, awkward smiles will be exchanged and I'm not sure I will be able to look anyone in the eye.

Will they think this is so apropos of Kyle Houston, who just couldn't let his own father have a proper burial? How it's selfish of me to want to be with my family on this day, to embrace people who care about me as I agonize on the inside knowing I will never get the chance to show my father that I *did* listen all those years; and that, despite the jumpsuit, I am determined to become a shining testimony of the effort he put into me ever since the first day he tried to love me?

And my chest aches knowing he will never see me happy and free and not wearing the orange jumpsuit. We will never build anything together again—a model airplane or a company or a shelf in my mother's kitchen. We will never have a beer and trade jokes and talk about the father and son moments that were always almost there. But that's not a reason to show up and embarrass the entire family, is it?

I mean, it's not like he's going to sit across a table and have a conversation where he tells me I'm forgiven, where we discuss all the things we've learned while we've been apart. So why is it so important to see the skin and bones, the stardust, that will soon be enclosed in that expensive box buried six feet underground?

I don't know, it just is.

I simply want to feel the embrace of family members on the day we all say goodbye, together, while we wipe the tears from our faces and sob in unity. As a family. Is that too much to ask?

But I can't help but imagine that my presence will create a memory, not of Tom Runge's funeral but of the day that Kyle Houston showed up at a funeral parlor chained and bound like an animal. How selfish. How thoughtless. How perfectly me.

You know what God, maybe it isn't the best idea for me to go. I'm torn on this one, right down the middle. How do you put up with me, being so wishy-washy all the time? Should I feel embarrassed? Should I feel ungrateful? Should I just accept that my prayers don't matter anyway?

And now we're in Kansas City and they are unloading the van, herding us through multiple doors, buzzing us in from a switchboard we can't see. I imagine my mother is on the other side of the city weeping, trying to figure out how to live without the man she loves. I am being stripped down, naked and cold, and shoved into a holding cell filled with criminals. While someone else consoles my mother, I am being instructed to squat and cough in front of a strange man, surrounded by other strange men who are also naked and lonely and angry.

But this is my life and that is hers.

Now, more than ever before, I am as much an outsider to Mom's life as she is to mine. She will never know the indignities I endure on a daily basis just like I hope I never know what it's like to be alone in a bed where your spouse's side will never be warm again. Where the scent on his pillow, now fades with every day as she lies with her back turned to where he once laid, wishing with the same intensity that splits atoms, that she will turn and Dad will be there one last time.

And I see clearly now, that in life—even in the moments we share—we experience each one uniquely; where in a moment like a loved one's death, one amongst us misses the warmth in the sheets and another is naked in a federal holding facility unable to grieve or say, "I love you, Dad." Death will always be that non-negotiable thing that tells you time was wasted, that life really was perfect, but only after it's too late.

A U.S. Marshal separates me from the pack, tells me to get dressed and go into the holding area by myself. My pulse races and I can't wait. Will I be given street clothes? Who will I see first when I get there? Will I have the nerve to face the people from my past? Will I be able to hug my mother?

"Houston. Let's go," a large man yells at me.

He escorts me, still just me, to a van in a dark, secured garage. I get in, thanking God, finding it hard to believe this is really happening. Maybe this is the answering of a prayer or one of the wonders of the Universe. What do I know? And who am I to question whether I want to be there?

I wonder again if this cost my mother money. Wonder again who it is that they know. Who could make this happen?

I'm coming, Mom and Dad.

Thank you, God, for knowing what was best, for sifting through my prayers and giving me this gift. Because I really needed this. It's been a shitty ride, God, a sorry couple of years, but I am so grateful that I won't have to carry the sorrow of not getting closure on my father's death for the rest of my life.

Maybe hope isn't such a foolish thing after all.

The marshal radios that the van is leaving the garage. Thirteenth Street looks alive as we pull out and make our way to Grain Valley. We're mere blocks from the building where I had my carpet store, not so long ago; where, if I could've made different decisions, I wouldn't be headed to a funeral in chains. He stops at a light. One way takes us further into the city and the other to my family.

"Where are we headed?" I ask.

The guard meets my gaze in the rearview mirror. "I guess I can tell you, now," he says. "We're taking you to Cameron. Back to state prison."

"Oh." I say, trying to keep the bile of reality from rising in my throat. But it doesn't surprise me. Because I knew—*I knew*—what happens to a convict who dares to hope and trust and let down his guard. Yet still I was the idiot who believed.

As the sun beams through the window on this warm spring morning, I listen to the engine and feel a salty sting in my eyes. Once again alone, left out, and missing someone I love.

Kelly told me Dad died shortly after he got off the phone with me the other night, as if he was waiting for my goodbye. And although it isn't much, that's what I'll hold onto as the proof that possibly nothing is left undone.

I hope this day is peaceful for him as he passes over without me in the room, to a place where my mistakes can't bother him anymore. And today I'll try to be strong as I shove the loneliness further down in those hard to find places. Because this is the moment when I teach myself a new life's lesson on how a boy in prison quietly mourns the death of his father.

As this U.S. Marshal and I barrel down 1-70, and my heart slowly dies.

71

Today is a day I'd rather be sleeping. Not sure if it's the weather or the time of year, since I haven't been outside in over a month. Loneliness has become my constant companion, a familiar voice inside my head. She reminds me that I am financially and emotionally broke at the age of thirty-two, that I am like a weathered and broken piece of timber dying in the middle of the forest, sentenced to spend eternity in this lifeless setting. That I am nothing at this point in my life. Nothing but alone and praying that I won't be forgotten.

With all due respect, God, Your love and grace aren't going to be enough today. I need something more so I can pretend I once had a different destiny. Because what are any of us without the people who share our memories?

So have at it, God. Lift my spirit. Isn't that why You're here?

Maybe faith is just a waste of energy and asking the universe to ease your suffering, to answer your prayers is like playing turkey bingo at the VFW—you never know who's going to get one. Or maybe I'm just not the type that deserves the favor of the Almighty. But today I am asking for a little fucking relief, any way I can get it, because I'm feeling pretty pissy, like I've been a sucker this entire time.

And I think about hell and how I've had it so wrong all these years. It's not fire and brimstone; it's the constant erosion of my spirit through loneliness with no one to hug, no one to listen, no one to share old memories. Hell is this prison. And I am scared that this is where I lose the person I really am, the person I've tried valiantly to hold onto this entire time. Because right now, desperate and desolate, I'm barely holding onto my sanity.

A guard enters the cellblock. In a continuous circle of same shit, different day, this is a small break in the boredom. "Mail call," he yells and the heavy metal door slams behind him. He carries in the white handled tote, sets it on the table, and starts to pick out envelopes.

The volume on the TVs get turned down. Cuban men with tattoos and gold teeth stop doing push-ups, put their shirts on, and amble to the table. The showers squeak off and start to drip. Naked men wrap towels around their waists and head to their cells. Some of them are covered with color and ink and images that took years to collect; some are covered in scars like oversized zippers down the center of their chest or flesh-colored putty slapped over bullet holes, but it all tells a story if anyone cares to listen.

The guard holds up an envelope. "Williams."

"Here!"

"Jackson A., Jackson L."

"Here!"

"Here!"

The sounds fade into the background. I have my back to the crowd, and I'm staring at a chessboard. I have been playing chess all morning with a guy who is in for armed robbery of several jewelry stores on The Plaza. We play often but say very little, at least not anything important. He's clever and very good at chess, which leads me to believe he's a savvy thief.

Behind me, I hear men laughing. Some comments about money, some comments about "bitches"—two subjects I always ignore. Money and women are the fishing stories of prison life. And the convicts talking the loudest about the one that got away are the son of a bitches that never had a fucking thing.

The showers go back on, the guard's voice lowers. He tells a joke, I think, because the men are all laughing. I try to contain my disappointment and pretend all I care about is where I'm going to move my rook.

If you do enough time, you get good at drowning things out, focusing only on what's in front of you. Blocking out the noise becomes an art, a game of survival, always keeping something insignificant in front of you because that's where you're safest––a chess game, a book, a radio station. Whether it's the sadness, the outside world, or these fucking convicts, it only becomes dangerous if you rear your head and look around. Until one day, it all goes quiet and you just know that's a bad thing, but never really know why.

"Oh yeah," I hear the guard say. "I've got one more. Houston."

And like a resting dog sleeping quietly on the front porch who hears a noise and barks, "Here," I say and feel my mood instantly change.

I stride across the common area like it's no big deal that the guard is holding an envelope that doesn't look like legal mail, for once.

I can see that it is a man's writing—messy, hurried, with no large looping letters. I wonder who it is. And as I snatch the envelope from the guard, practically taking his hand with it, I see the name: T. Murrell. I am curious. I am anxious. I'm scared to read this letter.

"Who is it, Houston? One of those fine, white bitches you be telling me about?" a guy named T-Red calls out.

"Yeah, you know me. Too many to keep up with," I tell him, but even I know I sound fake.

The crowd slowly breaks up. Men in orange pants and white T-shirts wander over to the television, their fingers tucked into the elastic waistband of their pants. The guard grabs the box and smiles at me. I smile back, but only out of courtesy. My mind is on this letter.

Tim Murrell was a friend—is a friend, I'm not sure; it's been a really long time—of mine from grade school. We graduated high school and played on the same football and track teams together, but we really didn't run in the same crowds. I was an odd duck who didn't really belong to just one crowd and Tim always knew where he fit in. But in grade school, it was different. In grade school you couldn't separate the two of us. Best friends, 'pals' as Tim would say, but that seems so long ago from where I now sit.

I close the door to my cell, sit on the cold metal bench attached to the wall, and slowly pull the letter from the envelope. It is typed and single spaced and full of thoughts, full of emotions. The kind men don't talk about, the kind that are hard to share, hard to explain. The kind men leave between the lines but there just the same.

And he starts with: *I'll bet you didn't wake up this morning expecting to get a letter from me.*

And he's right, why would I? You could have given me a thousand guesses and I would have gotten this one wrong. But I anchor in and prepare myself for where this goes and secretly pray it doesn't hurt.

He acknowledges our "parting of ways" in high school, the fork in the path, which is just how life is. And he tells me that where I'm at doesn't change his opinion of me, that I'm one of the smartest people he ever knew, and that he thought I could use some encouragement before I got lost in some crazy battle with who I really am.

And that hits me like a punch to the chest because I've been caught in that crazy battle for a very long time.

He uses phrases like "water under the bridge" and "no matter how long it's been" and "once a pal always a pal" and memories hit me hard: him and I wearing matching bibbed overalls and orange *Dukes of Hazzard* shirts, to the skating rink on Friday nights. Listening to Styx *Renegade* on his sisters' stereo all night long. Being in his house, a space full of love and understanding and joy and attention. And I could live vicariously through Tim, whose parents spent time with him, passing along things like how to hunt, and tradition, and self-worth. With Tim, I was just a small-town boy like him, the kind of friend he could laugh with until the early morning sunlight.

He brings up Franco Harris and the trading cards we used to sell and cinnamon toothpicks, and girls we kissed. He brings up the club we had and our club house, and it all feels like a million years ago.

The two of us unfolded in a tiny town that knew our names, knew our daddies, knew our intentions. And even though I got lost and ended up here, ours is a bond as strong as family. A real small-town thing. Like Sunday service and baseball diamonds. Like gravel roads and keg parties. Like a rustic, weathered barn just outside of town, seen from a blacktop as the centerpiece of a picturesque countryside. Time might be linear but true friendship is not.

The irony is he's a cop and I'm a convict. But not everybody sees it like Tim, like me. In that letter, between the lines, I see that in his mind there is no space between us. We have history, we have memories in our hearts, we have done our own time together many years ago. And he will probably never know that, on this day, he was the answer to a lingering and painful prayer. A prayer that someone might remember me dearly and it would be enough to save my life. That I could somehow remain in their heart as a human with worth, as a person with potential, as a real and cherished friend.

As a Pal.

And then his P.S. at the bottom: *Do they let you have visits?*

I hold the letter tight and realize what has frightened me ever since I tore open the envelope. That my old friend will see who I am now and be disappointed.

72

I'm seventeen now and although I don't realize it, this is the fork in the road, the proverbial Robert Frost choice to go right or left. I've always felt I didn't belong in a small town in Missouri, my thoughts are perpetually strangled by how people thought about what people thought other people thought (stew on that one for a while). But it is all I know. I have been here my whole life, after all, and every new thought I conjure up is being measured against this one—I can't wait to get out.

Don't get me wrong, I am sad—or something like that. I mean, I have lots of memories here. I love the people I grew up with. I love so much about this town, but living here just isn't something that has ever fulfilled me, even as a child. And nothing will ever change here, so I will hold onto that dearly as I go out and find the change I am looking for.

It's my senior year and I feel it—life has severed me from my identity. I got mono two weeks before the football season started. Up until then, people, including me, thought we'd see college scouts at some of the games checking me out and I would be recruited, and I would go off and create the life I dream of. But things have not turned out according to plan. Because of the mono, I've missed four out of ten games and with those kinds of stats, I'm not on any college's radar. Due to no fault of my own, my life went left instead of right. The number three that Coach saved for me has gone to waste; my football career is over before it started. Every dream I ever had evaporated.

I'm not sure what I'm going to do now once this year is over, but I do know I'm leaving and that I am deeply sad about that. In the wee hours of the night, while the town is asleep, I have been sneaking out so I can walk around and say goodbye. Emotionally, with my spirit.

I have this sense of melancholy but don't know why. All I know is I miss this town already as I walk down the quiet, moonlit streets, or sit underneath the scoreboard that overlooks the football field, or lie on my back on the quiet practice field and stare up at the stars, listening to the sounds that a small town makes when everyone's asleep. Or maybe it's more that I'm missing the future that could have been. The doors that were once open.

And I know it will never change, something I'm counting on as I go out into the world. But, although my heart has always wandered, a piece of me stays right here...forever.

My roots planted firmly in the soil of this small town.

73

The United States versus Kyle Dean Houston.

No matter how many times I see the words, they still hit me like a punch to the throat. To think, the most powerful country on the planet has a small posse of U.S. district attorneys who were more than likely top of their class in law school, with the unfair advantage of impossible laws, bent on tallying up drug convictions on some imaginary scorecard. Versus me, a sorry sack of shit who wears an orange jumpsuit, is lucky to afford ramen noodle soups, and has already pled guilty to possession of a shit ton of chemicals in my state case. AKA the only evidence a federal prosecutor needs to prove I'm guilty.

Turns out the real world isn't going to be like an episode of *Law and Order*. At least, not for me. In my world, you *can* technically get tried for the same crime twice. Nobody is concerned with what's right or what's wrong. These heartless bastards won't think twice about locking you up and throwing away the key. And not because it's justice, because the law allows it. Because they can.

And the first attorney to represent my case, with his arrogant smug face and a checkered bowtie, told me my only defense was to cooperate. Before we looked at the paperwork, before we talked about charges, before we even discussed a shred of evidence, he was already talking about cooperation.

So, I fired him.

Second attorney: no smug looks, no bowtie, but the exact same strategy. With a specific and effective bedside manner, he warned me to never discuss my case with anyone, "Not even your mother." Because everybody, EV-AH-REE-BODY, in the federal system is desperate to shave off some time.

"Don't hate the player, hate the game, kid." He quotes Snoop Dogg and it sounds so unnatural coming from this guy. "You either play this game or you die in federal prison." Then he adds that the prosecutors, judges, and Lady Justice don't care about ruining lives and families. Because, in short, "Nobody gives a fuck about you," And that sounded natural enough.

So, I fired him, too.

My third attorney, who is female, told me the same story with all the hyperbole and grave consequences. But at this point I needed to trust someone, so this plain looking bookworm of a lady with socially awkward mannerisms became the one I chose. And when she told me Preston—yes, *that* Preston, the fella who gave me my very first shot—was turning evidence against me, she offered me an option—do the same to him. I not only agreed but eventually became his cellie.

He and I worked it out, agreed to spill enough beans to help each other's cases. What did we have to lose? And as we made our deal with the devil at the crossroads, we bonded in a way other people will never understand. He was like a brother I needed desperately, a friendship that will inevitably last a lifetime. And I'm grateful that at least one other person stands right beside me, knee-deep in this impossible fucking pile of shit. I love that guy.

Because this week I needed him. This entire week, I've been on edge. I haven't been talking much, just trying to meditate and do lots of push-ups. Patricia and I have gone over the playbook, dissected our opponent, and agonized over all the ways things might turn out. She is a good person and cares about me in a way that makes me wonder if she's like this with other clients. Her small acts of kindness remind me that I'm human. She asks me how my mother is doing, or how I actually feel. Something nobody else in here would ever think to do. Because in my day-to-day life, nobody gives a shit about a convict.

At thirty-two years old I am, once again, being sentenced. This time, the difference between a five or ten-year sentence is literally the chance to have a family, a career, and possibly ever hold my mother again.

Because Mom isn't taking Dad's passing with dignity and grace. Her suicide attempts have become Kelly's full-time job. Watching her cycles, not allowing Mom to be alone, was all new to Kelly. And, although it made me feel sad and helpless, I would never say I didn't get it.

The mom I knew, who was always ready to fight, is broken and lost and without the man who had been committed to putting up with her shit. Not that he loved her flaws, but he was devoted—the perfect partner in crime—and he kept their secrets hidden, like sunken skeletons in some swampy marsh.

Once Dad was gone, she had lost the only person who knew her and still held a tender place in his heart for this fragile, beautiful creature. Mom's life was gone—gone from her movements, gone from her will, gone from her eyes. The only fight we could get from her was the fight to convince everyone it was over.

So, Patricia's thoughtful questions are a gentle reminder that some people still might give a shit. And maybe she sees me for the person I was before the shackled ankles, before the broken laws, before the goddamn meth. She is in my corner, rooting for me to have a better life, cheering for me to get my second chance at something amazing or fair or at least better than all this. And I choose to believe she cares about my future because, in ways I can't explain, that makes me feel better about who I am.

"We're going to suggest that they not count the gun because, although you admitted it was yours, it was never a charge," Patricia tells me. We are waiting in a holding room in the courthouse.

"Do you think they'll go for it?"

"They should see it our way." Patricia is intelligent, astute and by the book, but she lacks the "go-getter" mentality that would make me feel more comfortable. She clearly entered the field of law because she had good grades, not because she liked to argue. She is quirky and a little subdued, but honest. And in my life, with the amount of time the federal prosecutors are dishing out, I need to know the truth.

"We're also going to ask for five years," she adds, "and remind them that your state cases should not count toward your minimum mandatory sentencing."

"Now we're talking," I say. Her confidence soothes me. "Should I get my hopes up?"

She stands up before she answers. Her thick, wool, plaid skirt unwrinkles as she pulls it back down below her knees. "It's hard to say. Our judge is a seasoned vet on the bench. He's good at following the law."

"I'm sorry, was there an answer in there?"

"Well, I believe we have a great shot at all of them." She stares at me, then adds, "Okay, we should get them all."

"That's what I wanted to hear," I say. I think I see her smile.

The floor is cold and hard beneath the flimsy soles of my shoes. My orange jumpsuit is clean and pressed—I kept it between two hardback dictionaries all night—and the collar of my T-shirt still has good elastic, as if any of this will matter with the minimum mandatory sentencing guidelines of the federal justice system.

"There's one more thing, Kyle." She bites her bottom lip, as if she's choosing her words carefully. "I hope you don't mind, but I filed something this morning before I could get a chance to ask you."

"Uh-huh." The muscles in my neck and legs tense. A fractured sliver of my heart senses pain. *Not another thing, God. Come on.*

"Please don't get your hopes up," she says.

"Just tell me." The words come out sharp and hot.

She takes a deep breath. "Because of what's going on with your family, I filed what's called a Temporary Release."

What's going on with my family is a polite way of rephrasing that I have a dead father and a mother who clearly wants to join him. Because, in addition to a severely broken heart, my mom is also bipolar—although when I was a kid, I had a different name for it. The cycles in her moods, her arguments, her need to dominate were easy to see; but, honestly, I just thought she was a bitch. I love my mother and I know she did the best she could with the biology she was given; but still, my upbringing—at times—was more like hand-to-hand combat than a nurturing environment to unfold in. The game was to strike first and crush your opponent with words and I was, by far, her most astute pupil.

I'm not sure how much the illness played into our relationship, but it made her predictable, easy to affect. And, although I never saw it back then, in retrospect, I see the moments when the disease would hide things from her, important things like hope and joy and love. The very things she is struggling to believe in now.

And I remember that time in high school when I pushed the envelope too hard. She screamed and backed into the wall, her gaze searching for something only she could see. Instantly I stopped the insolence and pulled her into my arms, but she writhed and fought like a cold and loveless stranger. And it scared the shit out of me because there was no anger. And, back then, if we didn't have the insults, or the pain or any of the insecurity between us, then what else did we possibly have?

But now, in our visits, Mom was all mine—listening, not forceful or making faces or telling me to act like someone I wasn't. Just the two of us, getting to know each other, being ourselves, vulnerable, scarred, open.

It's what I always wanted. What I wished for… *But I should have added a caveat, God. I never wanted it like this.*

So, at thirty-two I'm being sentenced again. My father's death was fresh and my ability to hold down pain, like a drowning victim in a shallow pool, was powerful. But now my mother wanted to tap out and I was useless, locked away where I couldn't hug her or help her or even pick a fight if I wanted to. A son's duty isn't that difficult—show up the few times in life when your parents need you. That's it. And the best I could give to anyone now was to emphatically pretend that I would be okay without them. A thing I had never done before.

At least not without the drugs.

"What is this temporary thing?" I ask.

"It's basically a furlough," Patricia explains, "for thirty days."

"Wait. You mean freedom? What are my chances?" I think of a soft mattress, my mother's hugs, my home.

I think of Dylan.

Patricia puts up a hand and cautions me to remember that the judge is conservative, one of the oldest in the district, and he has never granted one of these requests. Because of the loss of my father and my mother's mental health concerns, she personally thought asking for this month of mercy, essentially, was "appropriate".

"I'll come back when the judge is ready." She hesitates, standing in the threshold with her back still to me, and says, "My hopes aren't high for the furlough, Kyle, but try to hold tight. Okay?"

I tell myself, she's right, that I can't afford to be vulnerable again. But hope is a dangerous and unhealthy affliction. No matter how impossible, even for the smartest and most practical human heart, sometimes we will cling to hope; even at the risk of never believing again.

Thank God for Preston this week. In so many ways, sharing an eight by six cell with a convict who knows your feelings, knows your stories, knows who in your family hurts you the most during the most frightening and dangerous time of your life, is the closest you'll ever get to another human being. And I didn't need him to be soft or to sing Kumbaya around the campfire and agree that my life isn't fair. When life goes this badly, with pressure this intense, what I needed was for him to care enough to tell me to quit being a pussy. In this world, only the people who really give a shit know that the sincerest form of compassion is a swift kick in the ass.

And I hate to admit it, but there's nothing unique about any of this. I'm not new to being sentenced, not new to being nervous, not new to being lonely and worried in front of a judge. I'm not new to the indignity of people in a courtroom judging me as another one of those filthy and dangerous members of society who need to be locked away from the good people of the world. I'm not new to feeling an unjustified amount of hatred coming from the prosecution, that there are people on this planet who wish for bad things to happen to Kyle Houston.

I mean, I'm not such a bad guy if you simply remove just two tiny, little years from my life. Twenty-four lousy months where I entered the world of methamphetamine, unaware and over my head. If the prosecutor could simply overlook that, then he and I could drink scotch and talk shit all night about the fucked-up people he puts in jail. And we could stand in a den with dark mahogany bookshelves, arms wrapped around one another, smoking stogies and discussing how he sticks it to every one of these fucking junkies because they deserve it, because they're not as good as him and me. That could be the kind of life I live if I could just get one small do-over, one tiny mulligan.

And I wonder what any of the judgmental people in the courtroom would think if they found out that twenty-four months is all that stands between this moment and a lifetime of Sunday tee times, Cabo vacations, and the prosecutor's first born carrying my name. Wouldn't that shift a few paradigms? To know that I could be them and they could be me—the fucking junkie. That it is way too easy—frighteningly too easy—for any one of us to drop into this insanity and to end up right here, on the wrong side of this courtroom. But, no matter how I try to explain it away, there will always be those twenty-four months dropped into the middle of my life like bird shit on my face when I'm sunbathing on a warm sandy beach.

So, although there is nothing that I am going to witness that will surprise me today, I still hate this moment. Just another afternoon spent listening to people who speak into amplified microphones, recounting the events that will haunt me for the rest of my life.

Patricia comes into the small office again and I rise from the table. The U.S. Marshal comes in, cuffs my hands and tightens the shackles, then mentions, "We usually don't see a lot of people for sentencing."

Before I can figure out what that means, Patricia pokes her head in to announce we are next. She reminds me of the routine—what I should say, when I should say it, the facial expressions that mean the most.

The U.S. Marshal takes me by the arm and we exit the room. I smell fresh paint and the chemical scent of new carpet. My stomach is in knots as Patricia, the U.S. Marshal, and I shuffle in tandem down the hall. I try to keep in step with them, but fail.

"Is Tim here, yet?" I ask to break the silence.

"In his uniform," Patricia answers. "Did you ask anyone else to come?"

"I don't know anybody else, Patricia," I answer and focus on what I might say if I'm given the floor. I also wonder if I'm going to have to fight any of the other damned convicts here for court today because Tim is in uniform. Are they going to think I'm a snitch? But then I dismiss the thought because everybody in the federal system is a snitch one way or another.

As I walk in, seeing Tim gives me a little jolt because half of me expected him to figure out I wasn't worth his time. When he visited months ago, he seemed so excited to see me; so anxious to make sure I wasn't alone in the world. His words were from the heart, filled with loyalty and brotherhood and nostalgia—exactly what I needed. And it was thoughtful, and it was perfect, and it might've moved me to tears had I not been so consumed with worry. I was worried how I looked to him, how I acted, how I might *be* different yet unable to see it.

So, I apologized a lot; I might've experienced a minor anxiety attack and couldn't wait for the relationship to move back to pen and paper. Instead of being rejuvenated, I was exhausted; instead of being lifted up, I was dragged down by the weight of the humiliation of being a locked-up meth junkie in front of an old friend.

Yet he volunteered to speak on my behalf, as an officer of the law, as a friend who knows what I'm capable of becoming. And I didn't have the heart to tell him there was nothing he could ever do or say to make a difference in the outcome of my case.

This stuff is cut and dry, my friend. You're simply wasting your time. With this system you can't sway opinions, you can't tip the scales, you can't influence anything. My fate is etched in time.

But good or bad, there's no stopping Tim. He's all heart. Because no matter how deep you find yourself in shit, if you're pals with Tim Murrell, you can count on him to grab a bucket and start bailing right beside you. To see him here, now, and the little smile of encouragement he gives me as I walk by, tells me he's got that bucket ready.

And I know Patricia told me not to get my hopes up about this temporary release, but are you fucking kidding me? Telling me not to get my hopes up over something as amazing as this is like telling me not to think about pink elephants. Suddenly, it is the *only* thing I can think about.

I see my mom, my sister and my aunt, all sitting in the front row dressed in dark colors, probably left over from my dad's funeral. Tim is talking to my mom. I see her smile and the words, "Thank you, Timmy," as they cross her lips. I see my sister reach over and squeeze his shoulder and look at him warmly. To the left of them, two law-enforcement agents sit with crossed arms and serious expressions as they wait for the proceedings to begin. The prosecution checks their files and straightens papers, whispering closely to one another and nodding their heads. It's two diametric opposites—the people who love me and the ones who want to see me destroyed.

And then, in some *Tie a Yellow Ribbon* kind of moment, I see the rest of them. Old friends, connections to my past, who wave at me and smile brightly and are there to support me. Instead of joy, my first reaction is shame. My orange uniform and the loud rattling chains all make me feel exposed and open and wondering if I deserve these people's friendship.

There's my dear friend who helped me paint my father's fence when we were just boys. He chose to stand in the sun with me that summer and slap white paint on the pickets when he could've done anything else. There's the girl I was in love with off and on, but never at the right time. Another who is like a sister, another who was an older neighbor, and there's the girl I stuck up for when she was being bullied in the halls of our high school. And another who was a cheerleader for the football team, always lifting me up, always raising my spirits. They are here, like my own personal cheering squad, doing the same thing now as they had done when we were kids.

And it's all so weird because I don't know how to handle this moment. I don't know how a convict greets old friends. I don't know if I should wave and smile or say thank you or tell them that they shouldn't have come. All I know is I feel ecstatic and warm and self-conscious at the exact same time. And I wish I could hide the fear and embarrassment on my face, but I can't. All I can do is sit and prepare for the hearing while I mentally send love into the universe toward each and every one of them.

The proceedings begin, the arguments ensue, and the entire hearing is long and uninspiring and painful as I'm forced to absorb the soundbites that my friends all have to hear. The ugly, distorted but true picture the prosecution paints of Kyle Houston at his abso-fucking-lutely worst.

Then Tim is asked to speak.

He proudly stands at the microphone and tells the courtroom about who I was to him growing up, that I was important, that in many ways we shaped one another. He talks about the bond that is forged through small towns and little boys' hearts. And he shares his background, how he is qualified to speak, that not only is meth a horrible drug that continues to be the scourge of the backwoods and rural counties of this state, but equally that my story is a tragedy he never saw coming. And what he says is heartfelt and touching in a way that is hard for me to explain.

He turns to walk away, then stops and turns back. "And Your Honor, if I may, before I step down—because it's been made clear to me that what I say won't make a difference anyway..." he says, and I can see that his eyes are glistening. "To the officers sitting behind me, I just want to say thank you."

There's a long pause as he lowers his head, then raises it back up. "... Because you did your job, fellas. You saved my friend's life. And maybe it's strange to say this, up here in front of the judge at a time like this, but I'm always going to just be me... call it like I see it. You see, I may not know everything about the details of Kyle's case, but I do know he was gone, checked out, convinced his best two options were an overdose or suicide. Without his arrest, I would've lost my friend forever. And no matter what happens today, knowing he is still here is something I'm not ever going to take for granted again. If you've ever had a friend like Kyle, you'd know why."

He gives the judge a final nod, then walks back to his seat. In a world full of elaborate explanations and fifty-dollar words, Tim is a reminder that it ain't that complicated. He's not going to argue whether there's a place in this world for psychology and group discussions and a deep understanding of the past. But when all else fails, his philosophy is simple—there is love and there is friendship.

The judge thanks him and assures everyone that Tim's words and the ten-page letter I wrote in preparation will all be considered. He then swiftly sentences me to seven years in a federal institution. The words pronounced so quickly; I barely hear them. They have almost no impact because I had expected it.

Everyone is confused now, leaning forward as if they heard wrong, and they are looking at each other with questions in their eyes. A murmur is starting to build.

"Which brings us now to the matter of a temporary release," the judge says and the room goes quiet.

He asks me to stand and come forward with my counsel. He shuffles the papers, reading the words as if there is something he may have missed. "Counsel," he says, peering out into the court above the rims of his wire-framed glasses. "Never in my twenty-five years on this bench have I granted a motion like this." He studies the papers again. "I realize Mister Houston has extenuating family circumstances, but I don't see how the district is served by giving him a release."

I had braced myself for his refusal, knew it was an impossible ask, but somehow this hits me harder than the seven years. I stand there and try to communicate with just my face that I would give anything to have this come true. I straighten up, try to look demure, try to look more respectful, or meek or sad yet cheerful. I try to appear as if you can trust me or pity me or whatever it takes to allow this to happen. I stand here in this moment firing off prayers to God, making deals, negotiating feverishly in the silence.

Please God, I'm not asking for you to show up for much. Just a tiny little miracle for a tired soul. And I'm livid toward Patricia for breaking my heart once again, for teaching me that hope is the enemy of the convict soul. For telling me not to think about pink elephants.

"But…" There's a pause that seems to last ten hours. "Mister Houston certainly seems to have community support."

I can't breathe. I can't move. Holy shit, is he actually considering this motion?

Take over, God. This moment represents everything to me about Your love, Your grace, the proof You still exist. My faith in humanity, my faith in justice, my renewed faith that love and friendship does make a difference. That acts of kindness, like the surprise visit of a group of friends, cannot only save one's life but also actually change the heart of a salty old judge.

Please, God, I need this single month more than anything I thought I needed before. These thirty days, if You grant them to me, could be the difference between losing my soul down the road and holding tightly to the boy these people all came to save. I need this, God. To believe, to hope, to heal.

"I'm going to grant this," the judge says, and Patricia squeezes my arm tightly and my sister erupts with a single squeal. Kelly cries abruptly and loudly, trying unsuccessfully to contain her sobs, from the joy, from the pain, from the pure excitement of holding her baby brother once again. "He will be released at nine o'clock tomorrow morning." The judge bangs his gavel, stands up, and leaves.

The murmur has become a roar of conversation. And I stand here, my back to the room, and facing an empty podium where a judge just granted me a break, a reprieve, a miracle to find my way. The last four years come rushing through my mind—the things I've seen, the fears I've faced, the fights, the loneliness, the lost innocence, and in less than twenty-four hours I will be outside, unrestricted and free.

The room is packed and loud and full of energy, but I don't hear any of that. My hands are clasped, my eyes are closed and in this moment I am alone. Standing in the center of the universe, my back to the crowd, with tears rolling down my face.

Me, not broken after all, in this moment, scared to death to turn around.

74

WHEN I INVENTORY my memories of the longest, most sleepless nights of my life, this one belongs at the top of the list. Biting my tongue, pounding my chest, swelling, expanding, unable to touch the ground. Never have I felt this kind of electricity; like the strength and abandon of a thousand children on Christmas Eve, unable to be contained, bouncing from wall to wall.

And I imagine what it felt like for the people of East Berlin when the wall was torn down brick by brick. The anticipation of seeing freedom, of seeing the sun, of seeing the world for what felt like the very first time, is exactly how I feel tonight.

Coupled with an unshakable fear that if I actually was to pinch myself, I might wake up from this lucid and beautiful dream. Like a schoolboy, I am uncontrollable; like a schoolboy I am about to explode, and I desperately try to keep my cool, try to hold it all in, but I literally feel the seams of my spirit ripping, bursting, giving way to this foolish abandon expanding inside my chest.

And what did I do this time, God, to deserve any of this? Please let me know because I'll make it my daily routine. There's no condition, no deal that I can see. Especially since we both know I have nothing to give. I am grateful, Lord, I am humbled, I am in awe. And I will see this as nothing short of a miracle, as long as it comes true.

But I swear if You pull back, God, I don't know what I'll do. Because this is too close, this is too real, and not even the parting of the Red Sea could prove to me more that You really can answer a lonely convict's prayers. Like this one. The one I never knew I prayed until You answered it and I realized that this is what I have wanted the entire time.

Hope. Freedom. And love.

The drive to the courthouse seems to take hours. I wonder who will be there to meet me, to hug me, to pick me up today. The U.S. Marshals aren't particularly nice to me but that's not their style. Still, I'm surprised, because they should see I'm different as they escort me through the threshold that leads directly to nothing short of the first day of the rest of my life. And I don't understand these guards—how can they be so stoic, so listless when the world is so fucking alive?

The courtroom is emptier this time. There is a judge, a court reporter, my mom, my sister, and my anxious son, Dylan. The whole process is taking forever or merely ten minutes, but I can't tell you which because, at this point, they both feel exactly the same.

I wear street clothes and shoes that all feel counterfeit and forced, but I don't really give a shit because the paperwork is signed and Patricia is congratulating me and I am walking out the door and into sunshine and blue skies. I hold my son as Kelly and Mom huddle around us and laugh, and cry, and make comments that won't make sense when we replay them years from now. Once again, I think of my old carpet store around the corner, and think about all those decisions I made before…just before. Behind me is the courthouse that just yesterday seemed to strangle me, seemed immovable and cold, but now feels like a milestone on the path to redemption and some other man's shit to contend with.

Dylan squeezes me so tightly that I almost cry. I forgot who I am to him, who I have never been able to be. I lay my palm over the back of his head, bringing him into my chest, wrapping, pulling, kissing the top of his head. "I love you little guy," I tell him as Kelly and Mom cry with joy and heartache.

"I miss you, Daddy," he says back. And I clear my throat and tell him I'm here right now. And I am so grateful that finally, these words are true.

I feel Kelly's hand on my shoulder, on my back, as she gives us a moment. Just father and son.

"Where do you wanna go first?" she asks me. "We have a couple hours before our flight." And it's all so bizarre, what you really want in a moment like this. But standing at the top of the hill looking back on the last four years of my life, calculating the loss, calculating the things I missed and the things I will never, ever have again, I realize that what I want is right here within these three people in this moment.

"Let us know, the meter is running," Mom tells me.

I pause, because I know this is an answer that says something about my journey, something deep and meaningful about my life. I'm convinced that what comes out of my mouth next represents more about who I am than any spiritual battle I have ever plowed through in my entire life.

So, I put Dylan down and ask for the keys to the car. Then I look into their faces, their breath is held, anticipating the answer.

And I sigh and I smile and I say with more confidence than anything I can remember saying before, "Pizza. I just really want a good pizza."

PART FOUR

RELEASE

75

It seems like a lifetime ago that my daily routine was weaving in and out of dimly lit basements, rooms with locked doors and an unimaginable amount of trash collecting in piles. Now that I'm standing in Dylan's house, the kitchen to be exact, my stomach is churning almost as fast as my mind is spinning, I realize it's all still here, closer than I imagined. I'm here to get his things, to bring him home with me for this too-short thirty-day window of being a father. I stand here and think how strange and yet how familiar it all looks. The dilapidated landscape that was once a disturbingly unsanitary mirror image of the interior world of my life.

But I'm sober now—fog lifted; head cleared. And filled with guilt that I once kept spoons and needles and eight balls of crystal in a tiny walk-in closet where, if the kids in the house wanted to, they could walk in and find them. And I thought I had escaped, thought it was forever a thing of the past, but I now see how our children must live with the sins of their father.

I have so many thoughts firing off with nowhere to land. I've been here—well not this exact here, but once you've seen one meth hovel you've seen them all. My initial reaction is pity for how far Dylan's mom has fallen with the gray front tooth, the acne on her forehead, and the greasy, disheveled hair pulled back into a ponytail. But this is where empathy doesn't serve us well. Because this is my son, who I thought was on the outside looking in. So any of the understanding I might have had gives way to anger and disgust because Dylan is getting dragged through all this shit with her.

The cockroaches scattering across the countertop. The dishes in the sink and on the table. The McDonald's bags, the half-eaten fries and big Macs all over the floor. It all comes rushing back to me, only this time it's something I can't distance myself from because it slaps me with the cold, hard fact that I didn't do my job; I didn't protect my child. I allowed the meth in, allowed it to touch my firstborn. This fucking drug is killing us all.

And I don't hate his mother, although I'm sick to my stomach. Because this hellhole I've walked into has blindsided me, like walking in on your wife of twenty years going down on another man. I wasn't ready. I didn't have time to brace myself. And as I stand here looking through the doorway into the living room, into the bedrooms, I am experiencing everything from anger to compassion to hate. And, once again, a tremendous amount of "What the fuck?"

My heart aches for this talented brilliant child whose only crime is being conceived by two drug addicts. And, in all my missteps, I thought I had gathered insights on most sides of life. But who the fuck am I to pretend I know what it's like to be the kid in school who wears the same clothes every day? Who is late and unclean? Who am I to understand what this does to his fragile self-esteem because he has to get off the bus knowing that he's coming home to this? Who am I to guess what it's like to wait nervously on a friend's porch, hoping he'll be invited to eat a real meal there and worrying that somehow, in some way, he is perceived as a bad kid?

Even though I don't have the capacity to understand what any of this feels like, I imagine it must feel hijacked. What I do know, without question, is this life he's been living isn't going to foster the greatness locked inside him, this isn't going to give him the role model he needs to live a fulfilled life. This is never how it should've been, and it certainly isn't fair to my baby boy.

And it's absolutely all my fault.

"Where are your clothes, Dylan? We have a plane to catch." I say and grab a trash bag. In these piles of trash strung throughout the house I can see what I've done and who I've affected, and how forgiveness won't be as easy as just doing my time.

And with every ounce of energy I possess, I want to clean this house, to make things better, ease my conscience, somehow. But as I stand here, staring at the mess, I realize I have no idea where I'm ever going to start.

76

Kelly and I laugh when I'm pulled to the side and frisked by TSA. How I look so stiff and guilty standing there, arms out, like the most committed scarecrow ever, but what she doesn't understand is the anxiety of stepping out of line is real. The system has done a number on me, in addition to the insane amounts of drugs I've consumed, and I'm becoming aware that addiction is not the only thing I'll struggle with from here on out.

Out here, I'm scared of my own shadow, scared I'll be wrong, scared I'll be arrested and tried all over again. And although none of it makes a bit of sense, I can't say I'm surprised that parachuting back into the free world comes with consequences I never saw coming. But I have Dylan and I have my sister and I have my mother, although she wrings her hands a lot like they hurt from arthritis and seems to be nervous and I wonder if that has anything to do with me.

Tampa is hot and full of palm trees like a tropical postcard that you send to people up north when they're suffering through ten inches of snow. This is where they all live now—my mother, my brother, my grandma Mimi, Kelly and her family. And the place is as unfamiliar to me as jail was during my first forty-eight hours, and quite honestly, twice as scary. My hope is to purchase some headphones, find a used Walkman, and listen to all the lost music that might transport me back to 1995, to a world I understand and that feels far more familiar than this one.

And Kelly's kids all love me. They ride on my back, jump in my arms, and stare at me for long periods of time because, to them, I'm a stranger who abruptly entered their house. But they see their mother hug me, feel how she loves me, and although they don't know why, they know they are supposed to love me, too. This is the part that is comfortable, the part that is fluid and natural and falls deep into my wheelhouse. The children, the stranger, and the laughter that heals my soul.

Sean Michael is outside climbing a tree and I take Dylan to see him. For the first time. They look like opposite sides of the same gene pool. They both have blue eyes and equally sun-bleached blonde hair, but one is lanky and thin, the other stocky and short. And it's clear that I am the common denominator in this complicated equation.

And they stare at each other, unsure what to do, like puppies who see their reflections in the mirror. They circle for a moment; Dylan looks back at me and it becomes obvious they aren't sure what they are to one another. So, I walk over, pick Sean Michael up and hold him like a child who fell out of the swing, then I motion Dylan over and wrap my arms around him.

"Dylan, this is Sean Michael," I say as they look at each other some more.

"Hi, Sean Michael." Dylan says. But I don't say the truth, don't say this is his brother, because that's a hurdle I don't know how to cross, not yet. Sean Michael is oblivious and young, and just smiles at this new person.

"Hi, Dylan." Sean Michael looks up at me. "Uncle Kyle, can Dylan play with me?"

I nod and they hug uncomfortably, then they run through the yard and start tossing a ball back and forth. I stand there watching this moment, thinking how glad I am to be here, to be alive.

Because this is the future that was hiding from me back when I was convinced death was my only way to freedom.

And it's all so vindicating, so full circle, so it's a wonderful life, except I don't exactly feel like Jimmy Stewart. Because, as I watch my sons laugh and play and get to know one another, I realize that even this happiness is mired by the forever-stain of my goddamn past. There is a lie between us, in two tiny little words, and they damn near kill me every time I hear them: *Uncle Kyle.*

Because of prison, I can't be his Daddy. Because of prison, I have to lie. Because of prison it feels like fatherhood was ripped from my hands like notebook paper held high above a bully's head as I jump and scream and desperately try to get it back because it means something, because it's personal, because it's mine.

But I didn't give you up on purpose, Sean Michael. I had no other choice. It wasn't because I loved you less, or we didn't fit, or that I didn't ache to hug you for the rest of my life. It was all because I needed you to be here and to be safe. When I get out.

Even with my back against the wall, I love you. Even as a callous man, I love you. Even with scars and mistakes and a toy chest full of regrets, I love you, and I will bargain with everything I have to keep you. So, I released you like some pure white dove into the air, into the arms of your Aunt Kelly, because I knew, if there was no one else, she would be the one to love you.

This is what you get when your daddy is Kyle Houston. You get love, you get lies, you get your aunt and you call her Mommy. And because I love you, because I trust in Kelly, I gave everything to keep you warm and safe. I gave everything to keep you with me.

I gave her you.

And later that week, when we drive into Tampa so that I can report to the probation officer they assigned me, I watch Sean Michael in the rearview mirror. He's doing this thing with his arm, looking around the front seat to see how I hold mine. This is one of those moments I will remember forever, one of those moments when I realize how critical I am to this impressionable human being and his ability to evolve into an upstanding and good young man. One of those life-changing moments that I hope to repeat over and over and over, only I know I will soon be gone again.

And I'm smiling from ear to ear as I watch him but remaining quiet as to not disrupt his thought process. I know this might be my only moment like this with him for our entire lives. But after all the shit I've endured getting to this point, I'll take it.

Quietly I drive, quietly I hurt, quietly I watch this child do the little boy things that remind me of his grandfather. His gravelly voice, his broad shoulders, and the way he holds his arms back make me swear that, if you put a cigarette between his fingers, he'd be the spitting image of Jerry Sam. And seeing all this makes me love him in a way that only makes sense to my body, to my blood.

But my heart breaks every time I hear the word 'Uncle' in front of my name. But I'm seeing his frail blue eyes get brighter, that light inside him once again give heat, his smile starts to loosen up and I'm torn between knowing it's all for the best and wanting to scream.

This charade crushes me.

Still, even if I'm only on the sidelines of his life, I will be grateful and remember—it's more than I deserve.

But nobody knows how close I come to holding his face close to mine and whispering, "I'm your daddy," although that's against the rules. I want to lock eyes and explain it will be over soon. *Just hang on, kiddo I'll only be gone a little longer; I love you little dude.*

Instead, I will love him and protect him and try to shield this delicate child from more broken promises. He deserves somebody who makes him number one. Completely. Finally.

And that can't be me.

But whether I am an uncle or the voice on a prison phone, I'll still be the man in his life. And there is nothing anyone can do to stop that.

I'd like to see them try.

77

"Everything's fine, Keenan," Mom says. Her voice is calm with this soft, understanding tone like a hippie who just dropped acid and is now waiting for the trip. "You don't need to worry anymore."

Keenan paces the floor of my mother's bedroom, back and forth between her bed and the bathroom repeating phrases like, "What should we do?" and "What's wrong with you?" mixed in with unintelligible phrases. I stand in the doorway watching my depressed mother in her lonely, yet immaculate bedroom with one son who is losing his mind to an unexplainable condition while the other is just a stranger passing through on his way back to prison.

She lies down on her back, like she would in a coffin, arms folded in an "X" across her chest almost as if she's practicing. Then she stands up and meanders around with no purpose. I start to question if this is how she acts, but I haven't lived with her in years. As far as I know, this could be the way things are now. But she seems especially calm; too agreeable for my mother, as Keenan continues pacing and questioning her every move.

"What's going on?" I ask.

Keenan tells me, "She's acting weird."

"It's fine, honey," Mom repeats and I think her words are slurring but I can't be sure. Her demeanor is so relaxed, she might as well be using words like groovy and far out.

The room is crowded with my parents' old furniture and there are pictures everywhere, like a museum of my family's life with moments captured in time when life was simpler for her, before voids were created where people once stood.

She grabs a picture of Dad, clutches it against her chest and lies back down. "I'm fine, honey," she says again, but the words are slower, more labored.

Keenan comes charging out of the bathroom, holding an amber bottle. "God damnit, Mom! I know this was full!" He shakes the bottle at her. "How many did you take?"

"I don't know," she answers and then hesitates and for a moment I think she's falling asleep. "Two, I think. Maybe three."

"Bullshit! This was full. I know it was full." Keenan swipes his hand through his hair; his eyes are wide like a meth addict's. "At least I think it was full."

My mother just mumbles, "It's going to be fine, baby. Everything is fine."

And I'm starting to realize that I might be witnessing a suicide attempt but what do I know; I've never watched one from the bleachers. I only have mine to compare it to. But one thing is for sure, I never imagined someone killing themselves could be so emotionless, so patient. It never dawned on me that suicide could disguise itself as a silly moment where my mom clutches a framed photo of my father and fumbles with slow, arduous speech like a teenage girl who got into the family liquor cabinet after her boyfriend just broke up with her.

I panic, just a little, but not because it all feels dangerous; more because, for some reason, it doesn't.

"What the fuck, Mom?" Keenan screams from the bathroom again. "What's this?" He comes out holding sheets of notebook paper above his head. "Explain this."

Mom rolls over, hugs dad's photo tighter, and mumbles that she's going to sleep.

"What is it, Keenan?" I ask.

"Here. You read it," he says as he shoves the papers into my chest. "I know she took the entire bottle."

My mother's handwriting is beautiful: dark black ink, feminine but not overly-looped, as if it was written by a strong, confident woman. This is handwriting I've seen my entire life—on permission slips for school, on birthday cards, on notes in the fridge warning me to stay away from the pie. But these words are broken, pieced together in pity. She says she's sorry but she misses her husband, that we will all manage without her, but to please take care of Keenan. She promises to love us all no matter where we are, and it isn't quite clear to me who it is written to. But what is clear is that this is no cry for help—she has made her mind up to go and, for a brief moment, I question if saving her life is really the kindest thing I can do.

And there she is, so peaceful, so content, prepared to elegantly fade to the other side. And, although I can think of a million reasons why she should be happy, who the hell am I? How arrogant would I be to decide for her what's worth living for, what's worth dying for? Maybe her reasons are legitimate; maybe she's right. Suicide isn't always alarming or sudden or messy or whatever expectation you put on it. Sometimes it is gentle, like a friendly suggestion from someone who cares or a whisper from a familiar voice that sounds so safe in the moment.

So, in this moment, I have the common courtesy not to pass judgment on my mother's tormented soul. She lives without her husband and it hurts, it's lonely, and if anybody knows how that feels, it's me.

But as empathetic as I might be, I am also just selfish enough to want to keep her around. So, I fold up the note, dial 911, and do everything I can to save my mom's life.

And I secretly promise to try to make it up to her somehow.

78

I'M THIRTEEN NOW. I'm popular to some, infamous to others at my tiny junior high school. The fellas think I'm cool because I lost my virginity over the summer to a grown woman.

And Higginsville is as satisfying as it has ever been, although we are too small of a town to get MTV, yet, and there are nuclear missile sites less than five miles from my house that give me the uneasy knowledge of who will be the first to go in a nuclear war.

Often Mom and I ride to the city in her car listening to songs from the '60s. I know every word, every band, and she knows enough to sing along. Just the two of us singing as loud as we can, smiling and laughing and connected and happy. Just the two of us, with no concerns, no demands, and music that was her soundtrack twenty years earlier that brings us together in these moments. Just the two of us.

I watch her sing with passion and confidence. I hear her laughing when she screws up and then starts singing even louder. And we are, at least to me, the truest sense of a duet.

This is the 'good mom', the one I always wanted, the one I want to be so much better for. In these moments, she gets me. With the sounds and the smiles, she inspires my deepest loyalties; and, if she only knew how close these moments are to being perfect, she would have her recipe for controlling me like she needs to. She might even see that control might not be necessary.

I want to please her, to make her proud, and in these moments, I know I am a good kid. Because she tells me with her smile and the look in her eye and the unapologetic trust that going for the high notes is all that matters.

She is beautiful to me—the most beautiful any mother has ever been, and I don't have to share her with Tom or the business or my sister or brother or crazy mood swings. None of it has anything to do with these moments.

Driving down I-70 in the dark, dashboard lit, and singing like we are the only two in the world.

The easiest it will ever be.

79

THE RIDE IN the ambulance seemed uneventful, except that Mom almost died. No one hollered out codes or got excited, not even me. It was more like the slow-burning fuse of a bomb as I held her hand and rubbed her hair and felt her fading into the dark. And as she lay there in the moving ambulance—which made me uncomfortable with its siren and swirling lights like cop cars in a chase—I knew she was a woman with issues, a woman with skeletons, but still the one I always loved.

Finally, in the hospital, she lies unconscious in her bed, like a little girl sleeping, dreaming, safe and peaceful. The constant hum of machines that pump and beep and keep her alive ruin the illusion. There is a diaphragm, like an accordion, that pumps and releases air—what I imagine her lungs have tried to do—and something grotesque that looks like coagulated fleshy lard collects in a see-through container at the side of her bed. I don't ask what it is, nor do I care to know.

For brief moments, it looks like she wants to wake. Her eyes will flutter, moving beneath her eyelids, and her eyebrows rise like she hears me and wants to respond. So, I tell her that I'm here and promise it's okay to sleep. And then imagine that I'm making a difference but realize I have no idea how.

It's a bizarre sensation, watching my mother lying in a hospital bed, unconscious from an overdose, like watching the events of someone else's story. This pillar of piss and vinegar who spent a lifetime protecting me, controlling me, inadvertently molding me, now lies weak, almost lifeless, before me. Almost as if she's searching for my approval to go, like I'm a bouncer standing between two worlds, deciding who goes beyond the velvet ropes.

She was the first voice I ever heard, the most consistent of anyone in my misguided life. For every bruise, for every broken bone, for every moment I needed someone to wipe my face or to wax my cowlick back down, there was this woman, committed and unwavering, with love like shattered glass.

And although she might just be the cornerstone of all my rage, she is still my loving, beautiful mother lying before me as close to being dead as it gets.

And if she were awake, she'd rip me a new one. Call me every name in her arsenal to piss me off. I can see it all clearly, the finger in my face, the outward jaw, arms cocked back because I was the thoughtless asshole who interrupted a perfectly good suicide. Who do I think I am? Did anyone ask me for help? And she'll find a way to finish this suicide, so don't even waste your time "you little shit". Because Mom has a very strong will, in spite of how all this looks, and she'll be goddamned if one of her kids is going to decide if she lives or dies. Especially the know-it-all son of a bitch who wound up in prison.

If there's a silver lining in any of this, it's that I have been given an extension on my furlough. Another month to spend with family. And I'm sure if she was awake, she would call me ungrateful, but I can't help it. It doesn't feel like much of a gift when your life circumstances are so grave that even the criminal court system wants to give you a break.

Sleep well, Mama. Your baby boy is here for whatever you need. Pick a fight, take a swing, piss me off, I don't care, but someday maybe you will kiss my bumped head and say I'm precious and loved like I am three years old again. And maybe Jerry Sam missed it all, but you and I lived out those days where I was the most prized possession in the world.

And I will be that again someday, I swear, I promise as I listen to these machines do their best to keep you alive.

80

WE'RE TALKING ABOUT the weather, how the Chiefs might do this year, but it all seems little more than a waste of time. Keenan's eyes shift continuously, back and forth, never quite locking with mine. Where I come from, that usually means someone's lying but that's not the case with Keenan. At least, not on purpose. I try to slow him down, to focus on our conversation, but it's clear I don't mean much to this stranger in my brother's body. And the combinations of pharmaceuticals that the doctors continually throw at him, as if he's an experiment and not a human being, change him in ways that make me sadder. If that's even possible anymore.

At one time, in his eyes, I could do no wrong. He was that person who would defend me with courage and conviction, like a Marine standing watch on a wall at wartime. He believed in me, when possibly no one else could see why. And we stumbled through life adhering to the unspoken code of brotherhood, where love is your North Star and forgiveness the only law.

But now he's not happy that I'm here, not happy that I'm no longer locked up, not happy that I have survived the painful things that life dished out. And I would probably be extremely hurt if I wasn't so damn confused. When did my prison sentence become the reason for him to stop being himself?

Mom is home now and tries to explain it isn't me, that his "condition" does this to him. "Nothing personal." she swears.

But I don't always believe what she tells me. She's too close, too attached. Her job is to protect her children from the painful things of the world, not to tell the truth. She'll never know the responsibility of being a big brother, or how I can see his face sometimes in my dreams—crying, wanting me to help, to save, to shelter him from the cruelty of a world that can leave you with some ailment that comes and goes like a Jehovah's Witness in a suburban neighborhood. We all see 'em coming but if you stay quiet long enough, pay no attention, soon they will all go away. But you always know they're coming back.

And the word "schizophrenia" gets thrown around when Keenan isn't in the room. He'll never believe it; and who could blame him? No matter how many delusions, no matter how many demons lurk in the shadows, no matter how many dramatic narratives he creates in his interior world, he will resist the diagnosis because his reality doesn't align with everyone else's.

And you're right, Mom, it isn't me. I haven't done anything to make him dislike his brother. I've never done a thing to make him believe I don't love him, but that small detail does nothing to shovel dirt back into the hole in my life that my baby brother once filled.

I see this vacancy in his eyes when I try to bring up old times. I hear it in his recollections that we don't remember it the same way. Because in my story, we laughed, we loved, we were encouraged to be more than we could ever be without the other; and in his story, we simply got through it. I think. At least, that's the way it feels. And the pain isn't in the things I hear coming out of his mouth, it's in the things I don't. Like the times we held hands walking back from his babysitter, kicking rocks, stepping over the cracks in the sidewalk, and just being boys. Our silhouetted bodies casting shadows in front of us as we made our way home. Or all those sleepless nights in his room on Christmas Eve when we would laugh hysterically, all night long, at things that could only be funny to us, only be imagined by us, because we were built to get each other.

I tried to always give him something to look up to, but we all know I kind of got distracted. Still, I love him in a way that is as subconscious as it is obvious, punctuated every time I accidentally call my son by his name. I've done everything from change his diapers to drop hints about how to be a man, and I miss him in a visceral way. I am his big brother and I failed at the sacred duty of protecting him from what life threw his way.

And I can't imagine the loneliness, the confusion, the injustice I would feel if the precious memories that have continually guided me back to me were nowhere to be found. And I am sad because it appears as if they're gone for my baby brother, from his mind, from his memories, from his heart. Because it looks like I might get a second chance at a better life if I play my cards right; but, unless I convince him that I'm still that boy he looked up to years ago, I have to face the unsettling realization that he may not.

I'll be here, Keenan, waiting, if you ever make it back. I will protect our memories and keep them warm in this scrapbook deep within my chest. And when you're ready, they will all be here to laugh at, to cry over, to remind us of who we really are. No matter how far you go, I love you, Bubs. Because, although I never meant to, I lost you, and now it seems I may never get you back.

And once again, I arrive at the ancient wisdom that guides me through so many difficult moments, those four simple words continually defining themselves every time I need them. And this time it comes with a caveat:

This too shall pass. That is, unless you might just be afflicted with schizophrenia.

81

"DUDE, GET YOUR ass to Kansas City. You fucking convict."

I sigh and shake my head. "I want to, Sullivan."

"Really?" Garrett scoffs. "'Cause I can't tell. You kind of sound like a whiny little bitch."

"Your compassion overwhelms me."

"It's New Year's. Everybody from the 'Ville will be at Mason's party. Now go change your Kotex and get out here!"

Garrett is my friend, my best friend from Higginsville. Someone who has known me since we were unruly little boys on our bicycles riding all over town. I lived in town and Garrett lived outside the city limits, but we were inseparable and as thick as thieves. In high school, when I chose the path of a letter jacket and Friday nights on the field, he chose to have an afterschool job and make money. He had long hair; I had short. He was tall and lanky; I was stocky. In so many ways we couldn't have been more different, but it was going to take a lot more than opposing life decisions and miles of small-town geography to stand in the way of a life-long friendship. Because our common ground is vast and filled with memories, years we spent together growing up in that tiny little town. And his love runs deep, his concern overflows in every word he speaks, if you simply know where to look.

"Fuck you, you're a pussy," Garrett continues. "What's the worst they can do? Put you in jail?"

He laughs and then I laugh; and, somehow, we wind up making a joke about shitting our pants and spend the next five minutes trying to catch our breath.

With him, I am good. Like the confident boy from our youth. Right now, on the phone, he is my partner in crime and it is circa 1988 again. But what he doesn't know, that I do, is that that confident kid is missing. Maybe not on the phone, but everywhere else. I have these panic attacks. It's all so scary, so foreign, being around members of my past. Because I forgot how people act, I forgot how it all goes out here, and I'm self-conscious, I'm insecure, I'm afraid.

My world has turned inside out. I'm more comfortable around murderers and thieves; I have more in common with junkies and dealers than I do with normal people. I know the mechanics of how those people think; I know what those people say. But with normal people, I'm just throwing spaghetti at the wall. I'm reluctant to get close, to let them see that I've missed a step somewhere, that my addiction held me hostage during those formative years when everybody else learned the fundamentals of being grown-ups. And just as soon as we hang up, I'll want to shimmy right back up inside my head where no one can find me—alone, distant, secretly changed.

He's telling me to fly back to Missouri and show up at a party filled with people from my past, punctuating every sentence with the word "Rally". Which might only mean something to people from Higginsville. This is a town where if you wanted to have an impromptu party, you simply did two or three laps from Bucks Grocery Store to Dog N Suds Drive-Thru and you'd have dozens of people on their way out to Rock Hole for a kegger and a bonfire. A town where nothing was ever experienced alone—not a death, not a major remodeling project, and not a single holiday.

And somewhere inside all that, to me, is home.

There's a romantic charm to growing up in this town, an essence that created who I am deeply and completely, even if, at times, I never wanted it to. To me, this town is the comfort food of geography—the fried chicken and mashed potatoes of my life. Because, even though I know it doesn't necessarily agree with me, I realize I crave it at the oddest times and simply can't get it out of my mind.

Higginsville is where I got my poetic spirit. It's where I learned to lower my head in life, to fight for what I want. Where I walked a mile to kindergarten by myself and rode my bike clear across town when I was eight, as long as I was home before dark. Where I played for hours on the train tracks and my neighbors were allowed to discipline me if they saw fit. And, although it's the butt of so many jokes—*don't blink or you'll miss it when you're driving through*—it is this tiny dot on the map that taught me how to appreciate life.

And if I was given just one choice of where I would spend eternity, it might just be a Missouri autumn where the golden-red leaves still hang loosely to the maple trees on my block, when the air is brisk and thick, and people's faces have ruby cheeks and smiles. Where sweatshirts and warm drinks fill the bleachers on a Friday night to cheer on the hometown boys.

When you grow up in a place like Higginsville, you never really leave. Like Sunday brunch at your parent's dinner table, your place is always waiting and empty when you're not there.

If you didn't grow up in a small town, you just won't understand.

Garrett tells me to call everybody who was at my hearing. "Everybody's got twenty bucks to pitch in for your airfare," he says. He then tells me to let him know after the calls how much I still need and that he'll make up the difference. "You just show up with bells on, you son of a bitch."

And I hang up with equal parts fear and hope. Hope that I'll see everybody in my hometown, and they'll see me and understand and welcome me home and tell me it's going to be okay. And fear that I'll see everybody in my hometown, and they'll see me and understand, but I'll scare them all and freak them out, and they run me off and tell me to never come back. Fear that, even if I belonged to them once, I might never belong again.

Ever since my plane landed in Kansas City, I've been reminded of who I am. I've held the daughter of a dear friend, taken pictures with her plastic tea set, and learned about Clifford the Big Red Dog. I've sat in living rooms with old friends dressed in camouflage and ball caps that read "John Deere" or "Massey Ferguson", having beers and reminiscing about stories of train tracks with hidden forts, where we kept *Playboys* and buck knives and all the things that made us boys. We talked reverently about playing at McCord's Park when we were little football players who cussed like sailors because there were no grown-ups around and had fist fights when needed and shook hands when it was over because there were no hard feelings. Because a black eye or a bloody nose was shit that a boy came home with, but friendship was something we would keep forever.

And, as I stand here at the party Sullivan told me about—the traditional one that Mason throws every year—I know I am around my people. I watch everyone laughing, dancing, singing with bottles of Bud Light held like microphones; in this room with spinning lights from a disco ball and tapped kegs where we all converge and hug and disperse back out into the party. I am intoxicated on booze, intoxicated on life, intoxicated on freedom. No one gives a shit where I've been, they only love that I am here. And the whole experience feels like the Hot Wheels Skating Rink with its oversized fuzzy dice and nervous boys against the railing, and lady's choice. It feels like jukebox music and fountain drinks and foosball tables. This feels like *Paradise by the Dashboard Light* in the dark on a gravel road, singing at the top of your lungs. It feels like crashing on your best friend's couch and waking to his momma's biscuits and gravy.

Like forgiveness, like a clean slate—this feels like home.

"Houston," a friend of mine named Gator screams over the music as he slowly siphons beer from the keg. He smiles warmly. "Got any cool stories about prison sex?" he jokes. His words slightly slurred. His eyes on his cup.

"My favorite subject," I yell back. "I'm not sure where to begin."

He laughs and shakes his head. "I can't believe you got in that much trouble. Hell, I know a million people who smoke that shit."

I pump the keg a few times, smiling uncomfortably. He means well but has no idea how horrible my drug abuse truly was.

"I missed you, you tough son of a bitch." He puts his arm around my shoulders and pulls me in. "I'll bet those fucking convicts have no idea what hit 'em when they fuck with you."

"Something like that," I tell him.

"Hey," he says loudly. "Remember that time we skinny dipped with those girls from Waverly?" He laughs and I laugh and we take long, cold gulps from our beers. I throw my arm around his shoulder as we stand there looking out at the dance floor. I have known these people forever. Some I even started kindergarten with. Some are farmers, some business owners, some teachers, coaches, CPAs. And normally, by now, I would've been telling myself, "Thank God I left," but not tonight.

And I lean in and tell him sincerely, "I do now, Gator. Finally, I remember it all."

82

THE APPLE ORCHARD is vast, abandoned, unattended for years. With tightly grown rows of trees that give fruit and a winding gravel road that meanders through from the swinging, locked gate to an aluminum barn centralized within the orchard. There is a frozen creek and beat up farm equipment with rust and filth and wear and tear like all things eventually have. And I can see that history is all around me and I can imagine what it was like with migrant workers and their baskets and ladders and gratitude to be working out in the sunshine, in nature, in God's country.

Incidentally, I can see why Mason got it so cheap.

He's been dying to bring me out here, ever since I was at his party, wanting me to see his latest crazy purchase. We're standing out in the middle of bare, dying branches as far as the eye can see, and piles of wood, and rolling hills off into the landscape as puffs of frozen breath fill the air. The occasional wild turkey runs past us; they are big and unusual for me and remind me that, no matter whose name is on the deed of trust, it is my friend and I who are trespassing.

Off to the side, I see a pack of stray dogs. There are four of them, and they are dirty, unkept and an odd collection of mixed breeds. Some short, some tall, but running in a pack that lives like a single organism. Where one goes, they all go. When one barks, they all bark. And I'm reminded of the packs of men who run together in prison, but I refuse to think about that now.

"Do you have dogs, Mason?" I ask.

He answers, "They came with the orchard. I let them stay because they were here first." Then he looks at me and winks.

The dogs start barking and seem to be circling something, showing their teeth and snarling. Through the blades of tall grass, I see a small gray ball of fur dodging, zigzagging in and out, frantically seeking shelter. The dogs chase and snap and we realize there's a rabbit, scared and alone, frightened for its life.

"Come on," he says. "Let's go watch this. The dogs won't bother us." We jog over to a woodpile that is now surrounded by scratching, snarling dogs trying desperately to get this rabbit that is now trapped within the split logs and splintered branches.

The dogs are electric, galvanized by their thirst to kill. Set off by some innate desire for blood. And I watch and I know this is nature, I know this is life, where it's survival of the fittest, where the hound always gets the hare, but I can't shake the common ground I share with this furry creature. This tiny, unsuspecting creature who was doing nothing but minding its own business, trying to find its path back home, and now these fucking dogs want to rip it to shreds.

Through the timber I can see the rabbit, its breath going in and out, partly from terror, partly from racing through the orchard. The dogs lunge at the pile, rooting their noses, scratching at the wood feverishly, as I stand over the pile and empathize with this rabbit.

I know how you feel, little fella. I know what it's like to lose your way, to be trapped in a restricted world, with no way out. Alone, frightened to hope, willing to give anything to be somewhere other than here. To be in constant survival mode and unable to trace the scattered steps of your zigzag trail that brought you to this fucking dark, enclosed woodpile—panting, praying, agonizing over the what ifs, wondering where you might be if you could just do it all over again.

And look, I realize that this is how the cookie crumbles. I know that where I'm from they hunt rabbit and deer and even those wild turkeys that walk the orchard like madams at a whorehouse in their housecoat. It never bothered me before, but this time, something inside me feels different. Something inside me says all life is precious. At the very least, the rabbit shouldn't have to be frightened, with its heart pounding in its throat, waiting to be eaten by a desperate pack of dogs.

I realize this is the first time I've been able to gauge who I am, out in the world, since my awakening alone in that cell. I felt things shifting inside me that all sounded good on paper, but I have not been able to test any of it in the real world. I am different now. I possess empathy, understanding, respect. I see both sides of this equation—the dogs and the rabbit—and while I'm not mad at the dogs for being dogs (how could I?) I still want to wrap my arms around this creature and bring peace to its heart. I feel love for this animal so badly that I catch myself praying for its safety. That even though there might be a course that destiny has for all these creatures, I still want to burrow down inside this wood pile and take away the pain and suffering of this fragile, tiny life.

"Come on, man. Let's get out of here." Mason says as he starts to head back to his truck. "It's getting cold."

"Leave? What about the rabbit?"

"Fuck 'em," he tells me. "It's cold, dude."

We get in the truck and head down the road. "Cool orchard," I tell him and look behind to see if the dogs are still there. But we're already too far away for me to tell if the rabbit is safe or still pinned under a log.

"Yeah, it's a lot of work," he tells me. "It will probably set me back a couple of years. Pain in my ass."

I nod my head as if I understand, but the truth is I don't. I don't know how much money people make or what setting them back a couple of years really means. I don't know what cell phones or internet service or dental plans cost; or how much someone should have saved in a 401K at my age. What I know is how to do time, how to survive, and how to make sure I don't get surrounded by a pack of savage dogs.

Weeks from now, I will be in federal prison, anxious and confined, zigzagging through my own episode of life. A world my friends can't imagine, one we don't talk about, one full of rabbits, one full of dogs.

"Yeah, you wouldn't believe how difficult it is keeping up with all the payments," he tells me as he lights a cigarette, cracks the window and blows smoke toward the ceiling.

"Hmm," I grunt. I don't have anything else to add.

We exit the orchard, turn right and back onto the blacktop. "What are you thinking, dude?"

I settle back into my seat as the truck picks up speed. "What am I thinking?" I repeat the question and turn to stare out the passenger window. I pause for a moment and then say, "At least you're not that fucking rabbit."

83

MOM SAID IT was a beautiful tribute, Dad's funeral. The flowers were perfect, the weather just right, and there was a huge turnout. She had them play *In the Arms of an Angel* by Sarah McLachlan and I'm sure that was more a tribute to her feelings and hopes much more than Dad's taste. But who gives a shit? She's the one who has to live with the outcome, not him.

And as I stand out here in the dark, under this midwestern sky with stars all listening and Mason's truck idling behind me, the music that plays in my head is more like Simon and Garfunkel's *The Boxer*, or something from Peter, Paul, and Mary. Or better yet, a recording of Dad and the way he would come alive with his guitar, singing *They Call the Wind Mariah*, like some free spirit around a campfire, uninhibited, being a version of himself we rarely got to see.

It was Mason who tells me I should come out here. "Find closure, buddy," he says and even though I feel silly and didn't realize things needed to be closed, after a few beers I agreed; and, well, here I am wondering what to say to a gravestone standing ominously over this tiny plot of earth with my father's bones six feet underground. Now, let's see what closes.

I know the man, in ways no one else ever could. I got him when he was new, before the bind had been broken in or the pages crinkled. I got him when his trigger finger was still very itchy, and I took it all on the chin because that was my role—to teach that man love ain't always convenient.

Hey, Dad, speaking freely here. Please don't make me repeat anything, it's hard enough the first time around. Although we found each other at a time when neither of us were good for one another, I feel like we've covered that over the years, so no beating a dead horse. Cool? You know it's odd, but I don't feel the things that I imagined would be appropriate and normal, but I do miss you. I miss being able to talk to you and hear your deep wisdom. That is, when you finally spoke. It wasn't often. But you know that, I mean, you were there.

Anyway, love lives on, Dad.

Wait. Really? Love lives on? That's what I've got after all these years, all these scars, all these emotions? But I guess that's right…it feels real. Love lives on, Dad. I'm counting on it, cause what else do I have?

You taught me that hard work is noble, and honor is one of life's highest ideals. And despite the fact it was clear that love and tears and feelings weren't things that men shared openly, you eventually bent the rules for me. And isn't that as intimate as it ever gets between men—changing the rules, softening the edges to meet halfway? That is the most I could ever ask for and you gave it, Dad. Maybe it was because you knew I wasn't giving up until you changed, because I could certainly be a son of a bitch like that. Maybe it was me who changed. It doesn't matter.

And I remember this black and white photo of Tom and his older brother, Dave. I only saw my uncle a few times because he killed himself not too long after getting his PhD from Dartmouth.

They're boys in the picture, both under ten, and they have the most amazing cowboy costumes on—matching shirts with fringes, matching cowboy hats, pressed dark blue jeans with holsters on their hips, and plastic guns in hand. Dad looks so small, so vulnerable, as he is clearly following his big brother's lead, trying to keep up. Even in the still-frame, you can feel the reverence he has for his older brother as they pretend whatever the little boys pretended in the black and white photo days.

For whatever reason, that picture has remained vivid and fresh in my mind all these years. This black and white photo that I grew up secretly admiring had something about it that I was unable to just glance at it. I had to stare, to study, to get lost in an idea of what my stepfather was like when he was but a fragile, unprotected child. A sweet, friendly boy with dreams and excitement and make-believe moments that lasted even after his brother couldn't bear it any longer.

And what I know now, what's taken me almost thirty years to figure out, is that at the age of four, I scared the hell out of you. There was always something flawed deep inside me, maybe something before we met, or maybe because we met or even why we met, it doesn't matter. But we both know that if that four-year-old boy terrified you, you certainly returned the favor. Neither one of us was what the other had hoped for. Kind of like how I ended up in prison and you ended up dying before I came back. We both left, in spite of what we hoped for.

But I want to believe that, just like me, there was always love in your heart. That you saw me looking up at you with my tiny arm hugging your leg and, in your heart, I always mattered. And I'm sorry that we all got really good at hurting one another.

I just wish life could've caught up with the two of us sooner, but here we are, freezing our asses off. And I can't say I miss your hugs, because I can count how many we shared in life on both hands, but what I wouldn't give for one right now. I love you. And although I'm no Sarah McLachlan, that's for sure, as I stand out here with my hands buried in the pockets of this stiff leather coat, and I feel the tips of my ears burn from the cold, and the frozen grass crumbles beneath the weight of my feet, I want you to understand that my life will be a tribute to you.

So here we are as I share my eulogy for one. And for the record, it is your voice that guides me to make the tough decisions, to stay on the straight and narrow. We may not have gotten into this mess together but, by God, together we're getting out of it as a pair. Because you were a good man, whether you wanted me to know it or not. It was hard work and empathy and lending a hand to your neighbor that were the fruits of your soul.

You taught me to ride a bike because who else was going to do it? You taught me how to tie a tie, hold a fork, speak correctly, swing a hammer, drive a car, clean a fish, hunt for frogs—the list goes on and on, because you saw it as your duty. But I was the one who taught you that, no matter what you do to a boy, he'll always be around if you'll have him. So, as I stand out here alone, in the darkness, I want to thank you for being my father. As twisted as we had it at times, it's as good as it's ever going to be for you and I.

Oil and water. Father and son. Tom Runge and me.

Love. Lives. On.

And that's a hell of lot better than holding a grudge.

84

"HELLO?" WHEN SHE answers the phone, her voice is unsteady, weak, much older than when we last spoke but still her, a woman who has known me since I was four, since her son stepped into my life as my new daddy.

"Grandma?" I ask.

"Yes. Who is this please?"

"It's me. It's Kyle."

There is a prolonged silence.

I clear my throat. "Grandma? Are you there?"

"Yes. Yes, I'm here." She pauses for a moment and I feel, I don't know, surprised to say the least. Not sure what I expected, but I didn't expect this.

"Can I help you?" she finally asks

"Um, no. I mean, I don't need anything, Grandma," I say. "I'm in town. Your town. I wanted to see you."

"Huh," she says and I'm starting to get the sense that I have overwhelmed her. For the life of me, I can't remember her age; I'm not sure I ever knew.

"I'm sorry," I tell her. "I should've called before now."

"That might've been nice."

"It's just that everything is moving so—"

"Do you know what time it is?" she interrupts.

"Um yeah, sure… It's a quarter till eight."

"That's right."

"Come on, Grandma, it's me," I tell her, but I'm surprised. She hasn't seen me in years. Shouldn't she be more…I don't know, happy I called? "I thought I'd swing by to see you. I haven't heard from you in a long time. Maybe give you a hug?" I debate if I should get cute with her. "If you're lucky," I tell her. I can't help myself.

"I see," she replies. "Well, I'm in my PJs."

"Put on a robe," I tell her, and try not to sound desperate to see my own grandmother. "I don't think the neighbors will talk."

"I don't think so."

And I realize the people I adored as a child come with a price tag, a price tag equal to mine, because we have all hurt one another deeply, irreversibly.

I no longer have to wonder who did a number on Dad. Who taught him to explode, to be intolerant for your own in spite of what they taught on Sundays. I don't have to wonder who taught the little boy in that mesmerizing black and white picture to be mean and destructive. I only have to wonder how much he taught me.

And whether I'm better or worse than he ever was.

But still, I don't let go, not yet. I keep trying, like a bug in a jar who can't see the way out when the lid is removed.

"Okay. No problem. I can swing by tomorrow instead." There's more silence so I add, "Or sometime while I'm here. I have nine days."

She hesitates. By no means am I a stranger to disappointment. Hell, I'm not even oblivious to being surprised. But once again, I didn't see this coming. And as we wait in silence for what I think is her trying to find the right words, I'm already feeling the walls slowly go up, like a drawbridge across a moat. I hear loud voices telling me that I shouldn't care, she is judgmental and set in her ways, she doesn't matter. But the truth is, she does matter.

I want desperately to hear her tell me she's been praying for me, like the upstanding follower of Christ that she says she is. I want to hear she's in my corner, always has been, always will be, maybe even shed a tear as she tells me. I want to listen to her ramble on about those days when I was seven, maybe eight, and she would tend to her garden while I rode my Big Wheel up and down the driveway. Just her and I. I want to listen to how much she loves me and all the cherished memories she has as she watched me unfold as a beautiful innocent creature of God. I want to know that, although she doesn't approve a single bit of the things that I've done, she has still been worried, that she has been restless, that she has been waiting for my call, for my arrival, so she can wrap her arms around me and tell me it's going to be fine, that I'm safe and welcome in her house. Always.

And as the silence stretches on, my thoughts turn bitter. *I am your grandson, damn you. I am your youngest son's son. No matter what you say or try to turn your back on, that is what I am. It was the story that was sold to me my whole life. Now show up, make an impression, change my life for the better because that's what I need. At the very least, don't make it worse, don't treat me like a discarded piece of trash, because although it's hard for me to see why, I know I'm worth it, I know I have value. Don't make this the last time we talk. Ever. Don't make this moment resound in my mind for the rest of my life. Don't make all my memories as a boy mean nothing to me because they mean nothing to you. I believed in you. I trusted you. I bought the line of shit everybody sold.*

"What do you say, Grandma?" I finally ask.

She clears her throat and says, "I don't think so."

"Really?"

"I need to go to bed now." I think I hear sadness in her voice but maybe it's just an echo in the phone line.

"I understand," I tell her and we disconnect.

And I lie to myself and swear it doesn't matter. I have thick skin, I've been through worse, I will carry on and survive in spite of how she feels about me. But as I replay the last five minutes of my life, the only thing that is real to me is the pulsating busy tone pounding in my ear and the goodbye we will never get to say.

85

WHO'S GOT TIME for forgiveness when you're building walls around your heart? Who's got the energy to connect when you're hiding all these secrets? Who's got the stomach for love when you're scared, when you're fragile, when you're as little as you've ever been?

Me, that's who.

And I feel like a liar but I'm not sure I care. Letting everyone believe that I am strong, unphased, but what am I supposed to do? Although I am hurt, I won't cry. Although it is difficult, I won't quit. And, although I'm lonely, I won't stop believing that I'm worth someone's love.

The shape of the female body is salvation to me, now. The softness of skin, the vibration of my name from her lips and the smell of her prim, elegant neck is so much more than a one-night stand. It is the confidence to believe I'm going to be okay, it is the strength I need to put my past behind me, and it is the memory of what love can feel like someday. Even for me.

And though I know I'm leaving soon, this person has no idea that I will cherish her for the rest of my life.

Because she let me in—a dangerous criminal, a conniving convict? But what if she knew? What if she knew what lurks behind my blue eyes? What if she caught wind of my past? Would she still lie here awake in the dark sharing secrets with a stranger? What if she detected my fear in this moment, like a dog can smell on its prey? What if she asked me why I was shaking and I told her it's because I don't know what I'm doing? I can pretend, I can impersonate, but I'm simply doing what I think people did back when someone else wore my skin. This is a dance that I used to be good at, where I could improvise, but now I just count the steps.

Can she see my lips move—two, three, four? Can she see me tremble when she seems so willing? Can she sense my reluctance when she touches the places that no one has touched in years and years? The back of my neck, the palm of my hand when we interlock fingers, the sensitive skin she kisses below my belly button, does she feel that? When I recoil because I think there is something she might see that illuminates the stain, the traces of prison life, like DNA under a blacklight?

Does she see all that but not say a word?

In that moment, in the dark, with the feel and scent of a woman beside me, she has no idea how deeply I have craved love, affection, and the simple kind touch of another person. How I have ached in the silent, cold cells, wishing for a look, a kiss, a soft, sultry whisper.

Does she realize that, in this moment, she is everything to me? Me, a resourceful criminal, a tough convict. Does she feel my fingers fumble touching her warm places, her soft places? Because it all seems so uncomfortably foreign to the boy in this man's body. Can she sense that I might just stand up and confess, get it over with, to no longer wrestle with my insecurity? Would she recoil? Feel betrayed? Scared?

Or would she see through all of that and realize that I am a misguided spirit, a fractured soul who needs these moments, these secrets, to somehow heal.

And what if I whispered, "I love you?" Accidentally let it slip? And then assure her that, in my world, it's not weird or too soon, but I will leave nonetheless, don't worry. But if she doesn't mind, I will hang onto this moment, when she had the mercy to say my name with her legs locked around me, pulling me in closer, harder, until the moment was over. And I was gone forever. But she remains with me because the thought of these nights will lift my spirits, and become the inspiration for redemption, the muse for my dreams of the next woman—the one who will become far more permanent. The one who will see me, just me, in all the facets and parts and experiences that brought me to her.

This girl I'm with tonight will never know that she reminded me that two people can lie together alone and want nothing more than the pleasure of each other's company. She'll never know what that means to feel awkward and unworthy, and in a single moment dare to remember that you belong.

In a world I have imagined, I have constructed, I have missed, I will belong to somebody someday. Her smile, her acceptance encourage me to believe that's true. She is like therapy and shelter in one, healing the raw edges of my soul.

But would all of this be different if she knew the truth about the places I've been?

86

THOSE TEN DAYS in Higginsville were a lot more than a party and a rabbit and an airfare fund—they were a resurrection. Really. And I doubt my friends will ever know or even saw the shift within me or how much I owe them. How could they? It's not one of those things that people understand unless it happens to them. Like a near death experience, or a premonition, or being born again. My friends brought me back from the dead with their unsolicited kindness, their unexpected warmth, like a defibrillator to a dying patient. Clear!

I'm different, I'm renewed, and I'm forever in their debt as I arrive in Miami just a few hours before I turn myself in and serve another three years of my life. That's right, when the judge sentenced me to eighty-four months, he made sure it would run concurrent with all the time I had already served, including my state sentence. Since I had already served forty-eight months, that left only thirty-six more to do and I've got my life back. Maybe that judge wasn't so salty, after all.

As I step out of the airport, I feel something I don't recognize. It's not so much hope as it is the *courage* to hope. It doesn't seem foolish or at all irresponsible, here in this tropical paradise. And I suppose it's odd to feel so strong and emancipated knowing I'm going to be behind bars soon, in a higher security prison than I've been in before, where I have to figure out the rules, the power structure, the people I can talk to, the people I can't, all over again. But here I am, breathing in the salty air, taking in the sights of an exotic United States city that belongs to Spanish-speaking men and their beautiful, tan women.

The colors are all pastel blue, yellow and aqua. The feeling of the city is exactly the same.

My sister's father-in-law, Hernando, insisted I get a tour of the city before I hear those metal doors shut. And I'm touched that a relative stranger cares more about my loneliness and well-being than my own grandma of almost thirty years. He is Columbian, salt of the earth, and gives me hope that someone with a cross on a gold chain might understand that we are all in this together. His accent is new to a boy from Missouri, and it's sometimes difficult to follow, but somehow, we understand each other perfectly. He's genuine and compassionate and I could see myself honored to be standing beside him, protective, and ready to go to battle for this man.

The afternoon is bizarre as we drink Cuban coffee in a Cuban café, with the saucer and the too-small coffee cup, oddly reminiscent of the tea party with my friend's daughter back in Missouri. Hernando wants to give me a full nickel tour of the city, of a culture that is as foreign to me as walking up to a prison door and pounding on it, requesting they let me in. We eat rich food with complex flavors, and he asks if I want a beer and I think about it but decide it might not be the best idea. It might just be enough of an excuse to stay out here with my new friend, Hernando.

It's an amazing place. Where the girls all look so manicured and dressed up, like the wives of important people with disposable money and nothing to do on a weekday but wear short dresses that show their toned legs that they got from Pilates or yoga or some type of workout that women who don't have jobs do in the middle of the day.

I love it here. What fool wouldn't? Too bad I'm going to be doing hard time in less than thirty minutes—no, make that twenty-three minutes and fourteen seconds.

What a pair we make, Hernando and me. He's an immigrant who has provided for four sons in a foreign country where he has discovered freedom. And I am a white boy, born and raised in the center of this vast land, who lost the very thing Hernando came here to find. And he promises to visit, and although by now I know better than to believe what people tell me, something deep inside me says let's start here, with this person I barely know, in a city I don't understand. Let's open up, let's trust something, let's start to heal.

And now, as I walk toward the prison gates, I turn around. Hernando waves and watches me all the way in, like I was one of his own. I feel a weight has been lifted, some of the fear set aside, and I choose consciously to believe that Hernando's word is good. I think of my friends, I think of the girl who made love to me in her room for days, and I breathe in the humid tropical air. I think to myself what a cool city Miami really is and how I'd like to experience it again one of these days.

Then I walk through the doors of the bureau of prisons, FCI Miami, and brace myself to lose three more years of my life behind bars.

87

I AM NINETEEN now and angry and confused and lost, caught somewhere between the hopes of a youth and the regrets of a man. This is the time for higher learning, the time in your life when worldviews are being formed and critical thinking is being experimented with. This is a time in my life when my most existential conviction is the simple and unflappable feeling that there is so much runway to life that it is impossible for me to make a mistake that is insurmountable. Life is as long as forever, and I am going to be whatever I want to be as soon as I really want to be it. And this makes sense.

In the two short years I've been out of high school, I have enrolled in college and dropped out, mostly because I spent too much time at the keggers or hitting crack cocaine from a glass pipe I kept hidden in my room. I joined the Navy, incidentally, because I didn't want to spend any more money on coke or waste any more nights behind that pipe, with burnt black finger tips and huge swallowing pupils staring down into a gigantic mirror with yellowish rock chips and cotton balls and grain alcohol, wasting all my money because I really wasn't sure how to say no.

'Sucking the glass dick' is what they called it, so I joined the Navy and met people just like me who were trying to slow down their extracurricular activities, and failed miserably at being a good sailor. I left the Navy in less than ten months with an "other than honorable" discharge, but managed to fall into an LSD ring, learned how to trip my balls off and got a stupid tattoo on my chest.

It has been a very busy two years.

There are a lot of fond memories being built at this time as well—memories with incredible expressions of love and youth and unbridled energy. Where kindred spirits connect over late night cigarettes and the best music ever composed—alternative, before it became so mainstream—in candlelit living rooms with milk crates and futons and where conversations run deep into the next day.

Westport, a bar-riddled enclave in Kansas City, is full of history and character and upcoming music from people who have the guts to commit to their tattoos, the kind of tattoos that keep them from being employed in an office.

And I love the way it makes me feel free, alive, and part of something underground. And I'm accepted in the oddest places, an honorary member of groups I don't really understand, even though I look like a cop or a yuppie or the entitled prick whose letter jacket matches his personality. But I think I'm genuine and I think all these characters think I'm genuine, too. Like the bikers who take me in, underage, as a regular at the Dead End Saloon, off the beaten path, somewhere between Chicago and Milwaukee. Where the old heads slip me folded origami envelopes with speed or black tar and warn me, "Be careful, Houston, this ain't for rookies," as we take shots of a shitty local drink called 'the doctor'.

Or all the Black dudes with names like Chicago or Philly or Jamaica who ride into the suburbs with me—for reasons I will never know—outside of Kansas City, away from Prospect Avenue, and let me try the kind of drug that will explode your heart or your life, whichever comes first.

Or the female bartenders who have pretty eyes above sexy, low-cut T-shirts, and listless faces. They tell me they don't trust me but I see their smiles at the corners of their lips, hidden from everyone, including themselves. But not me. And I pretend I don't pay attention and it drives them crazy as I get free drinks all night, even though I'm underage. And one of the girls sells me weed with names like Lamb's Breath or Colombian Gold, but I don't care, it's all the same to me as long as I get high. And later we go back to her apartment around the corner with a small group of people who play in bands and work at other bars. And she tells me she can get me a pound of the "same shit" if I think I can sell it, and I think about it for a long time but finally decide no.

"I'm leaving as soon as the sun comes up," I tell her.

And she says she has some paper and has the day off tomorrow, so we send one of the dudes with a Yin Yang tattoo on his shoulder out to the liquor store to get orange juice and we drop acid. I'm here for two days, in the same clothes, and I forget how angry and confused I'm supposed to be at the age of nineteen.

88

HOLY SHIT, THE federal institutions are so much different from the state prisons I've been in. At least this one is. We have free weights here, although they are all tethered with thick cables to weight racks and benches to make it more difficult to crack somebody's skull with a twenty-five-pound plate—but still, free weights. And the food is better. I've heard rumors that we get the rejected food from the military. Whether this is true or not, I think military rejects sound pretty damn good to me. There's more fruit, bigger portions, and the meat is strangely the consistency of meat, which is so much different than it was in Missouri; where, ironically, they probably get this meat from in the first place.

The racial separation is different here, too. There are more cultures, more divisions and although "Black and white" still exists, not everybody white is *really* white. In Missouri, I am a honky; in Miami, I am a cracker. But in reality, I look like some of the Colombians, I look like some of the Cubans, and there is a weird racial thing that clearly has nothing to do with the color of my skin. It's not hard to understand, just difficult to explain, and I don't much give a shit what racial bucket I get lumped into, I'm just quickly growing tired of all the non-white inmates thinking I'm soft because of the color of my skin. Like, *really* tired of it.

But there is a story to be told about each of these inmates. They're historical figures, as famous as they are infamous. Like Manuel Noriega—yes, *the* Noriega, old pineapple face himself. He is in solitary confinement, but I have bumped into him at least three times so far when he was being escorted to a visit. He'll never know me or I him, but it's interesting how we can both be on the same compound, during the same period of time, and have zero idea what doing time is like for the other.

In this prison, history is all around me. And I am reading a fascinating book about the tracking of Pablo Escobar and his men. One day, while I was walking the track and explaining to my friend about the power and the connections and the influence that these men all had over people's lives, he turns to me and says, "Oh yeah, Lehder, that guy's right over there," as he points to Carlos Lehder, one of Escobar's co-founding partners of the Medellín Cartel. A true baller, in every sense of the word, now looking like a lowly peasant just lucky to be alive.

And there are these white-haired Philadelphia mob bosses and one of their enforcers. They run numbers on the yard and sell anything that isn't bolted down from the kitchen. They sit on a bench every morning, feeding ducks and talking about whatever mob bosses talk about, but they are also odd characters in a book written by an ex-FBI agent; a book I can check out anytime I want in the prison library. Like adding insult to injury, the book is here as a painful reminder of how life led them to this institution.

Broken, just like me. Doing hard time, just like me. Feeling time pass through the lives they were supposed to live, without them in it, just like me. Only, I'm going to leave one day.

But, by far, my favorite characters are the bikers, with their long goatees and ink on their skin—esoteric symbols significant only to them and the brotherhood they bleed for. These are the men I find to be the most genuine. I mean, I'm not oblivious to the fact that these people would stab me in the neck if I had it coming, but we're cool and they like me and I'm pretty good at not giving someone a reason to stab me in the neck. And I feel like passing the time with these guys is like listening to a good book narrated by a crazy uncle with a deep smoke-stained voice who only comes around once every two or three years for Christmas. The kind of uncle who shows up with the coolest presents but says "motherfucker" in front of the children while he passes out the gifts. These men exist in a parallel universe where, at any given moment, they will nonchalantly tell me how their seventy-year-old dad is still getting into knife fights in biker bars and then announce that they have to get ready for their visit with David Allan Coe or Johnny Paycheck.

But it is the cocaine trade, and the cartel members who run it, that fills the vast majority of the cells here. For God's sake, we are in Miami after all. And if you've ever seen the movie *Scarface,* you'll understand. The characters in the yard I lift weights in, the people I play football with, the men who serve my food, walk the track, play me in chess, are all the parts of those mesmerizing storylines that we never got to see. Shit you only get to see if you're in here, dressed in these clothes.

Almost anywhere we stand, thick steel cables crisscross above us, marked with bright red balls like oversized bobbers on a fishing line. Those balls are the single most telling reminder of how much power these guys yield. Because it's not the money they have for commissary or the books that mention them by name that show the magnitude of their influence, it's the hard-to-fathom fact that the Bureau of Prisons had to create a barrier—a pseudo-ceiling—over the prison yard in Miami to keep helicopters from landing in an attempt to orchestrate a prison break.

I walk the yard knowing how freakishly small-time I am compared to these men. Me, the small-town country boy who cooked a few pounds of meth and them, real Colombian drug lords who have hijacked commercial airplanes, built their own prisons, created a billion-dollar industry, and made enough money to potentially send a helicopter into a heavily guarded prison yard.

The sun is amazing down here, although it's still winter, so I reserve the right to change my mind in a couple of months. And once the sun hovers a little closer to the surface there will be mosquitos, aggressive and large like pterodactyls, as we swelter in steamy, muggy heat like an all-male sauna where you have to keep your clothes on.

And I can't deny that some of this sunshine might be coming from me. I feel different on the inside—stronger, less alone, and maybe that has something to do with my outlook. Whatever it is, I'm cool. Well, as cool as I can be doing time in a federal prison for three years of my life.

Make no mistake about it, Toto; we're not in Kansas anymore.

89

THE STAKE IS driven into the center of my chest, deeper with every word that passes from her lips. She is my sister, the one person I thought I could trust and now she has become a blunt instrument of life served cold. My legs are weak, my breath shallow, and I feel like I'm suffocating in an oxygen-starved environment; like I'm suffocating and need to scream my agony from the highest mountain. But, honestly, I don't know where the screaming would start and worse, I don't know where it would end.

So, I just listen.

Her words seem careless, deliberate, but I know better. I know she has thought this out, she has agonized over it, she has spent sleepless nights arriving at this decision. Still it doesn't feel any easier, any different when she tells me, "I'm so sorry, Kyle. We can't keep Sean Michael."

I am mad, I am crushed, I am confused, I am lonely, but who do I point the finger at? In my mind, I hear Tuck's voice say, "Instant, just like your karma," and I know that all roads lead right back to me.

She tells me things that I think are supposed to make me understand, but nothing coherent ever forms. Words like "so sorry" and "tough decision" and "wish it could be different" might as well be Greek because I don't understand. My mind scrambles for ways to fix this, for ways to control this, to manifest something different. But this news is so fresh, so abrupt, like a punch to the mouth in the middle of a long, passionate kiss. No, *worse*. It's more like someone coming up behind you on Christmas day and putting a plastic bag over your face while you're sitting among the presents, amongst your family, suffocating, kicking, clawing, while everyone just watches you suffer.

Like now, as I sit here on the phone—suffocating, suffocating, suffocating.

And something tells me I deserve it all. That, somehow, I deserve to have a child, my own flesh and blood, stripped from my life and adopted by nameless, faceless people, never to be seen by me again. I am not worth being spared from this unfathomable heartache, that this is what happens to boys who get hooked on meth and I should have known better when I got myself into this trouble. I should have seen it all coming... But I didn't.

So, now, I pray that Sean finds someone who loves him as much as I do. No matter how I feel, it's what I want for him. I hope they are good and true and the kind of parent I'll never get a chance to be. Maybe someday I'll see this is for the best, maybe this is some part of God's elaborate plan, or maybe it's just more bullshit I sell to myself while I break into a million more pieces after I was convinced it was impossible to ever break again.

In this moment, my heart beats like a loveless, cold, mechanical part, and all I can say to Kelly is, "Okay. I understand." I hang up and I walk to my bunk in my cell in federal fucking prison and I feel so...I don't know, disposable, as the light inside me grows dimmer. Is this what I deserve? Is this a natural part of my sentence? Is this justice?

Because not even a shitty, lowlife convict—whose biggest crime was getting tangled in the web of addiction—deserves this. Not even me, dear God. And the next time the universe wants to send me a message that I'm not worthy, that I'm not loved, that my heart is the stomping grounds for your amusement, don't send my sister to deliver it again.

Et tu, Brute?

Then the second phone call comes. The one I've been dreading, the one I hoped would somehow never have to become a reality—Sean Michael leaves Kelly's house today. I'm told it's what's best and I brace myself to endure another goodbye over a crackling, metal prison phone. He is so brave, so precocious, so young as he tells me, "I wanted to wait to be with you," as I shut my eyes and press my head hard against the cold cinder block wall, and then, "when you get out."

"Me too," I tell him and wonder if he believes me. I curse the path that brought me here, to this moment in time so far from my son when he needs me the most. I want to hug him through the phone, to tell him a thousand things, like how to ask a girl to prom, and how to know when to change your oil, and how heartbreak and failure will teach him more than anything else in life. I want to package decades of fatherhood into a single phone call and I'm sad, unbelievably fucking sad, that I can't at least do that.

I don't want to hang up, I don't want to say goodbye, but then too soon, Kelly's voice is on the phone, thick and fractured, telling him he has to go. Knowing her, she is wading through the heaviness of her decision and the knowledge that I am in an agony like no other. Both her little brother and a precious boy are dying on the inside because she is trying to do the right thing for everyone.

In this last moment on the phone with my son, I have to believe in something. I have to believe that my prayers will be answered and that Sean Michael will find love, find a family, and find healing. I have to believe that the universe will wrap its loving arms around this precious child and protect him from more of my life.

Maybe that is what this is—a way to put armor around this poor child who has already been through too much. I say goodbye and they hang up, then I listen to the static of an empty telephone line. There will always be an empty place inside me. Pain that most people will overlook. Because I'm a junkie, because I'm a convict, because I made my bed and now it's time to lie in it. But, right now, I'm just a human being with a broken heart, a daddy, who has lost a child. I fear his fate and mourn his loss just like anyone with freedom and better choices. Only I'm all alone.

I am forever sorry, Sean Michael. You deserved so much better. But never believe you weren't worthy or loved or that any part of your precious life was disposable, because my heart aches for the moments I lost. And, although I can't remember the exact moment when I gave you your last embrace, I will always remember this. The moment I said my last goodbye to you; the little boy who fit so perfectly in my lonely, loving arms.

Until we meet again.

90

I'VE BEEN WALKING through my waking days conjuring up these elaborate ways to sacrifice my life to save someone else's, like jumping into a pit of alligators, plummeting from hundred story buildings to save babies, to save nieces, to rescue worthy, albeit hypothetical, people from the grips of death. There's no rhyme or reason as to when they come up. I can be in line at the chow hall, or staring off into the clouds, or walking the track. I can be in the shower, the library, the shitter—it doesn't matter; almost anytime I have a few moments alone, without the insanity of base Spanish-speaking men yelling 'pinga' or 'maricón' at one another like they want to kick off the next Iran-Contra affair, I catch myself daydreaming of dying.

Not dying for morbid, depressing, suicidal reasons—although I'm usually eviscerated by sharks or impaled on the grill of a semi-truck—no, these glorious deaths are all for noble reasons, the things that seem to be missing from my life's story. These imaginary deaths will bring honor and reverence back to my name, to my legacy, to my son's memories of me. Not quite dying on the cross for the world's sins, but a shit ton worthier than hanging myself alone with an extension cord in a dusty, dreary basement in Northeast Kansas City.

I daydream that, in an instant, I can erase the shame and heartache and indignity from my history. My death could be the ultimate act of contrition, folks. I walk through a world of "what if's that seem to illuminate the super-Freudian shit that goes on inside my mind; and I dream about death. I'll let someone smarter than me figure all that out.

The scenarios are endless, yet all frightening, as my pulse races and stomach coagulates in knots. And, as I think about the fear I would have to endure, the courage and honor and pureness of spirit it would take to lay my life on the line to save someone, literally anyone, from the pain of loss, I put myself in that moment, there, and ask—could I really do it?

And the answer is not only a resounding, "Hell yes!" but I find myself trying to will any of it to happen.

My new existential theorem: All life is precious, with a slight twist—my life is only precious if I sacrifice it to save someone else's. If I can somehow do something that makes up for all this crap and everything that came before. In my head, there's a truth that hasn't changed from the days when I was shackled by my ankles to drug abuse.

My life is still worth more dead than alive.

91

I AM TWENTY-FOUR now and the phone rings and rings, trying to pull me from my sleep but it's useless. There's no one I want to talk to tonight. The answering machine picks up.

"Hey, it's Quinn," I hear my friend begin. "I hate to leave a message like this, but I can't get a hold of you. Nobody can." His voice is somber and cold, a tone I've never heard from him before. Reluctantly, I grunt and start the slow process of waking up. "Not sure if anyone has reached you yet but Cooper is..." There's a long hesitation until he says, "He's, um, gone; and I wanted—"

"Hello! I'm here. Quinn? It's me," I say as I fumble with the phone in the dark. The answering machine reverberates my words; feedback shrieks in the stillness of the house. "Damn it. Hold on."

I stumble to the kitchen and shut the machine off. The blinking red light from the machine bounces off the walls. Eight unread messages. Shit, I need to call Ana.

"I'm here, buddy," I say to Quinn now. "I'm up."

"Dude, where have you been?"

Where have I been? How about high? Unavailable? Fucking up my life? "Cooper, tell me about Cooper," I demand.

"So, you haven't heard?"

"No, I haven't." I search the drawers for a pack of cigarettes. "What'd he do this time?"

"He's gone," Quinn hesitates, clears his throat. "I'm sorry, man."

The word "gone", for a brief second, gives me hope. Hope that Cooper is struggling or off the radar, hope that I can still tell him I love him or hit him in the mouth. It all means the same.

"Gone? Gone how?" I ask, and brace myself, close my eyes.

"He...he hung himself."

I say nothing; the words don't make sense to me. Cooper would never do that. Where are my fucking cigarettes?

"Just wanted you to hear it from me," Quinn says.

"Yeah I know. That's the right thing to do," I tell him but I'm not sure why. "I'll call you later," I say and hang up.

I pull a cigarette from a crinkled pack lying in my junk drawer. I light it and then slowly drop to the floor, pinning the cigarette between my first two fingers. And then it hits me, and I feel like I'm going to fall apart. My best friend…gone?

A month or so ago, someone told me Cooper threatened to kill himself and that the fire department had come, which didn't make sense to me. It all sounded like bullshit, his bullshit. I could see a story where some prank got out of control and how the grapevine blew it all out of proportion and that we would be laughing about it just as soon as I got my hands on him. I'd been through too much with this guy for him to check out without telling me. He would tell me, I told myself, because I know him.

So, I confronted him one day at the house. "What's this silly shit I hear about you and a gun and—"

"Come on, man," he interrupts. "You know me better than that."

"I know you're a crazy son of a bitch," I say. "So why the fire trucks?"

I remember it now, how it seemed too rehearsed when he told me that it was his mom's fault. "She thought I was serious," he said with his signature smile and I believed him. Why wouldn't I? We didn't keep secrets, we didn't lie, at least not to each other. If there was anyone in this world I could trust, it was him. But whether I could have done more in that moment or not, clearly, I didn't do enough.

"I'm not suicidal," he swore, then hesitated. "I would tell you."

He averted his eyes and a shudder runs through me. "Listen to what I'm about to tell you, Cooper," I told him. No smile, intense eye contact. "Whatever is going on with you, I'm the guy who gives a shit. I'm the guy you come and talk to before you do anything stupid."

He laughed it off. "Huey, you're worse than my mom."

"Whatever. You're my best friend," I told him. "Deal with it."

"Classic Kyle Houston," he said and for a moment I thought he was going to say more, but he didn't.

"Fuck you. I love you like a brother," I told him as I lit two cigarettes and handed him one.

He took a drag, squinted his eye and looked directly at me. "You know what I like about you, Huey?"

"What's that?"

"Nothing," he told me and laughed. "You worry too much."

Those were the last words I remember. We were in this kitchen—it seems like last week, but what do I know? I'm the guy with eight unanswered messages on his answering machine. Still, I knew something was missing; he was in too big of a hurry to leave that day; and now as I sit here wondering what was really going through his mind, I want that moment back. I want my last words back; I want them to be different. I want to hug him now, tightly, maybe too long, maybe uncomfortably, but I don't give a shit. I want to make him hear me this time, make him stay, make him tell me what the hell is so bad in his life that he wanted to leave. I want him to cry and slobber and apologize and scream. I want him to take wild swings at me because I won't let him leave this time, no matter how mad he is, no matter what he says to hurt my feelings, to get me pissed. I want a simple fucking do-over because, this time, I know that the distance in our conversation is real and I will keep him right here, alive, with me.

My hands shake as I quickly dial the numbers. Please be there. Please be there. I think as the phone starts to ring. A tired voice on the other end answers. The person I need.

And then I say the words that will define my life for way too many years, "Do you know where to get some shit?"

92

THE DREAM ALWAYS seems to drag me down for days—the guilt, the fear, the deep foreboding feeling that I have lost something I will never get back. And it isn't something I talk about; it just affects me as I'm tying my shoes or eating alone or wanting to fucking scream into my pillow alone at night.

I've had this dream dozens of times and it always starts the same way. It's my last high school football game, senior year. We're playing Knob Noster and I only have thirty-eight rushing yards going into the second half. Coach continues to call my number and the quarterback feeds me the ball again and again but, no matter what I do, I can't get past the line of scrimmage. Can't budge that ball a single fucking yard. I bury my head, churn my legs, but every goddamn time I hit the line, I am stopped dead in my tracks.

And the desire is there and the talent is there and the experience and the support and the strategy is all there. But time is what I lack and what continues to tick away.

Although I know I shouldn't, I repeatedly look up at the scoreboard and the changing numbers that continue counting down. With the ball in my hands, I'm doing what I've always done, what normally breaks tackles and gets the yards but for some reason my old ways don't work.

I then harbor this overwhelming fear to not look at the clock because I know it's over, I know it's too late, I know I've lost something that I will never get back.

And then the final buzzer goes off. Game over.

My teammates just look at me and shake their heads in disbelief, utterly disappointed. As if I could have done something different, something more. As if they couldn't believe I fucked this up, too.

Sometimes I feel the guilt before I wake up, a heavy, suffocating feeling that lingers like an unwelcome guest. It's like a cocktail party filled with all my mistakes and all the disappointed faces of the people who love me. And the dream is so lucid—the colors, the smell, the passion, the regret. Feelings I already know are here to stay.

But the thought of disappointing my teammates—my coach, my family, and the people who have yet to come into my life—is too much sometimes. And, although I wish the regret could be the fuel that pushed me forward to the man I promised Dad I'd become, it crushes me; it drains my spirit and lingers for days, every time.

All I know is that I feel the pressure of expectations, of a ticking clock. It's as if every second of my life is the fourth quarter and I'm giving it all I've got. I've got to break these tackles, keep pumping these legs, keep pushing toward paydirt. And I'd give anything for a first and ten.

For a chance to start over.

93

January 1, 2005. It's a new year with new resolutions for a brand-new me.

Finally, I'm on the backstretch of incarceration; finally, staring straight into the light that appears at the end of this tunnel. Something that can be hard to do, sometimes, because my case manager is the most condescending individual I have ever dealt with, and I don't know if the proverbial tunnel that I peer through, with squinted eyes and a dirty face, is three months or six months long. They don't tell you.

But this is my year. This is my time. This is my chance at getting back to where I left off.

And I've read about the technology—how the internet seems to be changing the world, how "digital" seems to be sinking its teeth into everything audiovisual, how VHS has given way to something newer, sleeker. I feel like Buck Rogers in the twenty-fifth century, when my friends ask if they can email me. Not that I don't get the concept. It's just that I'll be thirty-five this year, potentially walking into the workforce, and I've never sent an email.

Rolling Stone is my window into the world. At least, the one that counts. And, although I don't really get how Napster worked, I do get that, because of the internet, people are sharing music from all over the planet. And here I sit, missing the only window of time where my music collection could multiply like gremlins in a pool of water. And I feel like a sucker locked outside the record store, peering through the window, while people who listen to *...Baby One More Time* by Britney Spears and *Steal My Sunshine* by Len capitalize on this once-in-a-lifetime mad grab for music.

I constantly daydream about the thirteen-year-old version of me who used to sit in a beanbag chair with bulky headphones and colorful album covers strung out across the bedroom floor, having access to this amount of music. I could see it all now, as my teenage self has his mind blown by the fact that a faceless kid in Japan or Great Britain or some tiny town in Alberta, shares the bootleg import of *London Calling* by the Clash or some insane live version of Dusty Springfield's *Son of a Preacher Man*.

And I catch myself stepping back from the lure of the shiny objects—the mesmerizing spell of technology—and realizing that, with the changing of the guard, we are all bidding farewell to important things. Like, where are all the beautiful album covers going to go? What does this do to the experience? What would *Bat Out of Hell* be like without the badass demonic figure on the motorcycle?

And if we lose that, what's next? What other art form is lost and dying? What else has the world discarded without me knowing? Am I a missing piece to some complicated human puzzle or just a square peg in a round hole? Where will I ever fit? My friends all have lives—enriched, thriving lives. They subscribe to their version of the American dream with large SUVs and baby seats and cup holders with venti skinny lattes and retirement plans. They don't have children out of wedlock or felonies or scars on their face from prison boots. They don't lack an education or have unexplainable gaps in their work history. They've never stuck needles in their arms or lain awake at night inside a prison cell wondering who could ever love them.

Where do I fit in? Where can I ever feel comfortable? Where do I go if I want to dream, if I want to get along, and feel special or feel safe and sound and cared for? It seems that all roads lead right back to here. Because this is the world I know, this is the world I have learned to survive, and, in an odd way, this is the world where I feel most comfortable.

And the closer I get to walking out of here, the further away it feels. My case manager mentions my file, and I realize that once again, there are a lot of boxes to check and judgments to pass before I can move forward.

But what if I'm not getting out? What if, out of mercy, they aren't telling me that the prosecution wants a second chance at the longer sentence? What if seven years isn't enough to appease the power-hungry fuckers back in Kansas City?

I've heard the stories of men packing up their clothes, turning in their bed rolls, giving away their belongings to the fellas in the yard and then getting served an indictment. I've spoken to men who have shown up at the gate and been served by the U.S. Marshals for something they thought had been swept under the rug. Maybe these prosecutors have felonies waiting, charges in the bank; like some skewed form of currency that they buy, trade, and sell arbitrarily and no one knows when they will use them. I actually shared a cell with a guy who got twenty-four months in the eleventh hour for a crime that was supposed to be a part of the forty-eight months he had just served. It's spineless, it's inhumane, it's ungodly to think about what they do to people like me.

And I pace the floors of my mind, wearing a groove in my thoughts, worried sick that I'm a part of this criminal lottery system. Because I have seen how this works, I have seen how they play; and so far, I haven't been the luckiest guy in the world.

Please God, let me know now. It's the right thing to do. Let me know if we are going to go through this again, if I need to hollow out my chest. Or better yet, what do I need to learn? What lesson have I failed? I'll cram, I'll test out, I'll even go to a fucking AA meeting if that's what it takes. I can't do this again; you know that. I can't suffer another betrayal. I can't swallow my courage or shed another tear or face my family one more time. This one will break me, this one might kill me, dim my lights for good. This one could be the lesson that shows me how to embrace the darkness.

Please God, don't let me always question "What if?" What if I had killed myself? What if I never asked for truth? Because I don't need truth or salvation or redemption, I just need headphones and a beanbag chair on the other side of this fence.

And I ring in the New Year sick to my stomach—terrorized by law, by justice, by arbitrary decisions with the power to run me through the meat grinder just to watch me bleed. And I grapple with my anxiety and the blatant reality that my number one fear is that I won't get released. That they find another charge that is impossible to beat and chalk up another couple of years. And my number two fear is that, somehow, I do get released and I'm in the free world where no one will want me, no one will understand me, and where peace is the shiny object Karma never lets me hold.

January 1, 2005. Same me. Same shovel. Same shit.

94

MOST PEOPLE WILL never understand how civilized people can build up an immunity to violence. But when you've been locked up for years and years, this slanted prison etiquette gets drilled into your psyche. When you've struggled to survive on the most primal side of life, and made the solemn vow to choose death before dishonor every single time because you refuse to spend years of your life pissed at yourself, obsessively replaying confrontational scenarios, fights are seen more as a responsibility than an act of violence. And it's not what I would teach my children or what the world should subscribe to, but this isn't the real world…this is prison.

And whoever says violence is "never" the answer has never tried to negotiate boundaries with a room full of murderers, cut-throats, and thieves. Unless they're Gandhi or Mother Teresa, I really don't want to hear their shit. Because most people who talk this way have never lain awake all night preparing to defend themselves against a three-hundred-pound killer or hell, even watched a room full of thugs bully a man on a daily basis for his lunch tray.

My philosophy is this: Love—mutual and unconditional—will solve any problem. That being said, sometimes a good ass whooping will do a lot for a person's character.

My character is either being built or destroyed depending on how I view it, but all I'm trying to do is survive inside federal prison.

And that makes sense to a convict.

Even if you're relatively smart and trying to be good and committed to something super Jesus-y like turning the other cheek, you always know that—to some degree—you think like a convict. When you lie around with dogs, you're bound to get fleas. And at this point, my sincerest hope is that I'm more than just a convict.

But dear God help me, because one of these simple motherfuckers just took all my clothes out of the dryer and put his in. And I've seen this piece of shit hundreds of times over the past two years, but I can't remember exchanging a single word. With all his hard looks aimed at me, I'm more than just an enemy, I'm a blue-eyed devil, I'm the scourge of the planet, I'm a virus that has been spread for centuries across the globe. And I know why he's doing it. It's not that complicated.

These men know my days are numbered. They might not know I'm supposed to be finally walking out these doors in less than seventy-two hours, but they know it's a matter of days, maybe weeks. That is, unless I somehow get indicted again.

To most people the decision is easy…walk away. But I can't. As much as I wish it wasn't true, I am not only an animal attuned to his primal instincts, but I'm also an animal in a cage. Not only am I an animal in a cage, but I might also be institutionalized. I might never become a person who solves problems without fighting. And not only am I potentially an institutionalized animal in a cage, but I'm also a grown ass man you don't just start shit with for no reason. I'm not walking away from that.

No matter what I look like, I've earned my stripes. If he wants to fuck with me, he damn well better pack a lunch. I had to be pulled off a three-hundred-pound killer, I have slept with weapons under my pillow, I got my ass kicked by three guys in a cell and still came out on top. I'm not new to this. Don't mistake a smile and proper English for someone who's had it easy, asshole. I babysat my mom while she was in a coma, I inadvertently gave up one of my children, and I really miss my dead dad a lot. At this point, you can't take away anything that hasn't already been taken.

Except maybe my outdate.

Shit! God, what am I doing?

Okay, asshole, I think to myself—tit for tat. I cross to the dryer, politely throw his clothes on the floor and put mine back in. Like a gentleman. The intelligent thing to do. Now the ball is in his court.

"Whatchu doing, boy?" he yells and I act like I don't hear him. He sounds surprised and pissed; and that, in itself, makes me feel better. "I'm talking to you."

"Oh." I reply.

"Don't you never touch my shit," he says.

"Then keep your shit out of my dryer." I hesitate, considering the consequences of my next word, considering deeply how close I am to getting out, to starting the long, arduous process of putting all this behind me. I think about how easy it would be to just put his clothes back and walk away. The voice in my head now negotiates with me, presenting all the ways I could save face. Things like angrily putting his clothes back in and yelling, "I have my outdate, motherfucker, you can have the dryer," or something super John Wayne like that.

And I search frantically for what everyone from Chuck Norris to Mister Rogers would do in this situation, although none of it matters because I've had enough and can't quite bring myself to eat another shit sandwich in this godforsaken hole in South Florida. The voice now screams, *don't say it, don't say it,* but I stick my chest out anyway, and with perfect diction punctuate my sentence with, "Bitch!"

And that's it. There's no backing out. Whether he wants to, or I want to, there's no backing out of this one. The gauntlet has been thrown, and if he doesn't pick it up then he's exactly what I just called him.

"All right, cracker, you like getting loud? We'll see about that, motherfucker." He turns and heads towards his cell.

I turn quickly and do the same. If there's going to be a fight, I'm not gonna be standing here alone, folding clothes in shower shoes. I've seen how that turns out.

95

I'm twenty-six now and I'm proud of how I've built my life. I work for myself, I own my own house, people report to me, work for me, rely on me; and, so far, none of them have been let down. I take responsibility very seriously. I can be an asshole, probably more often than I even see it, but if I say I'm going to do something, you can take it to the bank. Simply put, people count on me and believe in me—everybody from the local suppliers who extend my line of credit, to my business partners, to all my customers, to my five-year-old son, to the girl who moved to Chicago to follow her dream. "Trust" is the currency that gets exchanged in my world these days, and something that would kill me to lose.

And I believe in myself, too. I have natural instincts that seem to serve me well in moment to moment decisions. Although I don't understand what's so difficult about problem solving, I see now that it doesn't come easy for a lot of people; at least for the people around me. And I like to be in charge because shit seems to get done when I'm at the helm. But I have no patience, little understanding, and zero compassion for laziness. Work is easy, life is easy, and money seems to be a by-product of good decision making; or possibly luck. I'm making money hand over fist now and I can't wait to show Mom and Dad what a success I am.

Lately, I feel this...what...moral dilemma with how impatient I seem to always be with my employees and this cosmic wheel of fortune. And emotionally, it has become obvious that I don't possess whatever that thing is that connects the dots between disdain and gratitude.

A few weeks ago, I prayed for humility but do not hold out that I will ever get it. My spirit knows it's a noble pursuit, but my mind knows it's just not in my DNA. It's a waste of time, and inviting God into the picture will probably wind up biting me in the ass someday. I mean, come on, I'm not new to this. In the church of Kyle Houston, humility is only going to be found at the intersection of personal failure, a healthy dose of 'give a shit', and a sweet hint of ecstasy—the drug, not the emotion; but once you're on the drug, what's the fucking difference?

And I believe I am enlightened, and I read books by Norman Vincent Peale, and I secretly do methamphetamine more than I care to admit.

I believe it's under control, that bad things like addiction only happen to someone else, that I'm different from the weak people.

But this particular day has been very strange. Today has been a futile exercise of willpower and denial, of trying to ignore this feeling inside me that speaks loudly like a kick to the nuts. All afternoon, I have been telling myself that this deep, foreboding nervousness is normal as I wait to be introduced to a legitimate major connection in the meth game. She is the ex-wife of one of my carpet installers, she sleeps with the biggest meth cook in Kansas City, and she has a flair for boys like me—clean-cut, ambitious, full set of teeth. And the installer has been sent out to find her, to mention a stereo I'd like to sell, to bring her back to me where I fully intend to be charming, polite and high as hell. After all, if there is one thing I am good at, it's meeting new people.

And the idea of knowing where to find pure, uncut crystal excites me. It is dangerous, it is foolish, and it is the answer to a real problem on Friday nights. So, I pushed my guy out the door, paid him double for all his work, and did everything but personally drive him all over Jackson County to get my hands on his ex who exchanges sex for meth.

But something feels deeply and inherently wrong or dangerous but definitely permanent and I want to call it off, tell him not to bother, that I have no business meeting people like her, that not even I can be trusted with a girl and her bottomless bag of pure white flakes. No matter how much strength I think I possess, something about this feels stronger, something about this feels like it won't play fair.

I'm pacing the carpet in my living room, contemplating an entire universe of 'What ifs'. I am completely aware that a decision is being made here. The decision I make is to do nothing as I sit quietly and pray that she never shows up.

But the doorbell rings and I choose to answer the door. And that still quiet voice that knows better whispers goodbye to the boy from Higginsville, goodbye to Ana who I will always miss, goodbye to my worldview and the music and my simple way of looking at people and how they can be so weak.

Goodbye to the boy who could have made a better choice.

96

I'm in my cell, now, looking for my shoe. I'm pissed and disoriented—and, if I'm being honest, I'm extremely concerned. Not so much because of what he might do, although I'm sure this fight will involve a piece of metal. No, what I'm concerned about is me.

And where's that fucking shoe?

For reasons that aren't exactly clear, I am prepared to get stabbed. Really. I am prepared to take on a couple of holes as long as they aren't in my neck or face; and, for some irrational reason, I have no fear of that—as silly as it sounds.

So, I'm standing here throwing clothes, kicking clothes, searching through piles of clothes everywhere in this cluttered too-small cell. Me, getting ready to go to battle where I may or may not get stabbed. One shoe on, one shoe off like some sick sadistic nursery rhyme, searching for a shoe or a weapon or the pieces of me that I never wanted to lose in the first place.

Because I know what this says about me. This is yet another one of those glaring indications that perhaps I don't belong anywhere *but* prison. I walk out of here, whether I have both shoes or not, I go find this prick waiting for me, and we consummate this fucking dance. Whether I show up with a weapon or not, the fight will be serious. Whether I win or not, chances are I'm going to the hole. Whether I get over it or not, whether this guy and I are able to cohabitate on the yard or not, whether we both eventually exchange addresses and spend every Christmas together from here on out or not, if we fight, chances are I'm not walking out of here as scheduled.

What the fuck am I thinking?

I straddle this proverbial fence that divides two Kyles right now, no longer searching for my lost shoe but my lost humanity. If that's even what this is…humanity. Going out and squaring off with someone right now, so close to that revolving door of incarceration, will say so many things about who I am and who I will ever be able to become. It will be yet another line

I will never uncross. Not because it's a fight, not because he will have a weapon, but because it's now less than seventy-two hours from walking out of the shittiest seven years of my entire life and I'm what—getting ready to jeopardize it all over some federal issued underwear?

And there it is; my beat up, tossed around, dirty-ass white shoe in need of stitching, sitting on top of the locker. I'm lucky this guy hasn't shown up with five of his brothers. I know what happens when a white guy on this compound, spends far too much valuable time preparing for a fight. They graciously bring the fight to you. And, just like this shoe, I become the beat up, tossed around, dirty-ass white boy in need of stitching.

And the crazy thing is I wanted to do this. I wanted to throw hands with him so badly when I was down there in the laundry room, but now that I've had a few moments, now that this shoe dilemma has tilted my world back on its axis, I just want to make it out of here in a few days and go home. *God, did you do this? Did you hide my shoe? But we both know it's too late now. Death before dishonor, God…unless, of course, You have an outdate.*

I dart out the door with my head on a swivel. From across the long expanse of the housing unit, I see three men pointing up at my cell. They encircle him, holding him back, I think. Oh, and they're tucked away in a corner, a huge no-no for me.

But I stick my chest out and head that way.

In one hand, I have my lock, clutched tightly with my middle finger laced through it. Fuck, what have I gotten into? *God, I'm sure You're up there shaking Your head right now but maybe You could intervene on this one. I don't know, part a sea or send some locusts for the next three days until I get out of here. At the very least, make us invisible so the guards don't see this. Have You ever pulled a stunt like that?*

Oh, I know, how about make this guy a Christian, a good one, or at least one who is in the middle of a legal issue and is trying to act like a good one? You know, the kind who are always trying to trick You into some divine intervention.

The housing unit is two stories high and, since I measure everything in football fields, I'd say at least fifty yards long. In the middle is a common area with multiple TVs. Sitting in the chairs, mesmerized by what plays on these televisions all day, are men with gold chains and gold teeth who pat the tops of their heads so they don't unravel the cornrows in their hair.

As I make my way quickly through the groups of chairs, I see a large black man walking toward me. He has a book in his hand. His face is emotionless, his stride effortless and unrushed, but he's clearly coming toward me. There are two others about twenty feet behind him, staggered, but in his wake. The hair on my neck stands straight up, my muscles tense, but I show no signs of aggression. The element of surprise is always my best friend.

"House-ton," he says from a distance. "I need to ask you something before you continue." A faint island accent in his voice.

"It's Hue-stun," I tell him and then wonder why I care. "Who are you? Where's What's His Face?" I'm looking past this guy, trying to find the one who wants to kick my ass.

The man smiles, the gold teeth legit. After seven years, I can gauge status by the quality of a man's grill. I can tell that on the streets this guy was a shot caller.

"Let's focus on you," he says and stops. I tighten my grip on the lock in my hand. "I hear you leave this month."

"In the next three months," I lie and then wish I could take it back. I don't want fate to hear me and then manifest the bullshit that comes out of my mouth.

"Right," he continues. "You have your outdate." He pauses and looks pensive for a moment and I notice the men behind him aren't circling me, aren't trying to get behind me. They're just standing there, listening. "Do you know anything about Islam?" he asks.

Shit. I ball my fists, stagger my feet, and quickly look around.

"The teachings of the Quran are many things to many people," he continues, his accent getting thicker now. "But to me, to…" He pauses for a moment then smiles. "…to What's His Face, it's a path to a better life. You understand?"

I nod my head, trying to absorb what's going on. I thought I ordered a fake *Christian*, God.

"We are men, we have egos, we can be brutal." His smile drops, his eyes lock on mine. "We are brutal."

Here we go. I look around again. Brace myself, make sure that lock is good and secure in my fist.

The guy across from me keeps on talking. "This altercation is a test for my brother, one he hasn't failed yet. He knows that." His smile returns, "I don't know your path, your history, your future, but I know his. He's tired of breaking hearts; he wants a life outside these walls. One that many of us won't ever have. He wants…forgiveness. You understand, Kyle?"

"You know my name?"

He nods slowly, and half-closes his eyes. "I also know you are leaving this compound in three days. If you choose wisely and simply do one tiny thing." He holds his book out, it's the Quran and it looks worn and used. "Forgive," he tells me. "Forgive."

It's unbelievable how that single word penetrates me even now. I'm back in my cell, looking at my belongings strewn all over the place. Like poetry to a broken heart, like the opening notes of my favorite song, it is the answer to a question I didn't know I should be asking. *Forgive.*

Whether the other guy meant to be wise or he was just protecting his brother, the truth is it was the perfect word for the perfect moment. I felt a vibration.

And maybe it's because of what's going on in my life, or maybe it's because I already knew it, or maybe this guy is some sort of sorcerer with a high level of trickery. Doesn't matter. He's right. Because this fight wasn't about What's His Name and me. No, the only opponent I face is the asshole in my head. The only opponent I was ever facing—and ever will face—is right here inside me.

I thought I had the fucking answers, and now what? I considered shitting all over the life I've scratched and clawed to get back to. Like some wayward explorer on an African safari caught in quicksand, sinking for years, looking for my rope, my vine, whatever, to pull myself out; and now that I've grasped onto it, I just toss it aside so I can dive back in. How can someone so hungry for light be so attracted to the dark?

If I didn't know any better, I'd think I do belong here.

And that whole intervention with the Quran-bearing shot caller reminds me of my preacher when I was a child. He had this policy when boys were roughhousing, and if it got out of hand, he would ask us if we were done fighting and then make us apologize and shake hands. Solid leadership, but I don't think that's what this moment is. This is deeper; real self-realization shit.

This is about finding me in the equation and accepting that maybe I was a son of a bitch inside this, too. This is about finding culpability and acceptance and then seeing him as me and me as him and blurring the lines between us.

It's not about apologies or shaking hands. It's about understanding and oneness and… wait… Humility?

Holy shit, there's that word again.

And, right now, there's a lot swirling in my head—*oneness, humility, this too shall pass*—dancing like a carousel above a baby's crib. And I need to collect my convictions and answer the unanswered questions and find forgiveness or leaving here is a waste of time. Because I'll just come back.

And the memories come now, in fits and spurts, in ebbs and flows, in poetry, in vignettes, in thoughts. In lines that I wish I could uncross. Like cobblestones in a garden, they lead me backward to a sweet confused child, to a curious kid, to an inspired young man. It comes; it goes. Humility, understanding, forgiveness of self, it's all in there and I need to find it quickly, but I don't know where to begin. Every piece is so important.

This is where I dig deep because I'm in the fourth quarter and the clock is always ticking. I desperately need to find that small-town boy I lost years ago, or stupid-ass prison cells and guilty feelings will be the backdrop of the rest of my life. But the truth is I am light-years away from the gravel roads and cornfields of my youth, and I don't know where I would even begin to find that kid I've been trying to get back to since this all began.

In a way, I feel like my thirteen-year-old self—looking at albums, trying to decide, with the turntable spinning and the needle aching to make sound, to change me, to find me again. And I wait to hear the rich, warm crackle through the speakers and follow the grooves, back to a single decision, or maybe it's many, that if I could just have a do-over, I could change everything.

And my mind keeps circling back to that fire, the one in Sweeney's basement. Not exactly the beginning, but a moment when I think that boy still existed, was still struggling, was in over his head. I'm there now, in my mind. I'm on fire, and the whole dammed thing is out of control. And clearly, it wasn't enough to make me stop then, and it wasn't enough to head off what came afterward, but that's because I couldn't fathom the grip this drug would have around my throat. Who could? For most people, a moment like that would have been a giant STOP sign. But I'm a stubborn son of a bitch, the kind of kid who *had* to touch the stove when someone told me it was too hot. Because I needed to know, how hot. And here I sit, in this federal prison cell, with a complete panoramic view of how hot that stove can really get.

Yeah, this is where I have to start, that night at Sweeney's, because it could have all been different. Only this time I stop it—the addiction, the shame, the destruction. Just before my life got completely fucked up so quickly, so out of control. This is the story I force myself to relive, only this time I walk away from the house with my mother into the night.

And never talk to any of those people again.

97

I'M THIRTY-FOUR NOW and it's the morning of my release; and I liken it to some sort of rodent—a mole maybe—burrowing out of his hole and seeing sunlight for the first time, hoping the light doesn't hurt my eyes. *We made it, God. Actually, made it.*

And for some reason, I've been thinking about that rabbit trapped in the woodpile on Mason's farm. How I empathized with the little fella surrounded by bloodthirsty dogs. But lately I've been working out this slowly developing revelation, like one of those pictures you stare at and eventually see a three-dimensional image appear, and I empathize with the observer.

My heart goes out to You, God. I wanted so badly to intervene, wanted to chase the dogs off and lift the rabbit up, out from its nightmare. Which I guess is what You feel being omnipresent with love and understanding and all the answers. You peer down at all us scared rabbits and crazy dogs and woodpiles, and want to help, want to shelter, want to save but know that we have to do things for ourselves.

The image of Michelangelo's The Creation of Adam is so vivid in my mind. The muscular outstretched arm of, well, You, reaching down, only my white bearded version has pain in his eyes and tears rolling down His face—because this shit is tough to watch.

Because us rabbits have all fucked up—<u>ALL</u> fucked up—and we have to find a way out of our own woodpile. The recipe for true wisdom, so we never do it again. And I'll bet it breaks Your heart because it would break mine if I were in Your shoes, knowing You could snap Your fingers and make it all go away, but the best You can do is watch and hope until we rabbits finally look up from the rubble and realize the dogs hold no power.

It's fear and insecurity and hiding that entraps us.

And if it's nonstop for us then it must be nonstop for You. You watch all this shit. You witness our pain, our heartache, our confusion. You're with us in those moments just before we cut our wrists or pull the trigger or tighten the noose. When tears stream down our faces and we beg for forgiveness and You want to wrap Your arms around us and shush us and whisper, "I've got you little, fella. It's going to be okay." We are Your fragile, furry creatures zigzagging across the orchard, scared to death, being eaten alive.

And it's clear I'm different now. Not back to the kid I was before the drugs—I'm so much further evolved; better, maybe. New. Because I care much deeper, I'm sensitive to the pain of even that doomed, tiny rabbit. Maybe I'm getting closer to unconditional love and oneness. And, although it's no hit of ecstasy, I'll take empathy over selfishness and anger any day. Because even though it's vulnerable, I feel a connection to something bigger that I wasn't picking up before.

I'm getting something here, God. What it is, I'm not quite sure yet but it has something to do with light and darkness and our need for suffering and why nature seems to be such a motherfucker. I think.

Maybe, God, there is no right or wrong, there are only choices. Choices with consequences. Real consequences that need to be thrown up on scales that have truly been calibrated for real justice.

And whether those scales are karma or cause and effect or reap what you sow, what's it really matter? Because these laws are the physics of spirituality and, just like gravity, whether the earth pulls us down or it's all a consequence of spacetime curvature, at the end of the day if your choice is to jump from a ten-story apartment building the consequence is you become a mess on the sidewalk below.

Oh, and don't forget, God has to shed the tears.

Even after diving into my soul search like some convict vision quest, even after I replayed critical moments that have led me to here, I still had to question, could that really have been me?

But it was.

And I understand now. I'm fucked up, not evil. I'm unique but not a different species. I've been lost, but who the fuck hasn't?

Everyone has had their moments at the crossroads, each of us have endured our share of life's shitstorm and whatever anyone does or does not think about me has nothing to do with the fact that in another life they could be me and I them. And I suddenly see this tapestry that weaves in and out of each of us,

I'm so ready to be that guy who dreamed of taking on the world — the very same world that has me shitting in my pants now.

It's so clear that the next phase of my life isn't going to be easy. But I've got you God and—for whatever it matters in this vast, cosmic apple orchard—you've got me.

Stepping out from the woodpile. Ready to live free.

98

I USE DIFFERENT doors leaving than when I entered three years ago. There are no keys jingling, no mechanical levers or sounds of steel hinges and it's nothing like I could ever have imagined. I question if that disappoints me. These doors are glass, and open automatically as I cautiously walk outside into this sultry, humid South Florida climate, and something tells me these are the only doors that are going to open for me out here.

So, this is what freedom looks like. Impossibly blue skies that almost go unnoticed above the hauntingly quiet parking lot with pickup trucks and economy sedans and reserved sections with aluminum signs that cast shadows like a sundial in the front row. Freedom, to me, looks like painted lines over cracked concrete that make it clear where all things belong.

I have spent a total of seven years in at least eight different institutions and now I'm walking out into the sun, which seems to shine much brighter than the gray and callous skies on the other side of this razor wire.

I take a few more steps, the see-through doors close behind me and suddenly I am no longer caged. Nobody is watching me; no administrative people to bully me into believing that all I really want is to get one over on them, no guards to ignore my presence or stare me down like they want to fight, no predators stalking me for signs of weakness. And I feel strange, and I feel like I'm doing something wrong, and it makes me sad because even I know human beings shouldn't feel more comfortable being watched, stalked, or bullied.

God, please don't let me screw this up.

I am four months away from my thirty-fifth birthday and I'm walking out of prison with no skills, no college degree, and at least a decade of heartache, loss, and multiple felonies that don't quite fill in the gap in my work history. Where most convicts are happy, I am nervous. It's March 6, 2005 and I am tired, relieved, fragile, and scared shitless that the world doesn't have a place for a person like me.

And what is "a person like me" anyway? Therein lies the real question. Am I the hardened criminal who has been irreversibly shaped over these lost years in the system? Am I still the worthless junkie who shamefully watched himself spiral out of complete control and sobered up in jail only to find himself facing life in prison? Twice? Am I the small-town boy who was once kind and honorable, who cares deeply for a town that helped raise me to believe in the values that gave me something to hold onto while I was submerged in these nasty prisons and holding facilities? Am I still the friendly, caring person who actually gave a shit about any of this or did my last decade of tragic events desensitize me to the harsh realities of life's never-ending beatdown?

I don't know. Or maybe I am just a sorry sack of shit who has lost everything.

The truth is, I'm all of them. I'm a patchwork of every good and every bad. A quilt made out of old T-shirts and too-small jeans and memories. They are the incongruous parts of who I really am, this person who sits in the driver's seat of my life.

And I carry so much shame but there has to be more to me than my mistakes, and I'm going to find that person. I'm going to remember. I'm going to become who I really am. A patchwork of experiences that will complete who I am. That will make sense of me someday. But until that day, I hope I can find people who will look the other way. Or at the very least, listen and try to understand.

I can only hope that, although my experience was ugly, my decisions will be forever rooted in empathy. And I'm sure there's a blessing buried somewhere deep in that shit pile.

I promise to keep digging.

And standing here looking out at the vast wide open of my new future, I can't tell you what's more frightening—going into the system or walking out. I'm forever mortified over the years I've lost. Without knowing it, I have slowly witnessed the death of things most people take for granted. So, I stand here taking in yet another surreal event in my life, trying to assess what's dead inside me, what's salvageable, and knowing that it all comes with time.

I close my eyes as the sun warms my face. "Here we go," I whisper, then I open my eyes and continue towards whatever life is going to be. And knowing that somewhere underneath the sadness, I am still good.

Across the parking lot, I see Kelly's silhouette walking towards me with Loren, her youngest, on her hip. They are off in the horizon where hot air fumes blur the landscape and asphalt gets spongy from the unbearable heat and, for a brief moment, I'm not sure what comes next. I think of Sean-Michael and wonder where he's at and how safe I might feel if he was here, on *my* hip.

I walk in their direction. And I won't turn around, I won't look back because I'm afraid something will pull me back in, like somehow this was a mistake or a sick joke, and now I don't get to leave because I was brazen enough to actually look back. Like Sodom and Gomorrah in a Miami parking lot.

And I stare at my sister as she grows bigger with each step and try to gauge what's behind me through her expressions, but she reveals nothing, which I think is a good sign.

I have survived the things behind me. Those things that feel forever ago, already, though it's only been a few minutes, a few steps, when I said goodbye and hugged the fellas. The men I did my time with, the men I called my friends, who have all given me the unspoken permission to forget them once I get to the parking lot. And I felt I could never forget them, but now they slowly slip from my mind, like an Etch-a-Sketch™ being shaken with every step. Through this quiet crowded lot where I walk between the rows of cars, the worn-out vehicles of guards, counselors, cooks, and the warden. The vehicles that bring them here to this prison for dangerous men, full of drug lords and killers and mob bosses and hitmen and bikers.

But no longer me.

The closer I get to Kelly, the more I fear the moment and wonder what to say. Can I hug her and my niece? Will I show my appreciation enough? Will my wayward past come through too loudly and make my sister not want me around? There is no protocol for this, there is no manual; or believe me, I would have memorized every word.

"Hi," Kelly says. Her voice cracks and her face contorts, tears are already running down her cheeks. She sniffles and forces a smile. "How does it feel?"

Loren, confused and worried, looks up at her mommy crying, then at the man she doesn't know, yet.

"Not sure," I lie.

"Not sure?" Kelly asks with a laugh. "Come here."

And we embrace and I clench my eyes and I try my best not to cry. She sobs and I squeeze tighter, which makes her cry even more. "I'm sorry," I whisper but I don't know why.

Maybe I am saying sorry for her needing to drive eight hours with her young daughter, my niece, to come get me. Maybe I am sorry that I am so scared of being free that I can't express my gratitude in the right way. Maybe I am sorry for committing crimes, or worrying our mother, or the black mark I put on our family's name. Maybe it is because she has been left alone to deal with our mother's four additional suicide attempts over the last few years. Maybe I am saying it because she knows what I'm capable of, knows my potential, and believes in me to a fault; yet, here I am being picked up from prison at thirty-five.

Or maybe I'm saying it to myself.

I know how these kinds of things happen to boys like me, now; that I might have accidentally asked for all this trouble, when I wanted the truth, to awaken, and something ominous tells me those lessons aren't quite over yet.

And after I climb into Kelly's minivan, I close my eyes and feel the sun on my face and take a deep breath and release…

This too shall pass.

Kelly's minivan pulls out of the parking lot and heads north and I watch the prison grow more insignificant in the rearview mirror. And, in this moment, I make a promise to God and myself that, no matter how difficult the road ahead will be or what the gloomy statistics show, no matter who believes or who has given up, no matter how hard my past tries to pull me back in, I'm stronger than that. And you better fucking believe one thing…

I ain't never coming back.

ACKNOWLEDGMENTS

Writing this book has made me a more complete and better human being. This work is beyond a labor of love. It is a chance to liberate my conscience and find purpose inside my mistakes and ultimate tragedies. With the incredible amounts of shit that we all carry around with us as we go through life, I can't begin to express how amazing it feels to step back into my life without the guilt and shame of this story. There are many people who have played important roles in the completion of this project and I'd like to mention a few.

To Tom Runge, thank you for instilling integrity and honor into my life. You are my father and you will always be missed. You deserve to be remembered as a great man who sincerely cared about people's lives and well-being. Wherever you are, I hope they have model airplanes and eager little boys to fetch them.

Thank you to Jen, Harper, and McKenna for allowing me to uproot our lives and drive across country so daddy can "save the world". All three of you roll with the punches and give meaning to my life in a way I never thought was possible. You are my redemption.

To my mother, thank you for finding me underneath all the debris. You were always able to see the child you loved inside me, even when I couldn't.

To my sister, Kelly, thank you for believing in your little brother and seeing the goodness in me, even when I hid it from myself. You are the purest example of blood being thicker than water, and one of my greatest blessings has been that God made us brother and sister. Thank you for never allowing me to be alone.

Thank you, Denny Affolter, for being my biggest fan as far back as I can remember. I will always want to make you proud. You have taught me more than you will ever know.

Thank you, Copper, for being the best dog in the history of the world and my single source of unconditional love during a time in my life when

I no longer wanted to live. You didn't make into the book, big fella, but you know what you meant to me. P.S.: Thank you for taking care of Denny until your final days. Glad you got that last rabbit.

To Tim Murrell, thank you for seeing friendship the way you do. You are everything I said you are in this book and more. A lot of people talk about "friends for life" but you are the truest expression of what it means. The world needs more Tim Murrells in it. I love you, man.

To Rachelle Chartrand, you are an inspiration to both watch and work with. I feel so blessed that the universe brought us together when it was time to actually put this book together. Your ability to see the story in your head and arrange it so beautifully, is an experience I will probably never get to have again. Working with you helped me to evolve well beyond my writing, so thank you. This book will always be our book.

To Tracy Thatcher, thank you for being the first real fan of my writing. Without you, the world may not have gotten the story this raw. It was your countless hours of listening to my insanity, insecurity and fear that kept this train moving. Your constant reminders that the world doesn't need another polished, sugar-coated version of a tragic story is what helped make this book so special. Your friendship and love have been a huge part of my strength. Thank you for getting me.

To my in-laws, Martha and Bill Spencer, thank you for raising such a kind and compassionate daughter. Thank you also for letting us all disrupt your life and crash at your house so I could have a peaceful place to right this damn book.

To Chris and Danielle Reites, your contribution to this project is something I could never measure. The feedback and overwhelming support have given me the confidence that maybe I really am an author. Thank you for keeping me in the fold, even after you read the details.

To Steve Sumner, you are severely missed, my friend. Thank you for always accepting me for who I am and who I was. You were one of the first people I confessed this crazy story to, and I never would have guessed that I could connect so strongly with someone by releasing my past. Our friendship was as important as it was unique. And it is the many hours we've spent talking about the loss of your brother that has inspired me to tell my story to everyone. I hope, wherever you're at, you're able to have beers with your brother and are talking about me now. Keep supporting me, man. I need you.

Thank you, Dave and Jackie Schuler, for being immediate friends to our family. Getting feedback and support from a core group of people whom I trust and respect has given me peace during this project and encouragement that I'm doing the right thing. You will never know how important you both are to me and this book.

Thank you, Shirley Jump, for not only bringing an incredible amount of talent and experience to the editing process but equally the patience to put up with all the questions. You are the first person to ever take me under her wing and teach me the fundamentals of good writing. I'm so lucky to have such a seasoned vet take a deep and personal interest in my story. You are a special person to me and clearly driven to help save lives.

To Mark Creamer, thank you for seeing something special in me and having the energy and compassion to bring it out. You are an integral part of my healing process and someone I know God placed in my life for a reason. Still not sure what you did so awful to deserve me.

To Roger Taylor and James Nichols, you both are like brothers to me. Thank you for being the friendships I needed during the most lonely and heartbreaking times of my life. Most people will never understand how close two people can become when you endure the insanity of prison life together. I've got your backs for life.

To Hernando, thank you for coming to visit me in Miami when I was still a relative stranger. Your heart has always been in the right place with me.

To my brother Keenan, I love you, bubs.

To Chad Rankin, Terry Bogue, Monica Vincent, Kristy Gash, Amie Tracy, there in not enough space in this book to describe what you mean to me and what you did for me the day you showed up at my federal sentencing. I love each of you and owe you a great deal.

Thank you, Daren Mattson, for being the friend I needed on my visit back to Higginsville so many years ago. And for coming to see me when I was in Miami.

To Higginsville, thank you for never changing. In my darkest hour, it was the memory of the cornfields, the football games, the small-town values and the goodness of the people that reminded me of who I really am. In so many moments, you were the strength, the reason, the example and the beacon light that gave me hope that I was going to make it back in one piece—the person you all remembered me to be.

To all my San Ramon peeps, thank you for listening to my story and not turning your backs on me. You listened, loved and respected me in spite of the crazy story I had to share. It would have been so easy to walk away.

And to all the people who are struggling with addiction, understanding addiction, or are suffering the consequences of what addiction has done to your lives—my heart is with you. There are people who believe in you and want the best for you, I promise. I know I do. No one said it is going to be easy, but I'm telling you it's worth it.

ABOUT THE AUTHOR

Kyle's life mission is to bring hope and understanding to a world full of intolerance yet yearning for change. A testimony to his commitment is the courageous act of walking away from the safety of his corporate career to tell a story that has been hidden for over twenty years. Kyle believes that if his work can blur the lines of separation between all of us then we can open the door to unconditional love and oneness.

Kyle's words are put out into the world to challenge us all, to shift consciousness by confronting conventional ways of thinking, in an attempt to inspire empathy, solidarity, and tolerance. Spoken from a man who knows—no mistake is too big to be forgiven and nobody deserves to be alone or without hope.

We are all in this together.

For more on his life's work visit www.kyledeanhouston.com. Connect with him on social media @KyleDeanHouston